DARK FEELINGS, GRIM THOUGHTS

DARK FEELINGS, GRIM THOUGHTS

Experience and Reflection in Camus and Sartre

Robert C. Solomon

OXFORD
UNIVERSITY PRESS

2006

OXFORD
UNIVERSITY PRESS

Oxford University Press, Inc., publishes works that further
Oxford University's objective of excellence
in research, scholarship, and education.

Oxford   New York
Auckland   Cape Town   Dar es Salaam   Hong Kong   Karachi
Kuala Lumpur   Madrid   Melbourne   Mexico City   Nairobi
New Delhi   Shanghai   Taipei   Toronto

With offices in
Argentina   Austria   Brazil   Chile   Czech Republic   France   Greece
Guatemala   Hungary   Italy   Japan   Poland   Portugal   Singapore
South Korea   Switzerland   Thailand   Turkey   Ukraine   Vietnam

Copyright © 2006 by Oxford University Press, Inc.

Published by Oxford University Press, Inc.
198 Madison Avenue, New York, New York 10016

www.oup.com

Oxford is a registered trademark of Oxford University Press

Library of Congress Cataloging-in-Publication Data
Solomon, Robert C.
Dark feelings, grim thoughts: experience and reflection in Camus and Sartre / Robert
C. Solomon.
p.   cm.
Includes bibliographical references and index.
ISBN-13 978-0-19-518157-9
ISBN 0-19-518157-3
1. Camus, Albert, 1913–1960—Criticism and interpretation.   2. Sartre, Jean Paul,
1905–Criticism and interpretation.   I. Title.
PQ2605.A3734Z736255 2006
840.9'00914—dc22   2005040198

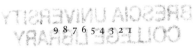

9 8 7 6 5 4 3 2 1

Printed in the United States of America
on acid-free paper

For David Sherman and Clanay Martin,
and especially, for Frithjof Bergmann

CONTENTS

DARK FEELINGS, GRIM THOUGHTS

INTRODUCTION

Camus and Sartre

Albert Camus and Jean-Paul Sartre, their famous differences aside, shared a "phenomenological" sensibility. They were both philosophers who described personal experience in exquisite and excruciating detail and reflected on the meaning of this experience with sensitivity and insight. That is the focus of this book: Camus' and Sartre's descriptions of personal experience and their reflections on the meaning of this experience. They also reflected, with some skepticism, on the nature of reflection. The thematic problem of the book is the relationship between experience and reflection. Both Camus and Sartre set them against one another, sometimes dramatically. Camus, in his best-known novel, *The Stranger,* as well as in some of his lyrical essays, suggested their radical independence, even opposition. In his more philosophical reflections, he sometimes hinted that reflection was a kind of affliction, not so different in kind from the torments of his mythical hero Sisyphus. ("If the myth is tragic, that is because its hero is conscious.") In this he joined a distinguished list of thinkers, among them Kierkegaard, Dostoevsky, and Nietzsche, all of whom also juxtaposed consciousness and happiness. To think too much and to be all too aware of the complexities of life is already to foreclose its simple, unreflective joys. Sartre, too, from his earliest essays, insisted on the distinction between prereflective "lived experience" and self-conscious reflection, and he often deferred to the former as more basic and of primary significance to human existence. How experience and

3

reflection relate to one another is one of the puzzles that pervades his early philosophy.

To be sure, the experiences described by Camus and Sartre are not, for the most part, of the "normal" quotidian variety. They are often dark, perverse, bordering on the obscene and pathological. In the case of Camus' character Meursault, in *The Stranger*, the pathology is one of vacuousness, the absence of experiences, emotional experiences in particular, where we would certainly expect them (a mother's death, love, a lethal confrontation). In Sartre's *Nausea*, by contrast, we are appalled by the petty nastiness of his protagonist's perceptions of other people, not to mention the depraved images he describes of faces, hands, postures, and some of his own body parts. Camus' Clamence in *The Fall*, by contrast again, describes experiences that are obscene and pathological in yet a different way: he is polished, seductive, sophisticated, but what he describes is no less disturbing. He gives us a grim portrait of human nature and experience. Both Camus and Sartre celebrated extreme experiences, life-and-death situations, impossible choices in war and in interpersonal conflict, life at the bottom, personal trauma, cynicism, and, on occasion, courage and hope. This was, first of all, appropriate to their historical situation. Writing in the midst of war and global catastrophe, they were not interested in the merely mundane but rather in the heroic, the not-so-heroic, and the downright cowardly. Second, I suppose, they were two eccentric and neurotic guys, each in his own distinctive way, and this inevitably gets expressed in their work.

But third and most important for this study, they were both interested in unusual experience because they were "phenomenologists"—explorers of consciousness. Sartre makes this quite explicit; Camus simply does phenomenology without the philosophical fanfare. But they were both fascinated by the liminal, the extreme, the foibles of human psychology, the outer edges of experience. Sartre's and Camus' early novels, *Nausea* and *The Stranger*, both featured truly weird protagonists who narrate in the first person. Sartre's later play, *No Exit*, dealt not only with life at its limit (namely, death) but also with the utter Hell of human relationships. Camus often wrote about the limits of life. His Meursault faces execution, and the people of his semifictional Oran face the fatality of the bubonic plague. Clamence in *The Fall* ends up raving that he is Jesus Christ, welcoming death. Sartre reveled in the exploration of experience, but for him the reflections were far more fascinating than the experiences themselves. Throughout his long career, Sartre thought deeply about the nature of consciousness and experience and obviously delighted in the activity of phenomenological reflection, too often separated from personal experience by the barbed-wire vocabulary he employed. Reading about his life (and marveling at his enormous output), one wonders, as has been said of his predecessor Kierkegaard, how he had time to eat and sleep.

Camus and Sartre: "Existentialists"

Camus and Sartre were the giants of twentieth-century "existentialism," although neither of them was comfortable with that title. They were an odd duo, to be sure. Their political differences made headlines in Paris for many months in the late 1950s. Their seemingly opposed personalities—Camus the *bon homme*, Sartre the somber Stalinist—kept literary critics and biographers in business for years. Camus was and is best known for his lyrical writing, his novels and essays. Sartre remains best known for his gargantuan *Being and Nothingness*, a technical philosophy book that is rightly recognized as an attempt to out-Teutonize even the Germans. And to exaggerate their differences even more, the French press made a scandal out of Camus' and Sartre's much-publicized personal falling out in the 1950s. The secondary literature that followed, accordingly, was almost always "Camus versus Sartre." The two philosophers came to represent two opposite poles of the intellectual debates of the time: in politics, on questions of literary style, on the purpose of writing, on the strategies of living, and, of course, in philosophy. That debate is again resurfacing as Camus and Sartre find themselves back onstage in French and American intellectual life, but it is the point of this book to show that Camus and Sartre are much better understood as kindred spirits who shared a sense of personal philosophy. Against the intellectualist, rationalist, and empiricist ("positivist") traditions in philosophy, they fully appreciated the importance of lived experience. One might even say, despite their often grim reflections, that Camus and Sartre exemplified a weird but palpable love of life. It shines clearly through even their most dreary political and moralistic prose.

Camus and Sartre wrote at a traumatic and difficult time in modern history and contemporary philosophy: just before, during, and after the Second World War, the Nazi occupation of France, the horrors of Stalinism, and the incipient Algerian war. The atmosphere in Europe was poisonous. Cities were in ruins, populations were humiliated, and the mood was despairingly pessimistic. The philosophical atmosphere (what Hegel called the explicit consciousness of the times or *Zeitgeist*) was exceedingly gloomy, too. Accordingly, the early works of Camus and Sartre are poisoned as well, albeit riddled with dark irony and humor. They betray a darkened but common consciousness, even if the "alienated" attitude that it inspired later became "cool" among a more pampered younger generation, especially in far-off, uninvaded America. There, too, they became a gloomy but immensely exciting literary phenomenon, required reading for the Beats and other avant-garde eccentrics in the New World. And their works remain on the reading lists of many American and other Anglophone university and college courses, long after their stars have faded in Paris.

But despite their continuous presence in American college courses, Camus and Sartre have been "lost" to us, at least until very, very recently.

They were lost (here as an active verb) first by the academic structuralists, who aggressively argued against and rejected them, then by the marginally academic poststructuralists (and more generally by the nonacademic post-modernists) who simply dismissed or ignored them. For two decades after (and at least a decade before) Sartre's death, a visitor to Paris or to many major universities might well have wondered what happened to those two French superheroes of the 1960s. But I think that Camus and Sartre were "lost" in a more profound sense, too, which is what that postmodernist patronizing attitude is about. To say that Camus and Sartre were "lost" in this sense is just to indicate what is so obvious in their early works: that they were alienated, uprooted, and disoriented young men. Their shared "existential" philosophy takes that attitude as something of a basic premise, which could not be more different from the ironic and often joking attitude of the new French philosophies. But the world is once again alienated, up-rooted, and disoriented. The young men, and the women, too, are restless and looking for a philosophy. The "existentialism" of Camus and Sartre, however dark, grim, and seemingly old-fashioned it may be, might be a good place to begin again.

Postmodern Eclipse

In the 1980s, after Sartre's death, Camus and Sartre all but disappeared from philosophy and from the shelves of the more "hip" bookstores and from "official" French philosophy. In a 1979 book by Vincent Descombes titled *Modern French Philosophy*, Camus gets barely a mention and Sartre doesn't even get a chapter, just an appendix—and that to a chapter on Kojeve!! The poststructuralists who totally eclipsed Camus and Sartre sometimes acted as if they had never even heard of them, although, of course, they were heavily influenced by, and even in awe of, them. Philosophers such as Roland Barthes, Michel Foucault, and Gilles Deleuze rarely even referred to Sartre although his example and his stature and his philosophy remained the model, or at least the target, for all of them. The public neglect was wholly disin-genuous. Meanwhile, Camus, already dead for thirty years, had virtually disappeared from the scene. The dramatic appearance of his last novel, *Le Premier Homme*, in Paris in 1994, salvaged from the car wreck that killed him and kept in protective custody by his daughter for more than three decades, only made evident how absent he had been those many years.

But if Sartre and Camus were rarely mentioned in postmodern academic philosophy, tens of thousands of students nevertheless continue to read *The Stranger* every year in introductory philosophy, classes on "existentialism," and second-year French courses, and the audience for Camus' other novels and for Sartre's accessible works, notably his plays, remained and remains enormous. Many students feel obliged to have a copy of *Being and Nothingness* on their shelves, whether or not they have ever opened it. And now, decades later, both philosophers are being resurrected and newly appreciated. Camus and Sartre, I am delighted to say, are back.[1]

Their reappearance is not hard to explain. Postmodernism went out of style, and poststructuralism revealed its ultimate vacuousness— particularly in the realms of personal experience, ethics, and social justice. Accordingly, Camus and Sartre are not only being reevaluated and newly appreciated; they also take on renewed significance. They, but not their successors, spoke passionately and (for the most part) sincerely about the pressing problems of personal and political life. For all of their differences, they now appear more in league with one another rather than opposed to one another. Despite their very different (and dramatically antagonistic) responses to the political questions of their day, they remain a natural pairing, as unrestrained moralists and as intense philosophers of personal phenomenology. This personal dimension of philosophy may not always be evident in some of the more tangled Teutonic bits of Sartre's overly ontological writing or in the lyrical casualness of much of Camus' prose, but it's there throughout their work and in their lives. In Sartre, it's there in his many public appearances, and in his sometimes embarrassingly eccentric and revealing examples. Thus I want to insist that Camus and Sartre are both exemplary philosophers of personal experience, a dimension of philosophy—I would say the essential dimension— that has been all but abandoned in the wake of post-postmodernism, overly analytic philosophy, and hypercognitive science.

The Philosophy of Personal Experience

Jean-Paul Sartre wrote twenty pages a day for his whole long working life. Many of his writings are embarrassing, and some of them virtually unreadable, the result of too much ideology and too many drugs ("bad ideas, bad chemistry, the yin and yang of craziness," according to Kurt Vonnegut). Sartre was, nevertheless, *the* great philosopher of our times. He could be stubborn to the point of absurdity, politically obtuse, and often misleading or in "bad faith" in his recollections and reinterpretations of his own work. So was Camus. Indeed, I will argue that some of Camus' interpretations of his own work are so remarkably off the mark that one might wonder if he ever read them. Sartre was an oddball, an egomaniac, sometimes a bastard, an unscrupulous libertine, and better at rationalization than at self-criticism or regret. He could be cruel, especially to those who loved him most. But I choose to ignore his faults and much of his bibliography as well as his biography. Camus, by contrast to Sartre, was generally recognized as a "good guy," if also a libertine and a bit overly prone to play the victim. But even Sartre recognized him as the supreme moralist of our time. Because Camus' life was cut so tragically short, it is hard to say how his philosophy would have continued. I am told (by his friend Raja Rao) that he had planned to go off to India. Had he done so, who can say what radical new turn his reflections and his experience would have taken?

In this study, I emphasize the personal and philosophical rather than the purely literary or political dimensions of the works of Camus and Sartre, and I treat their works selectively, without attempting to make overall pronouncements about or summary evaluations of "Albert Camus: 1920–1960" or "Jean-Paul Sartre: 1905–1980." (This is called "cherry-picking" when insurance companies do it, selecting and keeping the good bits and dispensing with the rest.) In this book, I admit to selecting and keeping what I think of as the best bits and ignoring the rest. And those best bits include, especially, the novels, but I subject these to philosophical rather than literary analysis. What I do not do—as I soon realized that this would require a much bigger book—is examine the systematic philosophy, that is, Sartre's *Being and Nothingness* (Camus never tried to write anything so philosophically or academically ambitious). To be sure, that great book appears in virtually every chapter of this volume and dominates several (especially the chapter on "Sartre's Bad Faith"), but I deal with Sartre's various philosophical problems in conjunction with his and Camus' other works and concerns. Thus I introduce Sartre's phenomenology in conjunction with *Nausea*, his Being-for-Others in conjunction with *No Exit*, and so on. Nevertheless, I attempt to produce a portrait of Sartre's philosophy that will emerge more clearly, I hope, than it might have in a commentary on his giant philosophical tome. In that sense, the literature provides the framework for the philosophy.

They may have differed vehemently in politics, but both Camus and Sartre were fundamentally moralists, and both of their philosophies (including their political positions) cannot be understood apart from their deep ethical commitments. To be sure, in Sartre's case especially, this is hidden behind a pseudo-Heideggerian emphasis on ontology and an absurd denial (in *Being and Nothingness*) that he is doing ethics. (He did include a promissory note to do that later. His various jottings were finally published in his barely coherent *Notebook for an Ethics* in 1983.) And Sartre's later writing, obscured in a haze of amphetamines and adolescent political ideology, renders the morality of his commitments rather dubious. Camus, too, caught up in the vicious politics of Cold War Paris, produced a defensive (and some would say rather pathetic) polemic titled *The Rebel* in 1955, which does not do justice to his basic moralism either. *The Rebel* is, I personally opine, a book that had better never been published at all.

The present volume, however, is not a study of the moral or political views of Sartre and Camus, much less a study of their personal lives or their curious friendship and dramatic breakup. I am, quite frankly, not interested in all of that, nor do I want to get into the ongoing Camus versus Sartre debate that began after their very public quarrel in the 1950s, imported into the American setting by Germain Brée and others, and now back in the literary and political magazines. Nor do I accept Camus' fairly typical dramatic dismissal, that he and Sartre have "nothing in common." Rather, I see Camus and Sartre as two of a kind, as brilliant practitioners of what I call the philosophy of personal experience. And that is something of a lost art, at least in academic philosophy.

In treating both authors selectively, I will focus almost entirely on Sartre's early work (before 1950), including two literary works, *Nausea* and his play *No Exit*, and on Camus' best-known novels, *The Stranger*, *The Plague*, and *The Fall*. My emphasis is on their phenomenology, which informs Camus' work as well as Sartre's, and the exquisite exploration of personal experience that phenomenology allows. Both philosophers also make an all-important distinction between lived experience and reflection. There is a pervasive question about how the two are related; how or whether reflection clarifies or rather distorts experience; and even whether it is possible or normal for adult human beings to have experience without reflection. In Sartre, these questions are evident in his early *Transcendence of the Ego* and in his *The Emotions*, where he introduces the terms "pre-reflective" and "reflective consciousness" (the distinction is employed throughout *Being and Nothingness*). In Camus, the distinction between lived experience and reflection functions as an organizational principle, most obviously in *The Stranger* (parts I and II) and in a more subtle sense in *The Fall* (in the contrast between Clamence's memories of his experiences in luminous Paris and his ongoing reflections in drizzly Amsterdam). I mention only briefly Camus' and Sartre's shared but hesitant affiliation with "existentialism," but I take their phenomenology very seriously as philosophy, and that is the running motif of the book. Experience and reflection are the twin tracks on which their phenomenology travels in order to illuminate what is both ordinary and extraordinary in our personal experience, in our "existence," and in our lives.

I make no pretense about trying to understand "Camus' philosophy" or "Sartre's philosophy," much less to understand Camus or Sartre themselves. I confessed from the beginning that I have a special fondness for these guys. I grew up with them, with their books and their ideas. But as with any deep affection, I see what I want to see, even as I acknowledge their serious flaws and faults, and even as I carefully pick and choose what I want to remember and think and teach about them and their works. Both philosophers and both men display a development or "dialectic" in their careers that I have chosen to ignore. My focus is restricted to their younger experience, expressions, and reflections (roughly before the age of forty, though that is when Camus died). Even among my limited choices, however, I have to admit that both authors were capable of writing dreary, tedious, and humorless novels (Camus' *The Plague* and Sartre's *Nausea*) and pretentious and overly dramatic philosophy treatises (Camus' *Myth*, not to mention *The Rebel*, and Sartre's *Being and Nothingness*, not to mention his *Critique of Dialectical Reason*).[2]

Nevertheless, no philosophers in the modern canon, excepting Nietzsche, have affected and influenced my own thinking and teaching more than Camus and Sartre. Moreover, in my mind, this book fulfills a long-standing ambition, completes a thirty-year project, and satisfies a fascination with "Continental" philosophy that I have had ever since being introduced to Hegel, Nietzsche, Sartre, and Camus back in graduate school. My teacher was Frithjof Bergmann, to whom I am forever indebted. The project formally began when I briefly took over Walter Kaufmann's "Hegel, Nietzsche, and Existentialism" course in 1967. This book, conjoined with my (equally selective) books *In the Spirit of Hegel* (New York: Oxford University Press, 1983) and *Living with Nietzsche* (New York: Oxford University Press, 2003), completes the trilogy.

In this book, I hope that I have given to Camus and Sartre the respect and credit that is certainly their due, though not without criticism. (That is how we philosophers show our fondness for one another.) But unlike many of the hatchet jobs that have been done to them over the years (including what they did to one another), this critique is, whatever else it is, appreciative criticism and an act of open affection. I do think that their descriptions of experience, their "phenomenologies," are among the most challenging in the philosophical literature. I say *philosophical* literature not so much to avoid competition and comparison with the more poetic and often more poignant examples readily found in novels and works not so clearly philosophical. But I think that it is worth emphasizing the very significant fact that behind their writings, including their novels and plays, are two profoundly personal and thoroughly philosophical temperaments, which pervade all of their work. With this in mind, I would like to study several selected works of Camus and Sartre, focusing on their descriptions of personal experience and their reflections on the meaning of this experience as well as of their reflections on the nature of such reflection. I have learned so much from them, living with them all of these years. My thanks to both of them.

Note: This is the third book in an informal trilogy on continental philosophy published by Oxford University Press. The first was *In the Spirit of Hegel* (1983), and the second was *Living with Nietzsche* (2003). Some of the chapters of this book have been previously published, but all have been thoroughly revised and rewritten. Chapter 1 and chapter 7 were both published originally in *Philosophy and Literature* 2 (October 1978) and 28 (Spring 2004), respectively. An essay on Camus' *Plague* will also appear in that same journal. Chapter 1 was also reprinted in my *From Hegel to Existentialism* (New York: Oxford University Press, 1987). Chapter 2 was originally published as chapter 2 of my book *The Passions* (New York: Doubleday Anchor, 1976), which was revised and reissued as *The Passions: Emotions and the Meaning of Life* (Indianapolis and Cambridge: Hackett, 1993). Chapter 5 first appeared in Paul Schilpp, ed., *Sartre* (in The Library of Living Philosophers series; La Salle, Ill.: Open Court, 1981), and was also reprinted in my *From Hegel to Existentialism*.

1

"TRUE TO HIS FEELINGS"

Phenomenology and Reflection in Camus' L'Étranger

The Stranger exploded on the scene in Paris in the early years of the German occupation, and it hit America during the height of the Cold War.[1] It marked, when I first read it in high school, one of those "existential" turning points in my life. Since then, I have read it dozens of times, taught it for more than thirty-five years, and watched it perplex and sometimes open the eyes of generations of American students in much the same way that it did me. In the 1960s, Camus' "strange" character Meursault was a role model for the alienated and disaffected. In the 1980s, he was considered a "nerd" by the more avaricious students of the Reagan era. In the new millennium, students still identify with him and react to him in all sorts of interesting ways, because his experience is, in some ill-defined way, their experience. What Camus has done, whatever else we may say about his book, is to capture an evasive truth about the personal experience of several generations of young people, at least in Europe and in the United States. It remains to be seen to what extent the book might also capture some similar truth about the personal experience of young people in general, at other times, and in other parts of the world.

The Stranger is an odd novel. It is very short. It features a character who has no character. It is written in the first person, almost entirely in the present tense. It describes to us, or rather, the narrator describes to us, the unfolding of a provincial world through the eyes of a protagonist who stands for nothing, has no discernible history, cares about very little, and thinks virtually not at all. He lives in a situation which we know was rife with interracial hostility, in a society on the brink of civil war, but we are given none of this, for it is no part of Meursault's experience. Indeed, what is striking is how little is part of Meursault's experience. We watch him going through several personal situations in which we would expect strong if not violent feelings—a mother's death, a new affair, a pimp's violence, a life-threatening confrontation, an arrest for murder, a trial for his life, an impending death sentence. But this is what the book is about: not these situations, nor even Meursault's reaction or response to these situations, but his *lack* of reaction or response to these situations. It is, one might say, a negative exercise in phenomenology, a detailed description of feelings not felt, thoughts not thought, experiences not experienced.

But, of course, there is no such thing as a negative phenomenology. Phenomenology describes what experiences one actually has, and Meursault has experiences continuously. He enjoys the sensuality of the sea and Marie's fresh smell. He suffers from the relentless heat of the North African sun. He savors a cup of coffee. Thus *The Stranger* is a book of phenomenology, but a book that is striking in its experiential absences.

It is, even more, a book that is striking in Meursault's virtual absence of reflection: thus the continuous present tense, and thus the near total absence of thought. There are occasional mentions of momentary memories, and there is an occasional reflective thought—usually borrowed from his mother or a simpleminded cliché. But there are virtually no reflections on his experience, no questions or thoughts about what something means, few "second thoughts" about whether an emotion—or the lack of an emotion— is good or bad, right or wrong, appropriate or inappropriate. (On the rare occasion when there is such a thought—for instance, concerning his lack of feeling of grief at his mother's funeral—we are struck by its utter banality.) So *The Stranger*, I want to suggest, is a book of phenomenology, but it is in particular a book about the problematic relationship between the phenomenology of experience and the phenomenology of reflection. Meursault, one might say, lives his experience, albeit shockingly limited, without reflection. This, I want to suggest, is what makes him so "strange" to us.

A Hero for the Truth?

> Lying is not only saying what is not true. It is also and especially saying more than is true and, as far as the human heart is concerned, saying more than one feels.
> —Albert Camus, 1955

What would it be—not to lie? Perhaps it is impossible. It is not difficult to avoid uttering falsehoods, of course. One can always keep silent. But what if lying is also not seeing the truth? For instance, not seeing the truth about oneself even in the name of "not lying"? What then would it be not to lie?—to see oneself and one's feelings as brute facts, as matters already fixed and settled? The very idea of not lying would then be . . . a lie.

The lie—it lies at the very heart of French existentialism. It is the infamy of the human condition for Sartre, the gravest sin for Camus. But where Sartre suspects that the lie—or what he calls *mauvaise foi*—is inescapable, Camus glorifies his characters—and apparently himself—as men without a lie. Meursault, Camus tells us in a retrospective interpretation, "refuses to lie . . . accepts death for the sake of truth."[2] Dr. Rieux of *The Plague* refuses to release information to Tarrou the reporter unless Tarrou reports "without qualification," and Rieux himself insists on taking an absurdly "objective" stance toward the plague and his reporting. Clamence of *The Fall* has been living a lie, so he is now in Purgatory (the seedy inner circles of Amsterdam), a judge—penitent: a judge, we come to see, of other people's hidden false-hoods, a penitent for his own past lie of a life. In *The Myth of Sisyphus*, it is "the absurd" that becomes the ascertainable truth, and it is the absurd hero who "keeps the absurd alive" with his defiant recognition of that truth. (By contrast, "philosophical suicide" is, in effect, a lie to oneself about the ulti-mate absurdity of life.) In the turmoil of French leftist politics through the Algerian crises and the Stalin show trials, Camus portrays himself in his *Notebooks* and in *The Rebel* as the "independent intellectual," the spokesman for the truth who refuses to accept the necessary political fabrications of the Left during a time of crisis and change. Accordingly, Camus has himself been interpreted and praised as the hero and martyr for the truth, as "Saint Just," the absurd hero and existential champion of honesty.

The Stranger is the best known of Camus' works, and it is on the basis of this early short novel that the interpretations of Camus' philosophy rea-sonably begin. (Its predecessor, *A Happy Death*, is generally considered a "test run." It was virtually "stillborn" until it was resurrected after years of *The Stranger*'s success.[3]) But virtually every interpretation of *The Stranger* has culminated in what I want to argue is a false claim—that Meursault is a totally honest man, the "stranger" who does not lie. In his own retrospective interpretation of *The Stranger*, Camus writes:

> The hero of the book is condemned because he doesn't play the game. In this sense he is a stranger to the society in which he lives; he drifts in the margin, in the suburb of private, solitary, sensual life. This is why some readers are tempted to consider him as a waif. You will have a more precise idea of this character, or one at all events in closer conformity with the intentions of the author, if you ask yourself in what way Meursault doesn't play the game. The answer is simple: He refuses to lie. Lying is not only saying what is not true. It is also and especially saying more than is true and, as far as the human heart is concerned, saying more than one feels. This is what we all do every day to simplify life. Meursault, despite appearances, does not wish to simplify life. He says what is true. He refuses to disguise his feelings and immediately society feels threatened. He is asked, for example, to say that he regrets his crime according to the ritual

formula. He replies that he feels about it more annoyance than real regret and this shade of meaning condemns him.

Meursault for me is then not a waif, but a man who is poor and naked, in love with the sun which leaves no shadows. Far from it being true that he lacks all sensibility, a deep tenacious passion animates him, a passion for the absolute and for truth. It is a still negative truth, the truth of being and of feeling, but one without which no victory over oneself and over the world will ever be possible. You would not be far wrong then in reading *The Stranger* as a story of a man who, without any heroics, accepts death for the sake of truth. I have some times said, and always paradoxically, that I have tried to portray in this character the only Christ we deserved. You will understand after these explanations that I said this without any intention of blasphemy and only with the slightly ironic affection which an artist has the right to feel towards the characters whom he has created.[4]

And throughout the standard interpretations, the same theme is routinely repeated; for example, "This indifferent man is intractable in his absolute respect for truth," and "His principal characteristic appears to be a kind of total sincerity which disconcerts us because it is virtually unknown in our world."[5]

This view has been challenged, but only in its scope, not in its essence. Notably, Conor Cruise O'Brien, in his *Camus*, argued that the "Meursault of the actual novel is not quite the same person as the Meursault of the commentaries. Meursault in the novel lies. He concocts for Raymond the letter that is designed to deceive the Arab girl and expose her to humiliation, and later he lies to the police to get Raymond discharged, . . . It is simply not true that Meursault is 'intractable in his absolute respect for the truth.' These episodes show him as indifferent to truth as he is to cruelty."[6] O'Brien continues to point out that Meursault, as the mirror of his author, is also indifferent to the reality of the hostility of the Arabs, the political tensions and sufferings of the Arab population, and the pretensions and arrogance of colonialism in which he plays an undisputed, even if unwitting, part. Perhaps O'Brien does not make enough of the distinction between lying and being simply indifferent to the truth, saying less than is true. In the passages in question, it is more indifference at stake than outright lying. For example, Meursault passes no judgment on Raymond's action apart from a banal appraisal of his means to an end: "I agreed it wasn't a bad plan—it would punish her all right" (40). And there is nothing in the description of the letter or his testimony before the police to make us certain that he has lied. But Camus, again in his commentary, explicitly points out that lying is not just saying what is not true. It is "also saying more than is true" and, we may safely extrapolate, saying less than is true as well. On this basis, we ought to agree with O'Brien that Meursault is, even if he does not lie outright, less than the ideal honest man. But ultimately, even O'Brien joins in the standard interpretation, qualifying it beyond the usual blanket judgment.

There is just one category of phenomena about which Meursault will not lie, and that is his own feelings. Neither to give pleasure to others nor to save them pain nor to save his own skin will he pretend that he feels something that he does not feel. Logically there is no reason why this should be so. There is no reason why he should not use lies to get himself out of the trouble which he got himself into by lies. Indeed, in the second case the motivation is (one could imagine) infinitely stronger than the first. Yet it is only the second he resists. The reason can only be that his own feelings, and his feeling about his feelings, are sacrosanct.[7]

But I want to argue that this standard interpretation in all its forms is unconvincing, not just in detail but in essence, and in spite of the seemingly authoritative fact that the author has endorsed it himself. The whole question of Meursault's "honesty" and the truth about his feelings should be replaced by an examination of the presuppositions of honesty and a very different kind of thinking about "feelings." For I want to argue that the character of Meursault is not to be located in the reflective realm of truth and falsity but exclusively in the prereflective realm of simple "seeing," "feeling," and "lived experience." On the basis of the phenomenological theories that circulated around Paris in the 1940s and with which Camus was surely familiar, I want to argue that Meursault neither lies nor tells the truth, because he never reaches that (meta-) level of consciousness where truth and falsity can be articulated. Moreover, he does not even have the feelings, much less feelings about his feelings, to which he is supposed to be so true.

Lived Experience as Prereflective Consciousness

If *The Stranger* has so often been defended as a celebration of pure and honest feelings, it has also been said that Meursault is "strange" because he has no feelings. This is certainly not true in one sense. He enjoys the warmth of the sun and Marie's company. He is annoyed—by the sun or by the fact that it's Sunday. What he lacks, and what shocks us, are appropriate emotions. He does not feel regret for his crime nor sorrow for his mother's death. He is confused when Marie asks him if he loves her, not because he is undecided, but because he does not understand the question. What Meursault does not do is make judgments, and judgments, I have argued elsewhere, are essential to emotions. As the narrator of the novel he factually describes, but he does not judge, the significance of his actions or the meaning of events. Nor does he even try to understand other people's feelings—or his own, for that matter. Accordingly, he does not reflect; he has few thoughts and is only minimally self-conscious. He cannot be true to his feelings, not only because he does not know what they are but also because, without judgments, he cannot even have them. His "true feelings," the feelings he actually has, are an emotionally emasculated and crippled version of normal human experience.

For those who construe Meursault as hero for the truth, his simple world of feelings must be treated as wholly autonomous, independent of reflection; his honesty is precisely the fact that he does not claim to be feeling anything more than what he actually feels. It is, in other words, as if the feelings were simply given and reflection merely commentary, a set of judgments about our feelings with which we, according to Camus, "simplify," and thereby lie about, life. In French phenomenology, which Camus knew well enough when he wrote *The Stranger*, this reflection-and-feeling duality was well summarized in Sartre's distinction between reflection and prereflective "lived experience" (*le vécu*), adapted from Heidegger's distinction between the "ontological" and the "ontic" and repeated by Merleau-Ponty. These distinctions provide the two-part structure of Camus' novel.

To state my interpretation baldly, Meursault is a philosophically fantastic character who, for the first part of the novel, is an ideal Sartrean prereflective consciousness, pure experience without reflection, always other than, but also nothing other than, what he is conscious of at the moment. He is a demonstration, even despite the author's intentions, of the poverty of consciousness, for it is only with judgments and reflection that the feelings we consider most human are possible. But then, in the second part of the novel, prison deprives him of his rich fund of continually engaging Mediterranean experiences, and then his trial robs him of his indifference to others' opinions of him, thereby forcing him to reflect on himself and providing him with such emotions as regret, guilt, and anger. The threat of immanent death finally forces him into a Heideggerian celebration of the "privilege of death" and the "happy death," which is a constant theme in Camus' novels (the last line of *The Plague*, the actual title of *La Mort heureuse*) but a clumsy paradox in his philosophical essays. In part II, Meursault begins to become a person, but only because he is condemned and scrutinized by other people and thus learns to reflect on his life and himself.

In his later writings, Camus employs the same duality. *The Myth of Sisyphus* explores the tenuous relation between experience (life) and the value of experience through reflection. Ultimately, Camus confusedly argues, it is only life that has value, but we can see the value of this value (in Nietzschean phrase) only by "keeping the absurd alive," that is, by reflectively accepting it. It is apparent that the "meta-value" becomes relevant only after reflection—one might add, inadequate reflection—has cheated the first of its value. Later, in *The Fall*, the delicate balance between experience and reflection is again destroyed by the absurd, and we meet Clamence, a character who is pure reflection and virtually indifferent to his experience; he barely tastes the gin he is always drinking, and he does not look at the painting he is hiding. He is only reflectively aware of its significance. Like Meursault at the end of *The Stranger*, Clamence refers to "the life which is no longer mine." This is the nightmare image of pure reflection. (Compare Kierkegaard, who often speaks of himself, because of his hyperreflectivity, as "one who has already died.") At the end of experience, there is only reflection on experience. "Experience," in this formulation, can only mean spontaneous and unreflective experience, and this—and this alone—is the meaning of life. This is Meursault's final realization, and consequently his only possible conception of an afterlife, as a literal reliving of this one (150).

So, in the first part of the book, Meursault does not reflect; he rarely even speaks. He does not think. Those sporadic occurrences where a thought does appear to him, like a weed that has surprisingly pushed its way through the concrete, only illustrate how unthinking he is; for example, "For some reason, I don't know what, I began thinking of mother" (50) and "Just in time, I remembered I killed a man" (78). This is not thinking, and certainly not reflecting. It is at most "having thoughts." But thinking and having thoughts are not opposed to feeling and having emotions. To the contrary, virtually all emotions (and many feelings), other than the most primitive, presuppose and often embrace thinking and thoughts, from schemes of revenge to raptures of love to replays of shame and embarrassment and the humiliating events that provoked them. Failure to reflect does not increase the power and intensity of emotion. Rather, it truncates and impoverishes emotion. So in order for Meursault to learn to have true feelings (emotions), he has to learn to reflect, to ask questions about himself, but first, to have some conception of himself apart from an abstract "I."

But there is a problem, alluded to earlier: Who is the narrator of part I, the abstract "I" who reports and describes Meursault's experiences? It cannot consistently be the same Meursault who is unreflectively experiencing. To "spell out" one's experiences, even by way of straight factual description, requires articulation and a certain degree of interpretation and comprehension. So it must be another Meursault, a reflective Meursault, a voice other than the subject of the experiences themselves. To be sure, the narrator has the special or "privileged" access to these experiences that is available only in the first person. Nevertheless it is arguably detached or one step removed from these experiences themselves. Philosophy, of course, abounds in such detached observational egos, from the *cogito* of Descartes to the "transcendental ego" of Kant and Husserl. It is this second Meursault who is the narrator, a necessarily reflective, even if not a particularly imaginative or philosophical, reporter. But notice that the report is not quite contemporaneous with the experience: even though the novel begins in the brutal present ("Aujourd'hui, Maman est morte"), it very soon (second paragraph) changes to the French present perfect tense and remains there. While the experiences are in ordinary temporal sequence, the reporting, occasionally, is not. On page 13, the narrator says, "But now I suspect that I was mistaken about this," and on page 70, "but probably I was mistaken about this." When are these implied reference points? When is the "now"? It can only be in the time interval of part II of the novel, in prison but (obviously) before the execution. On page 95 (in prison) the narrator reports, "It was then that the things I've never liked to talk about began."

If *The Stranger* were written from a third-person standpoint, Meursault would certainly not seem "strange," but he would certainly be a nondescript, most uninteresting character. It is from the first-person standpoint that Camus allows the Kantian or Husserlian ego to reveal the utter blandness of Meursault's prereflective consciousness as it matter-of-factly describes his world. Now, recalling Camus' warning, "Lying is not only saying what is not true. It is also saying and especially saying more than is true," this does not apply to the prereflective Meursault, who does not say enough to lie. But what of the reflective narrator? What is "true" for him would appear to be the flat, uninterpreted reporting of prereflective Meursault's experience, without addition or comment. But here we suspect that the entire first part of the book—however brilliant and sensitive—is a lie, for there can be no description of experience without conceptualization, interpretation, and some unavoidable, if minimal, commentary. Meursault of part I is an impossible character because he is both the reflective transcendental narrator and the unreflective bearer of experience. And if one finds just that same coupling in such luminary philosophers as Kant and Husserl, it was in the late 1930s and 1940s that this was starting to be rejected by philosophers in Europe (Sartre's *Transcendence of the Ego*, Wittgenstein's seminars at Cambridge, the circulation of Heidegger's work in France and Germany). When Maurice Merleau-Ponty pushed the question of whether distinctively *human* experience was possible without reflection and articulation, it started to become evident to philosophers that there was a real problem there. To be sure, animals have all sorts of experiences, without reflection and without being able to articulate those experiences, but for humans, the pure unreflective experience supposedly described as Meursault's is an impossibility.

Meursault is neither a hero nor an "antihero." He is more like the space from which the reader watches a world disclose itself. It is a simple world, without interpretation and without personality. Meursault is Sartre's nothingness of consciousness, John Barth's Jacob Horner (in *End of the Road*), but unlike Sartre or Horner, Meursault does not see himself as nothing, he simply is nothing; he does not see himself as anything at all. (It is impossible to be unhumorously grammatical in these matters.) Meursault might be described by others as "the man who . . . ," but he himself has no self-image until his trial, when he is for the first time forced to see himself as the "criminal." He says, "I too came under that description. Somehow it was an idea to which I could never get reconciled" (87). Compare Sartre describing the young Genet in "The Dizzying Word": "Someone has entered and is watching him. Beneath this gaze the child comes to himself. He who was not yet anyone suddenly becomes Jean Genet. . . . A voice declares publicly: 'You're a thief.' . . . It is revealed to him that he is a thief."[8] But Meursault is learning what it is to apply ascriptions to himself, to see himself as others see him in a social context. Early in the novel, in his flat, he says, "I glanced at the mirror and saw reflected in it the corner of my table" (30); like a vampire, he has no reflection, for reflections do not precede, but are consequent upon, concern with self-image. In prison, self-image becomes almost an obsession: he polishes his food tin to make a mirror, studies his face and his expression (101), does the same again later, and critically reflects upon his "seriousness."

Once, he hears his own voice, talking to himself. One can only imagine that to a person without self-consciousness, the sound of one's own thoughts might be understood only as the voice of another. In the mid-1960s, an enterprising psychologist named Julian Jaynes suggested that Socrates, before the latest stage in brain evolution, lacked self-consciousness in this integrative sense and therefore heard his own thoughts as the voices of others. Jaynes's evolutionary thesis may be outrageous, his brain theory may be science fiction, and his interpretation of Socrates is unbelievable, but he makes a good philosophical point about the ability to be conscious of oneself. It is a view that has been reiterated by many creative people—the poets Goethe and Hoerderlin, for example—in the personae of personal muses and "daemons" and the like. To actually speak from the first-person standpoint, as Meursault's narrator seems to do, is not the same as to *be* that person. The convolutions here are considerable, and I will save them until a much later chapter (on Sartre, who worries about such matters in depth). But the point, again, is that *The Stranger* is a novel narrated by a narrator who is not simply identical with the protagonist whose experiences he is reporting. There is a curious split between self and subject that would, a few decades later, be exploited to the full by some of the bolder poststructuralist thinkers.[9]

It is not as if Meursault has been deprived by his author of a single superfluous dimension of human existence. One might even argue that he has been deprived of *human* existence altogether. On this point, the pompous prosecutor is right, though we might too easily dismiss what he says because of his overloaded references to Meursault's "shameful orgies" (i.e., sleeping with Marie and watching a Fernandel film) and Meursault's being virtually guilty of parricide (the case to follow, for his lack of visible mourning for his mother). The prosecutor says that he looked into Meursault's "soul" and "found a blank, literally nothing," "nothing human," "not one of those moral qualities," and "devoid of the least spark of human feeling" (127, 129). From the first-person point of view, we quite naturally empathize with Meursault. (Indeed, that's what empathy is, sharing one's point of view.) Indeed, from the first-person point of view, we even empathize with Sartre's scoundrel narrator, Roquentin. But more "objectively," that is to say, from another point of view, we can appreciate that the prosecutor is in fact correct. Meursault is a blank, he is amoral, and he is without the feelings that make most of us human.

Meursault the character is a piece of flat, colorless glass, allowing us to sense the warmth of the sun and smell the brine on the pillow, to crave a cigarette or a cup of coffee, and to conjure up a vision of thin-haired, hunched-up, skin-blotched Salamano dragging his mulelike mangy dog. At the turning point of the novel, on the beach, we can feel the flash of light reflected from the blade of a knife "sear our eyelashes and gouge our eyeballs." We can imagine a having a curiously indifferent perception, in the midst of a life-and-death confrontation, of "a black speck on the sea that might be a ship." We can imagine being in bed with Marie and recognize the sea smell wafting from her hair. But we get no feeling for the *significance* of anything, not even enjoyment or disgust or fear. And it is judgments of significance that make most feelings possible. Meursault has no expectations, no desires other than his immediate needs and urges, no sense of responsibility and so no sense of guilt or regret, no ability to make moral judgments—and so he feels neither disgust nor alarm at the sight of cruelty or danger. He has no conception of either commitment or fidelity, so such notions as love, marriage, and honesty have no meaning to him. He has no ambition, no dissatisfactions. (Even in prison he says, "I have everything I want.") He can feel vexation or annoyance, an immediate feeling of malcontent, but not regret or even sorrow, which require a view of oneself and the past for which one is responsible. He can feel desire but not love; he feels fondness for his mother but not grief; he has thoughts but does not think; he exists but does not think of himself as existing. That is what makes him so strange, even to us as we read and identify with him.

Meursault in Love: Rationality, Emotions, and Empathy

Meursault lacks that human dimension that the Greeks had identified as "rationality" and that modern philosophy, since Descartes, has pinpointed in self-consciousness and reflection. For Meursault, there is no "I think," and there is not even an "I am"; he simply is. But without self-consciousness, Meursault also lacks emotions and, in an important sense, does not acknowledge other people because he cannot really empathize with them. Nor does he know his own feelings. Edmund Husserl, who best defined the phenomenological ideal of "pure description," was far more concerned with the analysis of knowledge and in particular formal (mathematical) knowledge than with the analysis of feeling, but when his reflective techniques are turned on the more "subjective" aspects of the soul, the consequences may be bizarre. Unlike the objects of knowledge and the eternal objects of mathematics, feelings, when examined, vanish like phantoms and pop like bubbles of froth. One of Husserl's best students, Max Scheler, wrote extensively on the phenomenology of feelings and emotions and about empathy (sympathy) as well, but he also made it clear that human feelings require reflection as well. And in Sartre's early analysis of the emotions (1938) and in his phenomenological works, *Transcendence of the Ego* and *Being and Nothingness*, he scrutinizes the "given-ness" of feelings and also watches them disappear like so many everyday illusions. Emotions, he tells us, are "magical transformations of the world." They are not primitive phenomenological givens but involve meanings, reflections, and interpretations. There are no emotions "in themselves," colorful bubbles adrift in the stream of consciousness to be simply felt and observed. Emotions—"feelings" in the grander sense—are reflections of a self-conscious subject on his or her position in the world. Accordingly, Meursault, who is not self-conscious, can have no such feelings, no emotions, and no reflections on his emotions.

It has always seemed curious to me that the standard interpretation of Meursault as a man faithful to his feelings should persist in the face of the embarrassing fact that, throughout part I of the novel, Meursault never has any significant feelings (that is, emotions), even where it seems obvious to us that he ought to feel something. There are blanks and gaps in the narration where emotions or feelings ought to be in the same way that there is an abyss where Meursault's "soul" ought to be. He is not disgusted by Salamano's treatment of his dog nor by Raymond's cruelty to the Arab woman; he is not frightened by the knife-wielding Arab nor moved by his mother's death nor by Marie, for whom his only "passion" appears to be the immediacy of sexual desire. Although there is at least one explicit instance of shared enjoyment, Meursault typically treats Marie as a source of sensations. Any hint of personality on her part appears to Meursault merely as a stimulus ("When she laughs I always want to kiss her" [44]). He shows no sign of jealousy when he sees Raymond flirting with her, and he is at most "curious" when Marie "has other plans for the evening." He never thinks of Marie when she is not with him until he is in prison—that is, when his thoughts are rather aimed at "some woman or other"—but even those primitive sexual desires apparently are satisfied by his "doing like the others."

In a rightfully famous and startling passage, Marie asks Meursault if he loves her. "I said that sort of question had no meaning, really: but I supposed I didn't" (44). (It is not clear whether the second phrase occurs in the conversation, that is, whether it is part of what he actually said, a thought occurring to Meursault at the time, or a reflective commentary.) When Raymond asks Meursault if he would like to be "pals," he responds with similar indifference. With love and friendship, as with his mother's death, "nothing in my life has changed." One would not expect Meursault to be an interesting lover, but we can see that he could not be a *lover* at all. It is not a matter of his not loving Marie in particular or a question of his not "saying more than is true." Meursault has no *concept* of love (or of friendship or family). If "love" would mean anything to him, it would have to be a sensation, something like the pleasure he feels from the warmth of Marie's body or the smell she leaves behind her. But love, as Camus must have been aware—if not from his own experience or from Sartre or at least from his early idol André Gide—is not simply a feeling but a system of judgments, meanings, expectations, intentions, regrets, reflections, fears, obsessions, needs and desires, abstract demands, and metaphysical longings. Of course there may also be pleasurable sensuous contact and feelings of animal warmth and comfort, but these are—however desirable—less essential than the more judgmental components of love, which necessarily involve conceptions of oneself with another person that Meursault simply does not have.

In *The Myth of Sisyphus*, Camus comments, "But of love I know only that mixture of desire, affection, and intelligence that binds me to this or that creature. That compound is not the same for another person. I do not have the right to cover all these experiences with the same name. But Camus the philosopher here makes the same error that he builds into his unreflective creation; love is not simply an experience or a set of experiences, however complex. It has a necessary dimension that one might call "commitment," not in any legal or moral sense, but in that series of demands, memories, intentions, expectations, and abstractions that add up to a relationship. And a relationship, unlike a feeling, cannot be simply "for the moment." (Consider the desperate ploy "Will you love me forever even if just for this weekend?") Meursault, who understands only his sensuous feelings, can have no concept of love that is not a sensuous feeling; nor can he understand friendship or the love of a son for his distant or deceased mother. One can have feelings for one's mother, to be sure. (They are usually very complex, according to Dr. Freud.) But one does not just have feelings. One has a from-birth attachment with all of the dependencies, duties, affections, and obligations that, recognized or not, accepted or not, such a relationship carries with it. One can claim indifference, but it is only in pathological cases that we have any reason to believe this. One can self-righteously insist that "no one has the right to cover all these experiences with the same name," as Nietzsche, too, suggests in *Zarathustra*. But we can rightly shrug at this bit of New Age intellectual sophistry. Love is not just a feeling, but neither is it unique and unnamable in every instance.

Since Meursault has no sense of commitment, we would expect that he would have an equally uncomprehending view of love's institutional variant, marriage:

> Marie came that evening and asked me if I'd marry her. I said I didn't mind; if she was keen on it, we'd get married. . . . I explained that it had no importance really, but if it would give her pleasure, we could get married right away. I pointed out that, anyhow, the suggestion came from her; as for me, I'd merely said, "Yes." Then she remarked that marriage was a serious matter. To which I answered, "No." She kept silent after that, staring at me in a curious way. Then she wondered whether she loved me or not. I, of course, couldn't enlighten her on that. (53)

For Meursault (and, one sometimes suspects, for Camus), only spontaneous experience ("life") is meaningful. But paradoxically, Meursault, who has only such experiences, can find no meaning in his experience. He cannot know love or friendship, nor grief for his mother nor regret for his crime. Experience and emotion are processes over time, not momentary episodes. Meursault is, as he tells us, all "too absorbed in the present or immediate future." He has no expectations, and consequently no fears or disappointments. In short, he has no feelings of consequence (and little conception of consequences). Unlike Roquentin, in Sartre's *Nausea*, he has no concept of an "adventure"; much less does he or could he have any. He has no feelings, only sensations, no emotions: only urges and preferences, like a cat or even a sensitive plant, but not like a rational, intelligent human being. It is entertaining to find commentators struggling to identify the "feelings" to which this "honest" man can be faithful. It is at least peculiar to call a man "honest" because he allows himself to enjoy the sun and the sea, the warmth of a woman's body, and café au lait, or because he doesn't go to a brothel on account of "not feeling like it," and if he refuses to call the cops because he "doesn't like police."

When Camus later praises his character for "refusing to simplify life," he seems to be thinking that the systematic interpretation of the innumerable feelings and judgments that compose our notions of "love" or "grief" or "anger" is "simplification." The underlying Faulknerian metaphor appears to be that feelings are incoherent collections of concrete flotsam in a Mississippi flood of consciousness. Consciousness and feelings are complex, but names ("love," "sadness," "anger") are simple. But it is unconceptualized consciousness, not our systematization of it, that is simple. Or rather, empty. (Kant: "Concepts without intuitions are empty: intuitions without concepts are blind.") And Meursault is as effective an illustration of that point as Hegel's labyrinthine arguments to the same end in the first famous chapter in the *Phenomenology of Spirit*.[10] Meursault's consciousness betrays an inability to go beyond the vacuous, while Camus seems to see it as fidelity to the complex. Human feeling and human experience come hand in hand with reflection. Of course, feeling and experience can be suffocated by an excess of reflection and overintellectualization, as in Dostoevsky's pathetic, hyperconscious Underground Man. But Camus' antireflective reaction is, as Kant said in the days before exhaust-fume—induced air pollution, like trying to avoid breathing impure air by not breathing at all.

O'Brien, agreeing with this part of Camus' interpretation, suggests that Meursault will not lie about his own feelings: "Neither to give pleasure to others or to gain pleasure himself ... will he pretend that he feels something that he does not feel." But the notion of "pretending" here, like its complementary notion of sincerity, is curiously out of place. When Meursault, who has already agreed to marry Marie, will not say that he loves her, that is not a matter of refusing to pretend but an inexplicable refusal to understand not only the word "love," but also a human relationship. To pretend, one must have some conception of what one actually does feel as opposed to what one feigns to feel. In the flourish of Anglo—American concern with "pretending" (J. L. Austin et al.[11]) and French concern with "sincerity" (the difference of interests may be of some cultural interest besides), a point jointly driven home by, among others, the curious troika of Austin, Gide, and Sartre, is that pretending to feel and feeling (where the feeling at stake is not a mere sensation) are not distinct and in many cases are identical. But this is because feelings are interpretations born in action, not the brute sensations that Camus uses as his paradigm. It is true that Meursault does not pretend to feel what he does not feel. But this no more makes him sincere than his awkward silence makes him honest. (Compare again John Barth in *The End of the Road*: "She had looked deeply into herself and found nothing. For such a person, the notion of sincerity makes little sense.")

One might hypothesize, in good philosophical tradition, that Meursault could not possibly sense feelings in others if he cannot comprehend them in himself. Quite right, but the logic of the argument—at least since Wittgenstein and Sartre—might better be reversed: It is only with an apprehension of feelings in others that one can have an apprehension of one's own feelings. And if understanding feelings is a necessary condition for having feelings, one can argue that unless one apprehends feelings in others, one cannot have them oneself. And so, too, for Meursault. His "indifference" to other people and his indifference in general are two aspects of the same impossible opacity: his inability to interpret, his unwillingness to judge, his consequent lack of emotion, and with this an inability to "say more than he feels" since he has no clue what he *ought* to feel in the various situations in which Camus places him.

Because Meursault lacks empathy (sympathy), people do not exist for him. He only "observes" other people, as he once suspected that some Arabs viewed him, "like blocks of stone or dead trees"—not without interest, but without compassion. At the vigil for his mother, Meursault watches the old people soundlessly usher themselves around the coffin: "Never in my life had I seen anyone so clearly as I saw these people; not a detail of their clothes or features escaped me. And yet I couldn't hear them, and it was hard to believe they really existed" (10). And then, insightfully but naively, he thinks "for a moment I had the absurd impression that they had come to sit in judgment of me" (11). But insofar as they are all "details of clothes and features," it is "absurd" to think that they can judge him. But, of course, they are judging him. Meursault sees that the old people cry, but he does not see them grieve. He sees Marie pout at his responses to her, but he does not see that she is hurt. He hears Raymond's girlfriend scream, but he does not see her pain. He sees Raymond bleed, but he does not sense his pain or his anger. The Arab whom Meursault shoots evidently feels or expresses nothing whatever, if we read only Meursault's (narrator's) description of the scene. They are all "little robots," like the woman seated opposite him in Celeste's restaurant. Meursault does not feel anything for them, and so he does not feel anything himself.

The Turning Point: Is This
the Phenomenology of a Murder?

It is the central plot device of the novel that Meursault murders a man. But what I have said in detail about feelings applies as well to the concept of "action." One can try—and occasionally succeed—in describing an action as a set of physical movements. But something is irretrievably lost in such a description: the concept of agency, and consequently the concept of action itself. But the breach between movement and action is again not "given" to experience, but is a matter of interpretation. Meursault has no feelings because he will only "feel" but not interpret. He is not aware of other people as people because he sees them as "details of clothes and features." Similarly, he is not aware of actions—including his own actions—because he will not interpret them as actions.

There is surprisingly little action in *The Stranger*. Much is implied, much is suggested: the violent racial hatred that pervades the society, Raymond's cruel treatment of his women. And then there is what Meursault does: he kills a man. But Meursault's crime is only barely an action, and as described it is not an action at all. In the brilliant description of that scene, Meursault is aware of the heat, the sun, the sea, a black speck that might be a ship, the wind, and the "keen blade of light flashing up from the knife scarring my eyelashes and gouging into my eyeballs" (75). He is aware of his bodily sensations; "everything reeled before me" and "all my being tensed" (or, in the more lyrical version, "every nerve in my body was like a steel spring"). But this is mechanical tension, not fear or anticipation. Then there is what we (and later the court) interpret as "the killing." But all we are told is "The trigger gave, and the smooth underbelly of the butt jogged my palm" (76). That is all. Not the slightest indication of his *doing* anything. He appears as much a Newtonian victim of the reaction of the revolver as the unnamed Arab is a victim of the action of the bullet. The whole event is impersonal, like an accident that happened to him, a mere "it" to be followed by another "it." "And so, with that crisp, whip crack sound, it all began" (76).

It is only then that Meursault performs any action at all, as an afterthought, as a reaction to what has already happened; "I shook off my sweat." And then, "I fired four shots more into the inert body" (76). He is unable to explain, either to the magistrate or to himself, why he fired those four extra shots. But the mystery that is not broached in the trial—or in Meursault's reflections—is not only why but even *whether* he fired the first shot and whether *he* committed a murder at all.

Killing Time: Meursault Grows
a Self through Reflection

The movement from part I to part II of *The Stranger* is a movement from innocence to guilty awareness, but not only in the "Christian" sense that has so often been pointed out. It is a movement from pure unreflective experience to reflection and philosophy. It is the second part of the book that carries us into the realm of *The Myth of Sisyphus*. It is not in his prereflective "indifference" or "honesty," but in his reflections before death, that Meursault becomes a semblance of the "absurd hero," like Sisyphus, whose tragedy and whose salvation lie in the fact that he is or, rather becomes, "conscious," that is, reflective, judgmental, morally aware, and fully self-conscious.

In the early stages of the indictment and interrogation, Meursault regards his case as "quite simple" (77). He is just beginning to characterize himself, to give himself an "essence" on the basis of his past and the "facts" about him, as Sartre would say. It is not his case but his reflections that are still "simple." As he learns to reflect on himself, his actions, and his past, he loses his former spontaneity; for example, at the prosecutor's office: "When leaving, I very nearly held out my hand and said 'Goodbye': just in time I remembered that I'd killed a man" (78). In part I, Meursault anonymously observes the little "robot woman" in the restaurant; in part II, at the trial, he notices only that she is looking at him. To reflect is to "see yourself," and to "see yourself" is to recognize that you are vulnerable to the look of others. In court, Meursault learns of the existence of other people, not as "details of features and clothing" but as his judges: "It was then that I noticed a row of faces opposite me. These people were staring hard at me, and I guessed they were the jury. But somehow I didn't see them as individuals. I felt as you do just after boarding a streetcar; and you're conscious of all the people on the opposite seat staring at you in the hope of finding something in your appearance to amuse them" (103).

Meursault develops an ego, a bit of French vanity. At first he is delighted at the attention he is receiving. Later he feels left out of the camaraderie of the courtroom, "de trop," "a gate crasher" (105), "excluded" (130). But finally, the looks take their effect: the prosecutor's "tone and the look of triumph on his face, as he glanced at me, were so marked that I felt as I hadn't felt in ages. I had a foolish desire to burst into tears. For the first time, I'd realized how all these people loathed me" (112); and then, "For the first time I understood that I was guilty" (112). "Guilt" here is not a premonition of the verdict, any more than the desire to burst into tears is a reaction of shame or fear. Nor is the sense of guilt here a feeling of guilt. This is, rather, a far more metaphysical claim: the loss of innocence, not for a particular crime and not before a particular human tribunal, but that loss of innocence that comes from being judged and recognizing oneself as vulnerable to being judged by anyone or anything.

It is Sartre's "look" (*le regard*) through which we become brutally aware of others. It is this "look," bursting upon Meursault's life as an unexpected and unwanted trauma, that is the foundation of Clamence's experience in *The Fall*. For him, after a lifetime of judgment (and freedom from judgment) in the French judicial system, the reality of other people's judgments, even the implied judgment in a sourceless laugh in the street or a merely possible judgment made by no one is sufficient to collapse the delicate structure of his unreflective if nevertheless sophisticated innocence. Meursault's guilt is Clamence's guilt, "Christian" guilt in the sense that mere awareness of oneself is in itself sufficient cause for condemnation. The device of the Kafkaesque trial, on this interpretation, is to force Meursault to reflect on his life, not to try him for murder. This is why the focus of the trial is not a plea of self-defense, which would have been reasonable and convincing (against an Arab with a knife who had already stabbed a friend, in a country exploding with anticolonial resentment and racial hatred). O'Brien (in his *Camus*) has made this political point most forcefully:

> In practice, French justice in Algeria would almost certainly not have condemned a European to death for shooting an Arab who had drawn a knife on him and who had shortly before stabbed another European. And most certainly Meursault's defense counsel would have made his central plea that of self-defense, turning on the frightening picture of the Arab with a knife. There is no reference to the use of any such defense or even to the bare possibility of an appeal to European solidarity in a case of this kind. This is as unreal as to suppose that in an American court, where a white man was charged with killing a black man who had pulled a knife, defense counsel would not evoke, or the court be moved by, white fear of blacks.[12]

Accordingly, it is artistically and philosophically (even if not legally) appropriate that Meursault is tried for not weeping for his mother, for his friendship with a pimp, for his "liaison" with a woman. In each case, he is forced to see for the first time what his unthinking habits and relations appear to be "from the outside" (e.g., "he kept referring to 'the prisoner's mistress,' whereas for me she was just 'Marie' " [125]). It is true that the trial is a political mockery, but its purpose is not to demonstrate some perverse injustice or to make a victim out of "innocent" Meursault. The trial of Meursault's uneventful life is a mirror, it is not a statement about justice or the lack of it. With reflection, Meursault begins to talk about his feelings, and his lack of feelings. Ironically, it is only at this point that he finally has feelings. At first they are simple feelings—boredom, vexation, hope (89), then annoyance and frustration (95), and finally, full-blown anger (151ff.). He begins to understand desire. In part I, all that he would want, he has. It is only with deprivation that he learns what it is to desire. When Marie visits him in prison, he still says he has everything that he wants (91). This is not a lie on his part, but a symptom of his still undeveloped ability to reflect, and consequently to want. A bit later, he realizes that he cannot smoke in prison. (We were hardly aware that he did smoke in part I.) At first he suffers faintness and nausea. Then he comes to understand that "this is part of my punishment . . . but by the time I understood, I'd lost the craving, so it had ceased to be a punishment" (97). Desire, as opposed to mere urges, requires imagination. Urges can be thwarted, but desires can be prolonged, delayed, made the basis of plans and schemes, creating long-term aims and goals. Desires, as opposed to urges, can be *rational*. Thus desire travels best in the company of reflection. Dumb urges, like the urge to smoke, are irrational not just because smoking is bad for you but also because it requires no intelligence at all. The only reflection is rationalization, about why one would give in to such a dumb desire.

It is with desire and its frustration that Meursault begins to be a philosopher. At first he is "hardly conscious of being in prison" (89), but he soon finds himself facing the breach between the concrete if vacuous reality of his former existence and the abstract but rich possibilities of thought. At first it is simple daydreaming, "my habit of thinking like a free man" (95), but soon imagination begins to take the place of lived experience, and imagination, as we know from Descartes, Kant, and of course from Sartre, is the beginning of all philosophical reflection. At first, Meursault's philosophy is imitative and adolescent, at best: "One of mother's pet ideas . . . in the long run one gets used to anything" (96). It is with his increasing frustration that his philosophy matures. In the half-humorous dialogue with his jailer, Meursault learns about freedom, which he has now lost. It is with the sudden deprivation of his everyday routines (Heidegger's "hurly-burly of everyday life," or the "wake, meal, streetcar, work, meal, work, streetcar, meal, Monday, Tuesday" of Camus' "Absurd Reasoning" [*Myth*, 10]) that reflection sets in. It is with the loss of the freedom that Meursault never knew he had that the "Why?" of philosophy begins. It is only with the frustration of his desires that he begins to ask what is worth desiring. It is only with the lack of life's routine that life becomes a problem ("how to kill time" [98]). It is only with his new void of experience and feeling that reflection, and with it genuine emotion, becomes possible.

To avoid frustration and boredom, Meursault invents a routine, a purely reflective routine. He practices remembering the contents of his room at home. And it is at this point that the most dramatic philosophical turn of the book occurs: "So I learned that even after a single day's experience of the outside world a man could easily live a hundred years in prison" (98). Here is the final twist: Reflection no longer serves experience, but experience serves reflection. One lives in order to be able to reflect, and now "life" is over ("A life which was mine no longer" [132]). Accordingly, Meursault's only conception of an afterlife is "a life in which I can remember this life on earth" (150). With the loss of freedom and the loss of "life" in this peculiar sense, Meursault can, like Sartre's damned trio in *No Exit*, review his life in its entirety. Like Clamence in his own "Hell" in an Amsterdam bar, he can pass judgment upon it. The fact that he is also condemned to death by the court becomes almost incidental, a vehicle to ensure that his reflections are not contaminated by hope, that his judgment is not affected by the possibility of "living" once again. Meursault's gain of self-consciousness is at the same time a transcending of self. Once he begins to reflect on life, it is not simply his life. It is life itself. And it is not his execution but the idea of execution that puzzles him. (Compare Camus' later "Reflections on the Guillotine," and the arguments that get repeated in *The Plague*.) And it is not his death that torments him, but the very idea of death itself.

The Emotional Climax: Raging against the God Machine

The climax of *The Stranger* is emotional, not just in the sense that it might well arouse sympathetic emotion in the reader, but in that it actually consists of a single, dramatic burst of emotion. The emotion is anger, or perhaps we should say rage, for it is very much beyond Meursault's control and comprehension ("Then, I don't know how it was, but something seemed to break inside me"). The provocation is the unannounced visit from the prison chaplain, just when Meursault has learned to accept his fate, or so he says. The priest disrupts his revelry, and then starts badgering him with a both too solicitous, then too aggressive, plea for Meursault's acceptance of a very different kind of fate. At first, Meursault is of the same mind that we have always expected from him, namely, that whether or not he believed (or was sure that he did not believe) was "a question of no importance" (145). What the chaplain had to say "didn't interest me at all" (146). But Meursault gets increasingly bored and irritated, and when the priest starts talking about sin and the afterlife, asking Meursault, "Do you really love these earthly things so very much?" the father starts to become truly "irksome." He asks Meursault if he has wished there was an afterlife, and this is where Meursault "fairly bawls at him" that his conception of an afterlife is just another life in which he can remember his life on earth (150).

It is now evident that Meursault's irritation and anger are rising, and it is then, he tells us, that something seems to "break" inside of him. He starts yelling at the top of his voice. He hurls insults at the priest. He enjoys "an ecstasy of joy and rage." He "pours out on him all the thoughts that had been simmering in my brain." He declares that he'd been right in how he had lived and he literally shouts out what is surely his longest (if not the only) speech in the entire book, aimed at the poor priest whom Meursault held "in his grip." The father leaves with tears in his eyes. As soon as he has gone, Meursault calms down, exhausted. He concludes only when he had been shouting so much that he'd lost his breath. It is in retrospect (a very short time later) that he reports that "that great rush of anger had washed me clean, emptied me of hope" (154).

Such powerful emotions are rare and dramatic enough in us ordinary folks. Most of our emotions are continuations of emotional trends and dispositions that we have nurtured over time, even a lifetime, and they are constrained by the context and our awareness of the "display rules" of our culture and the situation. But here is a man who has never had a real emotion, first of all because he has never had a real self, and second because he has never really cared about anything. If one doesn't care about anything, there is nothing to get angry about. But suddenly, Meursault discovers that there is something he cares deeply about, and that is life itself, the life he has lived (and is barely living still). It is the chaplain's questioning and implicit dismissal of that life that sends Meursault off on his rage. His alternative vision of an afterlife is itself an expression of his newly awakened passion for life. His anger is not against the priest but against the incomprehensible fact that his life is about to be taken from him. The promise of an afterlife, even if he could believe in it, is no salvation and no compensation. There is this life, and no other. Thus all of the chaplain's certainties were not worth "even a single strand of a woman's hair" (151).

Where one's whole existence hangs in the balance, there are no merely continuing passions, and there may be no constraints. Meursault has never before had a passion, because he has never felt himself to be engaged in life. He was engaged—one might say immersed—but that is different from being reflectively engaged in life and realizing that it can come to an end, that it is fragile. One of my students suggested that an explosion of rage is usually due to long accumulated and repressed emotion suddenly released, but I see no evidence of any such repressed passion in *The Stranger*. His anger is a burst of brand-new passion, and if it "washes him clean" I do not see that this is an expression of catharsis in Freud's dramatic sense. The cleanliness is the clarity that comes with insight, the confidence that Meursault expresses about his love of life, his love of life however he has lived it. And the cleansing agent is not so much the passion as the reflection that goes with it, that gives it structure and insight. The "ecstasy of joy and rage" is not unfamiliar to those of us who have on occasion enjoyed a true bout of unconstrained fury, not aimed at a particular person and not, needless to say, in the face of dire consequences, but a fury about the weirdness of life itself, the "primal scream" that expresses our most basic frustrations and disappointments.

Despite its reputation as a "negative" emotion (not to mention a "deadly" sin), anger can be a very positive and exhilarating emotion. (The cartoon philosopher Ren the Chihuahua says, "I love to get angry. It feels so good.") But it is not an emotion that just emerges in the unreflective situations of everyday life. True anger is not just seeing the world as offensive or frustrating. It is also the reflective endorsement of the feeling that the world is offensive or frustrating. For Meursault, as for all of us, it is emotion and reflection, not emotion and innocence, that go hand in hand. Reflection cannot be so cold and deliberate if it can climax in "a great rush of anger" and "wash a man clean."

Meursault Faces Being-unto-Death, Alone and with Everyone

In reflection, Meursault becomes, as Sartre once said of Camus, a "Cartesian of the absurd." In part I, Meursault had commented to his employer that "one life is as good as another" (52). Now, more philosophically, he argues, "I'd been right. I was still right, I was always right. I'd passed my life in a certain way, and I might have passed it in a different way, if I'd felt like it. I'd acted thus, and I hadn't acted otherwise. I hadn't done this, whereas I'd done that. And what did that mean? That, all the time, I'd been waiting for this present moment, for that dawn, tomorrow's or another day's, which was to justify me. Nothing, nothing had the least importance" (152). This curious notion of death as "justification" is as close to Heidegger's early philosophy as it is to Camus' own *Myth*. "What difference could they make to me, the deaths of others, or a mother's love, or his God, or the way a man chooses to live, the fate he thinks he chooses, since one and the same fate was bound to 'choose' not only me but billions of privileged people who, like him, called themselves my brother.... Every man alive was privileged; there was only one class of man, the privileged class. All alike would be condemned to die one day" (152).

Here is Heidegger's "Being-unto Death" with a vengeance, overwhelming all questions of value and worth. It is "that dark wind blowing from the future" that fogs over all ethics and chills all vanities. That one "brutal certitude" undermines Kierkegaardian "leaps" and Sartrean "projects." Here is a peculiar inversion of the central theme of the *Myth*, "whether life is or is not worth living." Death is the end (not just the termination, but the goal) of life: "Whether I died now or forty years hence, this business of dying had to be got through, inevitably" (143). In the shadow of death, Meursault's reflections tend toward, but inevitably fall short of, the suicidal conclusion that Camus attacks in *The Myth of Sisyphus*: "It is common knowledge that life isn't worth living anyhow" (142). For Meursault, the meaning of life resides only in the spontaneous and momentary lived experiences of part I. In part II, Meursault learns that his lost immediacies, the sun and sand, the smell of brine and Marie's hair, the taste of café au lait, were valuable in themselves ("I'd been right..."). To the chaplain, Meursault insists that all his certainties were not worth even a single strand of a woman's hair. The value of reflection, in its turn, is just this understanding, reflected in Meursault's conception of an afterlife as a life merely repeated. (Camus owes an obvious debt to Nietzsche here, for the concept of the "eternal recurrence.")

In other words, Meursault perversely sees that, on reflection, it can be seen that reflection is worthless. It is here that Meursault is more persuasive than his philosophical creator, for he has no pretensions of creating a second value—over and above "life"—in the very reflection within which life can be seen to be without value. Life is not of value for anything, yet it is worth living for itself. But Camus, not Meursault, adds another value, "keeping the absurd alive," "a matter of living in the state of the absurd" (*Myth*, 30). Because Meursault is condemned to death, he will not be in a position to live in defiance and revolt. For Camus, the loss of prereflective innocence appears to be as terrible as a sentence of death, and one should well react with rage. For Sisyphus and Clamence and, one might argue, for Camus himself, reflective defiance soon turns to scorn and resentment. It is deeply instructive that this is not Meursault's final reaction at all. Instead, the anger serves a higher end, as reflection climaxes in his great rush of anger, which washes him clean, empties him of hope.

It is in the impassioned hopelessness of reflection, just before his execution, that Meursault faces "the absurd" as a final revelation: "Gazing up at the dark sky spangled with its signs and stars, for the first time, I laid my heart open to the benign indifference of the universe [*la tendre indifférence du monde*]. To feel it so like myself, indeed, so brotherly, made me realize that I'd been happy, and that I was happy still" (154). How different is Meursault's "benign indifference of the universe" from Camus' "revolt of the flesh," and how different Meursault's acceptance of it from Sisyphus' scorn and struggle and Clamence's vicious bitterness. For Meursault, there is no "mind and world straining against each other," but a recognition of identity and brotherliness. The universe itself, like the innocent Meursault, is unreflectively "indifferent."

One might argue, perhaps, that this claim to innocence, as soon as Meursault himself states it, becomes self-refuting. Insisting that one is innocent, in this sense, is "one thought too many," in the words of Bernard Williams. Innocence by its very nature does not know itself as innocence. But the point, I would argue, is reflective life affirmation. This supplements— it does not undermine—the unreflective (and therefore uncelebrated) love of life that Meursault has displayed throughout the novel. Indeed, Meursault is perhaps the only character of Camus' creation, including the author himself, who knows the "happy death" that is his constant theme. "With death so near, Mother must have felt like someone on the brink of freedom, ready to start life all over again. . . . And I, too, felt ready to start life all over again" (154). But this invocation of rebirth, as opposed to Meursault's fanciful invocation of the eternal recurrence (in response to the prison chaplain's eternal vision) is unintelligible except, perhaps, as another reference to the cleansing his rage had afforded him. It is not as if Meursault has suddenly gotten religion, much less a belief in reincarnation. But Meursault, who has always been blissfully naive as he pursued his life, has become philosophically appreciative of what he is now about to lose.

But there is a shocking surprise to come just at the end of the novel. Giving up any hope of a reprieve, much less a rebirth, Meursault concludes, "All that remained to hope was that on the day of my execution there should be a huge crowd of spectators and that they should greet me with howls of execration" [*cris de haine*] (154). What in the world are we to make of this? I have struggled with it for decades, and, with the prodding of my excellent student David Sherman, I cannot seem to get away from the view that Meursault ends up in "bad faith."[13] Having learned by way of the trial to be self-conscious via the judgment and recognition of others, and thus having learned to see himself as *something*—namely, a remorseless criminal—he can see his way to a final recognition of himself only by way of the hatred, the "howls of execration," from the crowd at his execution. In Sartrean terms, he has not found his way to the autonomy and rebellion of turning against his accusers and insisting on his own conception of "being-for-itself" as opposed to the "being-for-others" imposed by the crowd.

Throughout part II, Meursault's development of a self has at the same time been a development of a sense of guilt, legal guilt, to be sure, but also his sense of moral guilt, at least to the point where he now recognizes what that is or would be. But part of our bewilderment in this novel and concerning this character is the fact that he seems to emerge without guilt. Meursault seems to salvage a strange sense of innocence out of the guilt of his crime. One might guess that this is just the not unusual reaction of condemned prisoners to their impending executions: to ignore their guilt and self-deceptively proclaim their innocence just in dread of what is to come. Some, of course, are condemned because of their remorselessness— precisely the accusation made against Meursault by the obnoxious prosecutor. But there is something else going on here, a kind of "transcendence," to use a dangerous word, in which Meursault sees his way through the details of life to a larger, clearly philosophical picture, one without God or Heaven or salvation or another life to live. I would now suggest that it is this glimmer of what Hegel and Nietzsche might call "naturalized" or "this-worldly" spirituality, even in the face of utter humiliation and death, that inspires and bewilders us.

2

CAMUS' *MYTH OF SISYPHUS*
AND THE MEANING OF LIFE

I have always found Camus' youthful essay *The Myth of Sisyphus* to be alternatively profound and whimsical, a puckish expression of despair. When I first composed this response (at about the same age as Camus was when he wrote *Myth*), I tried to approximate the same dark but playful spirit. Since then, after thirty-five years of teaching and thinking about the book, I have not found a more appropriate sort of rejoinder. The very idea of treating the essay analytically is—absurd.

—R.C.S.

"Life is absurd."

"No, it is not."

But our retort is unconvincing. It lacks intellectual conviction. Once raised, the complaint that "life is absurd" seems to be supported by the whole of human reason. Just look at the grotesque amount of injustice in the world and the delusional incompetents who are running some of the world's great powers. Consider the many good people who suffer without reason and the thousands of children who die every day. Many people turn to religion, but religion doesn't deny the absurdity of life. Quite the contrary, most religions affirm it and use that to sell their particular version of hope and rationalization. And contemporary philosophy surely doesn't help us out here. Analytic philosophers scoff at the very question of the meaning of life as meaningless. Existentialists take "the Absurd" as a mantra, beginning with Kierkegaard, Camus most famously. Sartre is well known for his bleak view that "man is a useless passion." And one shudders to think what response one would get from most of the postmodernists.

Indeed, the absence of values in "a world of facts" continues to block not only the idea that life is meaningful but also the reality of ideals and values of all kinds. If there are only facts, then the universe is "indifferent" to our needs and hopes. Our logic stays stuck on Hume's insistence that there is no deriving an "ought" from an "is," and therefore there is no rational justification for values. And beyond all logic, there is that ultimate personal offense: we are all going to die, and our projects, our good deeds, and our reputations will die with us, or soon after. All of our efforts, no matter how noble, come to naught. From the point of view of the universe, from an "objective" point of view, who cares? Life is indeed absurd. Our protest, "No, it is not," is but a momentary reaction, a false hope, perhaps the expression of a temporary good mood, or of stubbornness, a refusal to admit the obvious. The truth is that life is not fair, it has no ultimate meaning, and in the end we are unable to give any good reason for living, except, perhaps, that we have gotten used to it, sometimes enjoy it, and have a project or two in process that we would like to see through.

Nevertheless, despite persuasive philosophical arguments we have the sense that something is very wrong, not with life or its meanings but with the life and that sense of meaning that allows life to be meaningless or absurd. The intellectual integrity of the complaint itself, all but the epigram of our contemporary sensitivities, often goes unchallenged. Philosophers claim they have better things to do. They leave the field to religion and the gurus. But though the question of the meaning of life may be confused, there is no doubt that those who ask it—including most of our students— have genuine concerns. It is up to us philosophers—who else?—to appreciate and properly identify those concerns.

Many people would argue, then as now, that underlying the very notion of the Absurd is the widespread unbelief, "the death of God," the rejection of that which alone can give life meaning. But to those who would appeal to God for meaning (what Camus calls "philosophical suicide"), we should remind ourselves that it was Kierkegaard, a devout Christian, who first introduced "the Absurd" into existentialism. And as I said, religion doesn't deny the absurdity of life but rather uses it to sell its products. The weight falls on existentialism, and on Camus and Sartre in particular, to make some sense of the question and suggest something by way of an answer. We want to say that "life is meaningless" is itself meaningless. But what is it for life to have a meaning? What is the answer to the question Camus poses with his notion of "the Absurd"?

The Absurd

> There's not even a film.
> There's nothing . . . just nothing.
> What the hell's "sincerity" anyway?
> —Fellini, 8½ (1963)

Is life worth living? A familiar mistranslation of Socrates says that the unexamined life is not. But is the examined life worth living? What could it mean to answer no? What would it be to answer yes? Once we have begun examining our lives, once the philosophical question of "meaning" has been raised, we must be prepared for an unwelcome answer. One might be shouting into an abyss, neither expecting nor getting an intelligible reply. Yet we once seemed to know the answer—that is, until we asked the question. It seemed that we were sure: "Of course life has meaning—there is happiness, and one's friends, there is the laughter of little children, there is love, and there are life's little pleasures, there is art and entertainment, there are occasional examples of justice triumphant, and there is a promising party downtown this weekend." But when we ask about the meaning of life, we step back from living, just as one might step back from love to ask about love. It is often said that to ask "Do I really love her?" is already a setup for an unpleasant realization, an indication that one really might not love. Otherwise, why ask? And there is that quiet, ominous sound, like the ripping at the seams of a tightly fitting garment. We immediately recognize what we have done. Our step back has severed the intimacy that once served to answer our question, before it had been asked. Looking at love from a distance, it is easy to be skeptical, even cynical, about love. Kierkegaard makes much of the absurdity of watching *other* people make love (by which phrase he had a quainter and more innocent meaning than we do). Looking at life from a distance, it is easy to be skeptical, even cynical, about life. But the damage is done. We cannot mend the garment or recapture that innocent intimacy. We are like Jean-Luc Godard's Pierre le Fou, changing his mind after he has tightly strapped and ignited the explosives around his head.

Too late. From our now irremediable cynical, or at least skeptical, distance both life and love have lost their meaning. We thought that we would understand by asking "why?" but that "why?" has undermined everything. The price of our understanding is the loss of what we would understand. Now, our intimacies and affections seem like childish games; our struggles, nothing more than vain gestures. Everything remains as before, but deadened, emptied of meaning. The world is no longer ours: We observe it, alienated, the fading hues of vitality overshadowed by a cloud of our own creation. The old habits and ambitions keep us moving, even frenetically, through the paces of life, but we are no longer wholly engaged. The "why" has no answer, and that is the singular fact that now defines our existence. This "fact" is what Camus called "the Absurd." I believe that it is still the dominant philosophical conception of our time, at least among our students (who are by no means all cynical).

Indeed, modern philosophy has only made the problem more respectable. My former student and now colleague David Sherman traces the origins of the Absurd not just to Kierkegaard but also to, before him, Hume and Kant. Hume showed that truths about the world could not have the necessity of the truths of mathematics and logic, and Kant argued that knowledge had to make room for faith. Both together, following Descartes, were responsible for the heightened emphasis on "subjectivity," from which Kierkegaard took his cue, insisting that our belief in God and so, too, all our important life choices are absurd because they are inescapably subjective and nothing more than "leaps of faith."[1]

Why not just accept the Absurd as a fact of life? Or else dismiss it as no more than a philosophical perspective, one among many? But the idea that life is without meaning is intolerable. Our discomfort, however, is in the intellect, and because it is undeniable that thinking created the Absurd, a common reaction to the Absurd becomes a hostility to thought, perhaps along with a nostalgic appeal to innocence or a retreat to the passions of everyday life. That is certainly what gives Camus' *The Stranger* its enormous appeal. Routinely, philosophical questions are dismissed as jokes or indefinitely postponed. The problem of life is replaced by life's little problems. Bureaucratic absurdities eclipse the Absurd, and legal formalities take on newly motivated "seriousness." In Texas, another rise in the price of gasoline spurs much more moral indignation than a criminal's execution. Several of the most popular ads on television depict chimps in business suits playing the roles of business executives and political leaders. We do have a sense of humor about the absurdity of it all. But there is an air of desperation about us, as if we are trying too hard both to take ourselves seriously and not to take ourselves so seriously. Meanwhile, the intellect distracts itself by refocusing its attention on faux-cosmic questions—how to explain certain emanations from space, whether life requires an "intelligent design" for its explanation, how to resolve certain inconsistencies in Leibniz's logic. If the Absurd cannot be answered, it can always be avoided. Or so we would like to think (that is, by refusing to think about it).

But the Absurd is not a philosopher's invention. If "the Absurd" were only a philosopher's extravagance, a mere idea, it would be no more worthy of our attention than any number of other impressive but ultimately nonsensical concepts and conundrums that have intrigued thinkers from Plato to Wittgenstein and Derrida. But the Absurd, though created in thought, will not contain itself as "an idea." It poisons our everydayness and gives our every experience a tinge of futility—"nausea," Sartre calls it. In the shadow of the Absurd, our jokes take on the cast of gallows humor, a distracting playfulness, or a welcome viciousness. We find ourselves desperately trying to move more quickly, to nowhere; or we try to "entertain ourselves." Camus said that he was describing a "widespread sensitivity" during the early years of World War II. We can all sympathize with the ghastly plight of Europeans during those bad old days. Hayden Carruth introduces *Nausea* by calling existentialism "a great shift in human attitudes that has altered every aspect of life in our civilization."[2] It has been "independently invented by millions and millions of people simply responding to the emergency of life in the modern world." Listening to my nineteen-year-old students—our philosophical canaries in the increasingly cavelike atmosphere of the current zeitgeist—it is evident that it remains a widespread sensitivity in our own time, too. The Absurd permeates my students' perceptions of themselves, their future, their world. Their material and social aspirations only make the Absurd more obvious, and it does not seem at all diminished by the religious or spiritual veneer that many of them embrace as cover.

The Absurd follows with merciless logic from the most everyday thinking. Our frustrated expectations of fairness, the hope for global justice, our demands for deep understanding, the cold irresponsibility of global capitalism, our ruthless pragmatism, and our insistence on purposefulness and efficiency—all lead us more or less directly to the Absurd. Whether by that dramatic name or not, the Absurd is well known to us all. It is the horizon of meaninglessness that lies just beyond our immediate projects, compromising our successes as well as our failures, undermining our pride as well as underlining our humiliations. Yet it has not been understood. Camus' attempts to describe it are so varied and sometimes so incoherent that the Absurd remains an abstraction, even despite his sometimes poignant concrete examples. That is why, perhaps, readers have been so quick to identify the many varied themes of the *Myth of Sisyphus* with just the title character and his simple repetitive story. They also identify at least one theme of the *Myth* with the title character if not also with the plot of *The Stranger*, where the concept of the Absurd seems to get a concrete incarnation. Meursault is, on this reading, the "Absurd hero." But it is not as if Camus' aim in either book is to get us beyond the Absurd or cure us of its oppressiveness. He even insists, in the name of a curious mix of philosophical integrity, obstinacy, mock heroism, and defiance, that we "keep the Absurd alive." Nevertheless, the point is to go beyond it, which Meursault surely does not do. Can philosophical thinking, which has brought us to the Absurd, help us through it as well?

Camus' Absurd Reasoning

> There is but one serious philosophical problem, and that is suicide. Judging whether life is or is not worth living amounts to answering the fundamental question of philosophy.
> —Albert Camus, *The Myth of Sisyphus*

Camus begins *The Myth of Sisyphus* with what is arguably the most striking sentence in the history of philosophy, "There is but one serious philosophical problem, and that is suicide." Wow! What college sophomore, perhaps having recently struggled through a course in symbolic logic or epistemology, not to mention having entertained some personal thoughts of making a desperate exit, would not get hooked? Of course, the tremendous momentum of such dramatic beginnings is difficult to sustain. (After one of the great openings in modern classical music, Richard Strauss quickly allows his *Thus Spake Zarathustra* to slip into romantic kitsch, although one could meanly argue that Nietzsche does the same soon after his rousing Prologue to the same text.) Camus' essay begins to flounder (again, perhaps like *Zarathustra*) soon after insisting "These are facts the heart can feel, yet they call for careful study before they become clear to the intellect."

In attempting to give us a careful study of the facts, Camus gives us instead an "absurd reasoning," a supposedly ruthless pursuit of the truth through logic. (This is not a pretension unknown in French philosophy—flamboyant rhetoric, memorable lyricism, dramatic gestures, melodramatic examples, and many appeals to, but little actual use of, *la logique*.) In Camus' clumsy Cartesianism, in particular, the logic often gets lost and confused even though the arguments are familiar enough. In fact, we probably rehearsed them in high school. But I want to suggest that they are ultimately incoherent. Nevertheless, as I said of the "meaning of life" question, it is not enough to ridicule and dismiss this very real concern. It is up to us to understand it. I think that Camus' book is best understood as giving us a *phenomenology*, not a way of reasoning, and the power of the book is due to his seductive success in doing this. After all, he described the Absurd as "an absurd sensitivity." What remains after we have dismissed the bad logic is the phenomenology, a powerful appeal to our prephilosophical feelings.

But first, the arguments. There are quite a lot of arguments or suggestions of arguments in the *Myth*, few of which are pursued in any depth or detail. Several of them play on the dichotomy between "subjectivity" and "objectivity." For instance, right after his striking opening, Camus shifts to talking about objectivity in science and how ultimately irrelevant it is (that is, irrelevant to the One Serious Philosophical Problem). Galileo judged that the truth was not worth dying for, and, Camus says, he was right. Here is the opening salvo of Camus' anti-intellectualism. However, some of Camus' suggested arguments are fully philosophical and suitably abstract, and turn on the philosophically mind-blowing notion of *infinity*. From what Husserl called "the natural standpoint," namely, the approach of the natural sciences, it makes perfectly good sense to talk about the infinite universe and the age of our solar system or our galaxy, even the universe as such. But from the phenomenological standpoint, what are we to say? What becomes of our sense of ourselves and the significance of our lives from this cosmic viewpoint, the one Thomas Nagel calls "the view from nowhere"? It is, of course, a familiar phenomenological experience, the shock and rupture as one gets the sense of his or her own insignificance. Compare puny man with the infinity of the universe. Or compare our brief lifetimes with the span of eternity. Or think of our meager actions within the context of intergalactic collisions. Or compare our infinitesimal finitude to the Divine Infinity of God. The upshot of every such contrast is that we are virtually nothing, our actions and subjective feelings wholly insignificant.

This image of our own insignificance serves as an argument for the Absurd that is taken very seriously, for example, by Nagel in his reconsideration of Camus' problem (in "The Absurd," in his book *Mortal Questions*). Camus suggests this argument in *The Stranger* when he has Meursault momentarily look at his life through the wrong end of the telescope, diminishing all details but gaining that lethal sense of distance from which it appears that any details of his life are all but irrelevant. Meursault also ruminates on the scope and scale of the universe and its "benign indifference." (More on this in a moment.) In *Myth*, Camus also questions the relevance of "reality," whether as postulated by metaphysics or discovered by science. He suggests that metaphysics is merely a "game," and that "whether the earth or the sun revolves around the other is a matter of profound indifference." This is, perhaps, not an expression of hostility to science as such, but just another dramatic salvo in the service of holding up the suicide (meaning of life) question as the matter of first importance in philosophy. But it suggests a picture that is at the very heart of Camus' philosophy, namely, that what is lauded as "objectivity" in scientific and philosophical circles is a mixed blessing. As an ideal of getting beyond our limited viewpoints and experience in our search for the truth, it is disputed only by dogmatists with their own weirdo worldview to defend. But there may be such a thing as *too much* objectivity. If our cosmic or "God's eye" point of view is to transcend all perspectives, it may also lead us down the road of discounting all of our personal experiences, values, and concerns.

What is particularly modern about the widespread sensitivity of the Absurd that Camus finds in the present age is of a piece with the revolution in science, which began in the seventeenth century and culminated in the twentieth, that stripped the universe of its values in the name of science and then stripped it even of predictability and measure, thinking instead in terms of "chance" and "relativity." As our knowledge of the universe increased, one might argue, our sense of our own significance has diminished. As Freud famously said, Copernicus inflicted the first great blow, Darwin the second, and he himself had delivered the third. But that was before Einstein's work was well known, not to mention the mysteries of quantum mechanics. But, again, I do not think that this works as much of an argument. It is, rather, a powerful piece of phenomenology regarding the suprapersonal perspectives of which we have become capable.

Predictably, several of Camus' arguments in the *Myth* are shared with *The Stranger*. For instance, "that dark wind blowing from my future" that Meursault describes in the final pages is one that we all feel at some time or other, whether or not we are condemned to death in the straightforward and imminent manner that he was. Meursault follows this by thinking, "I had passed my life in a certain way, and I might have passed in a different way, if I'd felt like it.... And what did that mean?" The implication is that the dark wind obliterates the meaning of all choices. But this argument that death is the basis of the Absurd and makes our choices meaningless deserves a lot more scrutiny than Meursault or Camus gives it, for at least one of Camus' mentors, Martin Heidegger, thought that that same dark wind was instrumental and instructive regarding the meaning of one's life. Closer to home, the title character of Camus' own book, Sisyphus, is exemplary of the Absurd even though he is immortal.[3] Whatever the Absurd is, therefore, it does not depend on death and mortality. If life is meaningless, it would surely be no less meaningless if it were to go on forever.[4]

A second shared set of arguments also turns on the "did this, but could have done that" idea but has little to do with death. In its most outrageous formulation, it has to do with Camus' much-quoted comment (in the *Myth*) that it is only quantity of life that counts, not quality. This makes sense only in a minimal way, which Camus spells out by saying "there is no substitute for twenty years of life." True, perhaps, and this is something we have all thought from time to time—for instance, when some young and promising scholar, actor, or athlete dies a tragically early death. We might catch ourselves thinking, "better alive than talented but dead." But what does Camus mean by "no substitute"? The idea of *compensation* for a short life goes back to the Hebrew Bible—Solomon's stated preference of a short and wise life to a long one, and to Alexander (the Great), who asked the gods for a glorious life instead of a long life. Achilles, according to Homer in the *Iliad*, was given a similar choice. And more recently, there was the 1960s rock group the Who. They sang, in then-familiar postadolescent arrogance, "hope to die before I get old," and Jerry Rubin was going around telling everyone "not to trust anyone over thirty." The surviving members of the Who are now in their sixties, and Jerry Rubin (who has now passed on) moved to Wall Street soon after he reached thirty and was indeed no longer to be trusted. But what looks like a statement of the obvious, "there is no substitute for twenty years of life," turns out to be rather problematic, depending, perhaps, on the age of the person who utters it. I think back over my last thirty years, and I certainly wouldn't want to give them up. But at thirty my future was just a blur of possibilities, and while I wasn't ready to throw it away, I wouldn't have felt that it would have been much of a loss either. But Camus was under thirty when he wrote that, so I really wonder what he had in mind. (He writes, "Yet a day comes when a man notices or says that he is thirty. He belongs to time, and by the horror that seizes him, he recognizes his worst enemy. Tomorrow, he was longing for Tomorrow, whereas everything in him ought to reject it. That revolt of the flesh is the Absurd.") The Absurd, so considered, is a young man's game.

The most cosmologically ambitious argument for the Absurd also appears in *The Stranger*, although as much by way of what is *not* argued as by what is stated as such. The point is the one that Meursault blurts out in his epiphany of anger at the prison chaplain, where he rejects the promise of Heaven and the chaplain's "certainties" in favor of even just one day of *this* life or "one strand of a woman's hair." The premise of Camus' objection (and then of his rage) is a Nietzschean premise, *God is dead.* With that cosmic absence, according to the shocked and shaken priest, life would indeed be absurd. But Camus' stance, like Nietzsche's, is unapologetically "this-worldly." And from such a stance, the absence of God is an irrelevancy, not a loss, certainly not a tragedy. But here we see a confusion of feelings in Camus (as we will discern in Sartre, too). Raised in a pious household, he had gotten Christianity "under his skin." He suffers under what Nietzsche called "the shadow of God." And so his rage at the chaplain is not just irritation with the man's philosophy or his pious presence. Meursault (and Camus) seem to understand the chaplain's dread: that if there is no God, life would be absurd. So here we meet up with Kierkegaard as well as Nietzsche. Their shared argument is that life is absurd not because of God's absence but because of the futility of human existence. Without God, Kierkegaard would say, there is no hope in this futility. In Nietzsche's harsh diagnosis, the problem is not God's nonexistence but the shadows [He] casts: "we are weary of man," even "weary of life." In the light of God's grace, human beings are taught to feel that their lives are worth something. Without it, nothing.

I do not want to weigh into the theological questions raised here, but as I read Camus, it is not a matter of argument, "if there is no God, then. . . ." It is, rather, an insight into religious phenomenology, and the derivative phenomenology of late-blooming nonbelievers. (Nietzsche, too, was once devout, his father a Lutheran minister. He was raised by a family of pious women and as an adolescent intended to be a minister.) The perspective described, in both *The Stranger* and the *Myth*, is not theo-ontology but the horror of an infinite yet meaningless world. It is the perspective described by Kierkegaard, but Camus, like Nietzsche, refuses to make the "leap of faith." And Nietzsche, like Camus, tries to put a happy face on this horror. Both of them are caught up in "the shadows of God," their atheism at odds with their upbringing, their exuberant passion for life haunted by the memory of a vision of life that was much more innocent and once seemingly secure.

Finally, Camus offers us a more mundane set of arguments that are familiar to every student of philosophy: For every human desire, there is the "why?" of explanation or justification. "Why should you want that?" and "What will that get you?" and so on. And to every answer, there is a further "why?" and then another, ad infinitum, ad absurdum. That is why, to Meursault, it makes no difference what one does. That is how Camus can say that there is no meaningful "quality" to life. The ultimate " 'why?' has no answer," Nietzsche warns us (*Will to Power* #2). But of course not, if there is no ultimate "why?" the chain of justification is never completed, never anchored, and so all of our desires and our values remain unaccounted for, unjustified, mere vanities, and therefore absurd. Nevertheless, the absence of an anchor (in God or anywhere else) does not make our values absurd or our lives meaningless. The anchor, as Camus shows quite clearly in his lyrical essays, lies in our desires and satisfactions, in the passions of this life. Sartre, accordingly, is wrong when he says, melodramatically, "man is a useless passion." Our human passions need not have an ultimate "use," unless one takes on the eudaemonistic notion that their "use" is nothing other than a flourishing and meaningful life. But that, of course, is a value internal to this life as well as a suitable aim and measure of all that we do and desire. Sometimes, "because I enjoy it" or the bratty "because I want to" is all the "anchor" (or reason) that one needs. Camus' argument has a point: Once we start talking the language of explanation or justification, we feel compelled to finish the job. But the end of explanation and justification like the meaning of life, need not be found, and should not be sought beyond the joys, satisfactions, ultimate desires, and virtues of life.

The Meaning of Meaning

Insofar as the Absurd is the problem of the meaning of life, we need to ask, What is "meaning"? For Camus and in the above arguments, as well as for many philosophers, "meaning" means "reference beyond itself," external "appeal" (in Camus' terms). Thus Morris Raphael Cohen, an American logician and a contemporary of Camus, defined "meaning" as "anything [that] acquires meaning if it is connected with or indicates or refers to something beyond itself, so that its full nature points to and is revealed in that connection."[5] It is sometimes clear that this is the sense of "meaning" that Camus has in mind for "the meaning of life," whether or not it is God that we find beyond. (It is not clear what or who the other candidates might be.) This is the phenomenological picture that seems to be at stake in Camus' descriptions. If Meursault really remained an unreflective unbeliever (as he would seem to be throughout the novel), the thought of something outside of life would not occur to him at all. (It is the prison chaplain who raises the possibility of this Unthinkable, and Meursault responds with rage.) But it is Camus who asks, "Is it possible to live without appeal?"—that is, appeal to something or someone outside of life. That seems to me to be some kind of admission of an incomplete atheism. Or, thinking instead of Camus' occasional sense of fatalism, it could be interpreted as a less than convincing conception of fate, a sense that matters are preordained or serve some transcendent purpose. But is living without appeal living without meaning? This would again seem to assume that the meaning of life could be found only outside of life rather than *in* it.

But the demand is incoherent: In the name of his ruthless "logic," Camus insists that only meanings within our experience are allowed us—no unwarranted "leaps," no mystical "insights," no external "appeal." He tells us (reminiscent of Descartes), "My rule is to get along with the immediate evidence." But coupled with his externalist notion of meaning, namely, meaning as reference to some meaning-endowing source outside of our lives, it follows that our lives *cannot* have a meaning. Therefore Camus says that life is absurd. But, again, is living without meaning living the Absurd? Or is some sense of meaning necessary even to experience (and certainly to formulate and express) the Absurd? That would certainly seem to be the case for Camus' most convincing formulation of it (still to come).

It is worth noting, by way of analogy rather than argument, that the above notion of meaning has been discarded by a great many philosophers, linguists, critics, and poets, particularly since the later work of Wittgenstein. It has been increasingly evident, if not conclusively so, that the attempt to characterize meaning as "reference beyond itself" is applicable—if at all—

only to very small units within a semantic system. But the system itself does not "have a meaning," nor, however, is it meaningless. The word "loquacity" has a meaning in English, but what sense would it make to say that the English language has a meaning—or that it does not have one, apart from the fact that people do or once did speak it? Does life as such have to have a meaning in order for our lives to be meaningful? Does one's life have to have a meaning for things in life to have meaning? And does one's life have to have a meaning for it to be "worth living"? Perhaps one's life might not have meaning but yet not be absurd and still be worthwhile.

This fog of questions is due in no small part to Camus' rather varied and fanciful characterizations of the Absurd and his rather casual treatment of questions about meaning, meaningfulness, and meaninglessness. But Camus' self-stultifying quest for the meaning of life can be helped along in his own terms by taking seriously his suggestion that meaning can be found only in life and not outside of it. The meaning of our lives can be found in what we love, in what we take pride in. One can even find meaning in what we hate and oppose, in resentment, in "scorn and defiance" (although in Camus' telling of the myth, this is directed at the Greek gods, but they are clearly "in" Sisyphus's life). The meaning of our lives, in other words, resides in our passions, in our desires and affections. Thus Meursault's life is quite meaningful in *The Stranger*, even though he does not (until the end) reflect on it. Sisyphus's existence is meaningful, because he has his ongoing project. He also has his scorn for the gods. Camus in his lyrical essays celebrates the simple joys of young Arab boys playing on the beach. Their lives have meaning—as opposed, perhaps, to the life of a French philosopher who watches them with alienation and envy. The seductive message of *The Stranger*, too, is that the meaning of our lives is in our sensuous pleasures, our routine satisfactions, and (by the end of the novel) the passions of this life. Thus Pascal and Kierkegaard both make it clear that what gives meaning to life is not the actual existence of God beyond our lives but the passion that pervades our lives because of our belief. Even if one does believe that life is meaningful only because of "appeal," it is the meaning of our lives, not the being appealed to, that matters.

One can indeed "get along with the immediate evidence," but life, then, is not without meaning and, insofar as this is the same thing, it is not absurd. The Absurd creeps in only with reflection. It distances itself from our immediate experience and in so doing, loses its grip on the everyday meanings that give our lives meaning. It is in reflection, not in our experience, that the Absurd becomes a problem. But even in experience, some lives may be both without meaning and absurd. We will see one such life in the person of Roquentin, Sartre's curious protagonist in *Nausea*. And we will meet another in Camus' last novel, *The Fall*. There, Jean-Baptiste Clamence will give us a grim tour of a life lived in reflection, which has become (with some significant qualifications) devoid of meaning. A man robbed of his life and all of its pleasures, allowed now only reflection, like Meursault in prison, may find his life meaningless and absurd. But that is not what our lives are like, and that is not Meursault's conclusion. He concludes that he has always been happy, and so long as he is still alive, he continues to be. (So, too, the monster Caligula, in Camus' play, screams in something like hysterical delight [just before he dies], "I'm alive!") By contrast, Meursault's casual efforts to generalize his situation, however moving and even thought-provoking, are not very convincing. One's submersion in his or her life cannot be generalized.

The meaning of life may be found in our passions, but life itself is not, contrary to both Sartre and Camus, a passion. That "passion for life" that Camus and Nietzsche make so much of, may make good sense in contrast to a life-negating fascination with the "other-worldly," but it makes little sense as a meaningful emotion. Having a "passion for life," where it is not just an odd way of referring to someone's indiscriminate enthusiasm, sounds more like the desperation of someone who is about to *lose* his or her life. Where else in life does one get the chance to stand at the exit door of one's life and love it? At the exit door of life, facing imminent death, one might for a moment occupy such a peculiar position and have such an emotion. But the passions *in* life are not, except by extension (referring to generic enthusiasm), the passion *for* life. So long as we are passionate, not about life but about the things in our lives, our lives will be meaningful. I am for the moment glossing over what I have called the "demeaning" passions, those that make one's life pathetic—envy and resentment, for example. This, we can anticipate, is an argument against Camus' Sisyphus, as well as against his Clamence. But my unexamined thesis here, and Camus' as well, is that such passions nevertheless give life meaning, albeit a demeaning one. And so we need to turn to Camus' phenomenology, to see how it is that the meanings of our lives are constituted by us through our passions. It is these meanings that make or fail to make our lives worth living.

Camus' Phenomenology

Most of Camus' arguments, many commentators have pointed out, are no good. But the same has been argued of Plato, perhaps the greatest Western philosopher of all, so this should give us pause. Could it be, we should ask, that great philosophers do not always give arguments, at least not good arguments? They may be trying to do something else: to make us think, to give us a vision, to inspire us to change our lives by way of many different devices, only one of which is argument. Plato does this through dramatic dialogue, myth, and allegory. Camus does it by way of appeal to our "sensitivities." Thus virtually all of the arguments discussed above, few of which are very impressive *as arguments*, can be reinterpreted as provocative in a different way, especially when flowing one to another in the stream-of-consciousness essay form that is Camus' style. Thus I want to read most of

Camus' bad "arguments" as appeals to ordinary experiences of absurdity, in other words, as everyday phenomenology. Thus the observation that we are all going to die, that we are all "condemned to death," is not intended as the premise of an argument but as an awakening to the preciousness and urgency of life.[6] The argument that we are objectively insignificant in the eyes of the universe is a prompting to subjectivity, to make us appreciate the importance, if only "to me," of the pleasures and passions and values that make up my life. The overall "argument," that life is absurd, does not depend on the premise that there is no God or that we can't ultimately justify our desires. And there is no "therefore." Camus, rather, tries to impress on us, with image after image, that our lives, from various perspectives, don't seem to make sense. That provocation of a sense of profound disorientation, disillusionment, and dissatisfaction is what *The Myth of Sisyphus* is all about.

The idea that Camus is describing and appealing to our ordinary experiences of absurdity in everyday phenomenology brings into the foreground many of his examples that cannot possibly be construed as arguments or as "absurd reasoning." For example, he tells us, "A man is talking on the telephone behind a glass partition; you cannot hear him, but you see his incomprehensible dumb show: you wonder why he is alive." This is by no means intelligible as an argument. But it has its perverse appeal as an appeal to our experience of meaninglessness. Again, we think of Kierkegaard's rather nasty voyeuristic comment about the absurdity of watching others expressing their affections, and we think of those many experiences, when we are in a grumpy or cynical mood, perhaps, when we uncomprehendingly or unappreciatively observe the gestures of people we do not know. Meursault, in a more or less continuous mood that we would call neither grumpy nor cynical, watches others without empathy and so without understanding—or trying to understand. If one puts his mind to it, or if one has something seriously lacking in her character, or if one finds other people truly alienating and impossible to understand, the world might well seem absurd. But this is either a very temporary or a dangerously pathological condition.

A bit later in the *Myth*, Camus suggests, "Likewise the stranger who at a certain second comes to meet us in a mirror, the familiar and yet alarming brother we encounter in our own photographs is also the Absurd." Again, here is a bit of the absurdity in everyday phenomenology. Who among us has not had this reaction, at least once in a while if not often, of catching a glimpse of ourselves in a mirror and finding the image alien. (For instance, many people do not smile when they look at themselves in a mirror even though they might smile quite freely with other people and correctly think of themselves as cheerful. Thus they find their reflection strange. Or they force a smile, but forced smiles are not genuine ["Duchenne"] smiles, and so they look false.) So, too, we take a glance at a loved one's reflection in the mirror and her asymmetries are reversed. That, too, gives us a shiver of the Absurd, even when we are long used to it (given that most of the time we do not see our beloved in a mirror). We expect a mirror to give us a faithful as well as familiar reflection, but it may not. Such reflections or our appearance in a photograph may well momentarily jolt our sensibilities, at least raising the question whether we know ourselves or our loved ones as well as we think that we do, even on the most superficial level.

Colin Wilson, in his *Anti-Sartre* (in fact on both Sartre and Camus), objects that Camus (like Sartre) has cheated here and given us a piece of bad phenomenology. Wilson notes that "if you turn down the sound of the television set at a moment of high drama, the faces of the characters look 'absurd,' with their mouths opening and closing, their expressions tense or horrified. But this is because you have deliberately *robbed* them of a dimension of reality—a dimension necessary to grasp fully what is going on."[7] He goes on to suggest that the same argument applies to Camus' man in the phone booth. "He has been stripped of certain essential 'clues' that would enable you to complete the picture."[8] This is a deep argument that applies to a great deal of Camus' work. By abstracting away from the intimacy and values that animate people—Meursault is the bizarre embodiment of this mode of abstraction—Camus "robs" them (and us) of meaning or the "clues" that are necessary to appreciate what is going on.

When we look at other people and at the same time remove ourselves from their world to the extent that we cannot understand them, this is not good evidence for the Absurd or the absurdity of life. It is only good reason not to so remove oneself. But this, Camus seems to think, is what reflection does. It removes us from our own experience, takes a step out of our world as well as the intimate world of other people, and so we cannot understand them—or ourselves. The result is the seeming absurdity of life. The alternative is to remain engaged and compassionate, and not allow oneself that distance; and as a human being, that was Camus. But as a philosopher, he cheated at phenomenology by insisting on descriptions of the world that were far less than adequate and a conception of reflection that was not so much part of experience as antithetical to lived and engaged experience. The Absurd, on this account, is something cultivated, even manufactured, and hardly a natural sensitivity. "What you are seeing," Wilson says, "is *less* than your normal view." I think that Wilson is right, but this, I would argue, is not all there is to Camus' well-known concept.

Camus' suggestion that we experience the Absurd when we see ourselves in a mirror or in our own photographs is interesting phenomenology. It is not so much that we lose the context but rather that we experience ourselves in an unfamiliar way. Looking at a photograph of ourselves, we are often shocked (that is, unless we have mastered the art of posing and gotten used to the results) because pictures capture us in gestures and expressions that are surprisingly revealing. Candid "snapshots" are especially disconcerting, often because they involve "unnatural" gestures and expressions.

But, of course, those gestures and expressions are perfectly natural. We are just not used to seeing ourselves in the midst of unself-conscious activity, or we are surprised and embarrassed that our supposedly hidden contempt or nervousness or lust has been so well documented. Wilson notes, "You might see a thousand snapshots of a man and still know less of him than would be revealed in ten seconds of actually talking to him." Well, perhaps. But sometimes you might learn more about a person in a single timely snapshot (say, in one of those momentary "looks") than would be revealed in a lifetime of polite conversation.

But more to the point, a photograph of oneself yields a very different experience than photographs of anyone else, insofar as it makes you (more or less) *self-conscious*. Looking at oneself in a mirror, too, provokes self-consciousness. The mirror gives us an experience not simply *of* oneself but a *reflection* of oneself, and this is or can be extremely alienating. (Meursault, tellingly, does not notice himself in the mirror, suggesting his striking lack of self-consciousness.) Indeed, a good deal of Camus' phenomenology of the Absurd has to do with making us self-conscious in various ways. This, of course, makes perfectly good sense if he thinks that the Absurd, and our sense of meaninglessness, emerges only in reflection, not in experience itself. Self-consciousness, after all, is a species of reflection, or, at least, it is a step into reflection.[9] On reflection, even in the reflection in the mirror, we rarely appear to ourselves as "natural." We "catch" ourselves in the mirror. And we reflect on our reflection. Meursault notes, when he does see his reflection (in part II of *The Stranger*), that he seems grim. But don't we all? If one is trying to ascertain the meaning of life, unless one is blessedly superficial and totally enamored with his or her looks, looking in the mirror is not a good way to proceed. It is hard not to be confronted with that sense of "contingency" that haunted Sartre, or that sense of the Absurd that so fascinated Camus. Totally engaged in our experience, we do not wonder what we are doing, much less why we are here at all. Looking at ourselves in the mirror, even admiringly, it is difficult not to ask such questions. (Again, special considerations apply to those, like Sartre's Estelle in *No Exit*, who have their identity *in* the mirror, and actors and models who find their identity in their film or photographic images—or wholly in the reflections of their admirers.) It is reflection, possibly even in a mirror or a photograph, that triggers the experience of the Absurd.

But the mirror image and the photograph are momentary, often static. Indeed, that is what makes them so strange. (Acting or exercising in front of a mirror, or seeing a video or moving picture of oneself, alters this.) But a moving picture of oneself (or a series of gestures in front of the mirror) may well display something else, something even more absurd. It is not just one's contingency that becomes evident on reflection. It is the overall pointlessness of one's behavior. And this is nowhere more evident than in the repetition that is so routinely part of our lives.

Repetition and Absurdity:
Camus' Myth

> Boredom is the root of all evil. Strange that boredom, in itself so staid and solid, should have such power to set in motion. The influence it exerts is altogether magical, except that it is not the *cause* of attraction, but of repulsion.
> —Kierkegaard, "The Rotation Method" (*Either/Or*)

> The gods had condemned Sisyphus to ceaselessly rolling a rock to the top of a mountain, whence the stone would fall back of its own weight. They had thought with some reason that there is no more dreadful punishment than futile and hopeless labor. You have already grasped that Sisyphus is the absurd hero. He is, as much through his passions as through his torture. His scorn of the gods, his hatred of death, and his passion for life won him that unspeakable penalty in which the whole being is exerted toward accomplishing nothing. This is the price that must be paid for the passions of this earth. If this myth is tragic, that is because its hero is conscious. Where would his torture be, indeed, if at every step the hope of succeeding upheld him? The workman of today works every day in his life at the same tasks, and this fate is no less absurd. But it is tragic only at the rare moments when it becomes conscious. Sisyphus, proletarian of the gods, powerless and rebellious, knows the whole extent of his wretched condition: it is what he thinks of during his descent. The lucidity that was to constitute his torture at the same time crowns his victory. There is no fate that cannot be surmounted by scorn.
> —Camus, "The Myth of Sisyphus" (in *The Myth of Sisyphus*)

Robert Meagher, in his misleadingly titled *Albert Camus: The Essential Writings*,[10] defends the too clever thesis that Camus' philosophy is tied progressively to three Greek myths—Sisyphus, Prometheus, and Nemesis. I have doubts about the centrality or even the relevance of the latter two, but there is no doubt about the centrality of Sisyphus. That is a myth Camus grasps with both hands, the story of Sisyphus as a story of futile labor as punishment and of the absurdity of infinite repetition. This is nowhere more obvious than in his choice of Sisyphus to play the "absurd hero," the mythical representative of the Absurd. Repetition, of course, plays an odd role in nineteenth-century European philosophy. Fichte and Hegel both discuss it with the possibility of cosmic repetition in mind, the idea that history does not progress but simply repeats itself, over and over again. Both Fichte and Hegel found this suggestion repulsive, and in recoil celebrated escalating fantasies of human and cosmic progress, culminating in Absolute Spirit. Kierkegaard, reacting against Hegel, celebrated repetition instead, inventing a "rotation method" that depends on "change in its boundless infinity." He notes that "a prisoner in solitary confinement for life becomes very inventive, and a spider may furnish him with much entertainment." Immediately we should think of Camus' character Meursault, who is, of course, in solitary confinement for what little remains of his much-curtailed life. And he does indeed adopt Kierkegaard's method, finding on the walls of his cell considerable, if something less than infinite, variation.

Schopenhauer shared the thoughts of Fichte and Hegel (a "charlatan" and a "fraud," respectively, in his opinion), but he, unlike Fichte and Hegel, refused to evade what he deemed obvious: that life was repetitive and therefore meaningless. But his pessimism was a metaphysical expression of his also finding repetition repulsive. In biology, for example, he found plenty of examples of birth–life–reproduction–death cycles that are nothing but repetitive. Nietzsche, too, insisted that life was repetitive, but (reacting against Schopenhauer) he *celebrated* this in one of his proudest ideas, "the eternal recurrence of the same." It is worth quoting that famous passage (from *The Gay Science*) in full:

> The greatest stress. What if some day or night a demon were to sneak after you into your loneliest loneliness and say to you, "This life as you now live it and have lived it, you will have to live once more and innumerable times more; and there will be nothing new in it, but every pain and every joy and every thought and sigh and everything immeasurably small or great in your life must return to you—all in the same succession and sequence—even this spider and this moonlight between the trees, and even this moment and I myself. The eternal hourglass of existence is turned over and over, and you with it, a grain of dust." Would you not throw yourself down and gnash your teeth and curse the demon who spoke thus? Or did you once experience a tremendous moment when you would have answered him, "You are a god, and never have I heard anything more godly." If this thought were to gain possession of you, it would change you, as you are, or perhaps crush you. The question in each and every thing, "Do you want this once more and innumerable times more?" would weigh upon your actions as the greatest stress. Or how well disposed would you have to become to yourself and to life to crave nothing more fervently than this ultimate eternal confirmation and seal?[11]

But Camus will have none of this. He does not believe in progress, but he also does not think that repetition can be rationalized or made tolerable (that is, on reflection). Meursault's refusal to reflect makes him more or less immune to the absurdity of repetition (although he still suffers from boredom). But a self-conscious Sisyphus, reflecting on his situation, recognizes the absurdity of his repetitive task and so discovers the Absurd. Therefore, Camus suggests, it is reflection on repetition that reveals the Absurd. That is why it is Sisyphus, of all of the mythological martyrs that Camus might have chosen (Tantalus, Prometheus, Philoctetes), who represents the Absurd in human life. The others might be eternally tormented, but sheer repetition is distinctively absurd. Camus easily extends this absurdity, though not immortality, to all of us.

Sisyphus turns out to be the representative of a fate that faces all of us. "At any street corner," Camus writes, "the feeling of absurdity can hit a man in the face." A momentary break in our chain of daily gestures and adventures—"rising, streetcar, four hours of work in the office or factory, meal, streetcar, four hours of work, meal, sleep, and Monday, Tuesday, Wednesday, Thursday, Friday, and Saturday according to the same rhythm—...But one day the 'why' arises and everything begins with that weariness tinged with amazement." Once the "why" has arisen, in that "moment of lucidity" that marks all of philosophy, we wrench ourselves away from our everyday tasks and successes, our duties and our failures, our embarrassments and achievements alike, and we watch ourselves, as if from another room or from a distant nebula. We detachedly observe another couple making love; it is an absurd performance. Imagining ourselves from the same distance, our own lovemaking then seems absurd. We find ourselves in a political argument, view ourselves from a similar distance, still talking; we hear our words, but they now lack conviction. The performance is pure vanity, and we wonder, without breaking the flow of our argument, why we are doing this, perhaps even (just a passing thought) why we are alive. We similarly distance ourselves from every human performance, including our own, from our feelings and our thoughts and even from our thoughts about our thoughts. The world becomes a screen of meaningless movements and sounds. Every act becomes a Marcel Marceau mime, a comedy whose only significance lies in the artful familiarity of its senseless gestures.

The alienation captured in such experiences, brought on by various modes of reflection, permeates Camus' phenomenology. Camus' last novel, *The Fall*, introduces "John the Baptist" Clamence, a highly respected and successful lawyer and lecher, blessed with every advantage of health, wealth, achievement, and social position, who from his distance in exile (in Amsterdam, thinking about his former life in Paris) sees through it all as so much pretense and fraud, amounting to nothing. Similarly, Schopenhauer, a kindred spirit, despite a long life of fine dinners, good wines, sporadic if not wholly satisfactory affairs, and eventual literary success, complained as well that it all "amounts to nothing." So, too, of course, Ecclesiastes, "all is vanity." Any self-conscious creature, whether Sisyphus, "the Proletarian of the gods," or the gods themselves, whether the eminent Clamence or the axle-man proletarian of the Renault assembly plant in Lyons, is subject to this all-encompassing sense of absurdity. From moment to moment, we cannot imagine a greater difference than that which separates the toil of Sisyphus and the equally repetitive labors of another "absurd hero," Don Juan ("1003 in Spain alone"). But from that reflective philosophical perspective in which we demand that our lives have meaning, the erotic affairs of Don Juan amount to no more than the daily toils of Sisyphus, that is, they amount to nothing. (One can imagine Don Juan's mother complaining to him in just this fashion.)

What is essential to Camus' concept of the Absurd, I keep suggesting, is reflection, or what Camus somewhat misleadingly calls "being conscious." Repetition alone is not absurd. We can watch a machine, say, a jackhammer, doing what it does time after time after time, until someone turns it off or it runs out of fuel. We might, in a particularly giddy mood, be amused. But there is nothing absurd about it, unless, of course, we imaginatively endow the machine with self-consciousness. ("If this myth is tragic, that is because its hero is conscious.") Or consider the Texas roach racing across my floor in its usual aimless panic as it scurries to the molding. Its life could not lack meaning: it seems to do so through my eyes only. I try to imagine myself as a roach (but necessarily a self-conscious roach), and my imagined roach life seems meaningless—by human standards. But it is *my* life that I am judging, contrasting my own scurrying with that of a roach. Underlying the contrast are the too-obvious comparisons, and they do not escape my awareness.

What if at every step there was the hope of success? What if I thought that my life, unlike the roach's, would "add up to something"? But, of course, it does not, at least in the long "objective" view of the universe. In the much-abused words of Lord Keynes, "in the end we'll all be dead." Even the sought-after immortality of the Greek heroes of *The Iliad* is now no more than a story (most recently a Brad Pitt movie, make of that what you will). There is no hope of ultimate success, and so, Camus would argue, there is no ultimate hope. Thus the sense of the Absurd is well captured in the ancient myth of Sisyphus, especially as restated by Camus. For Sisyphus, there is no hope, not because in the end he will be dead but because he is immortal and so there will be no end. His futile task will go on forever, and his tragic consciousness, painfully aware of this repetition, provokes our own recognition of repetition and meaninglessness of our lives.

This is not to say that we cannot submerge ourselves in our experience and get "into the moment," ignoring the repetition. Sisyphus does this. He makes his rock "his thing," and therein lies one possible source of his alleged happiness, avoiding reflection and just appreciating the momentary experience and the challenge anew. We all know that, sometimes, if we just allow ourselves to fully engage our repetitive tasks without dwelling on the idea that they are repetitive, the tasks seem so much less oppressive. Imagine those medieval monks, copying bible after bible. Or the modern-day mechanic doing brake jobs all day. Engaged experience without reflection is not meaningless. It lends itself to Kierkegaard's "rotation method." It is reflection, reflection on the repetition as such, that makes repetition meaningless, so better not to reflect. Simone de Beauvoir has a character in one of her novels contemplate suicide as he thinks about how many times he has brushed his teeth in his life, and how many times he has to do so again in the future. But there is another way to think about this sort of repetitive engagement, one that is not without reflection but nevertheless sustains the meaningfulness of activity.

In a word, it is *ritual*. Rituals by their very nature tend to be repetitious. Ritual actions, also by their nature, tend to have little meaning just on their own, without some larger context or set of beliefs. Lighting a candle or saying a prayer in a language you may not even know may be meaningful just because these are actions repeated for a cause, say, a religion or a relationship that you believe in. Even repeated drudgery, say, hauling the stones for a cathedral, may be fully meaningful just because one has faith. (The ancient Hebrews hauling stones for their captors' pyramids probably felt their tasks were meaningful, not because they had any love for the pharaohs but because they saw their humiliating tasks as punishments from their God.) That is why Confucius, defending ritual (*li*) as one of the most important virtues, insists that ritual cannot be "just going through the motions" but must be fully engaged in and "heartfelt." It is the passion that gives the act its meaning. But this is to suggest, à la Colin Wilson's argument, that Camus has once again stripped the story of something that would make it meaningful. But at least Sisyphus "getting into" his task makes it something of a ritual and therefore makes it meaningful.

Camus does not stop the story there. He goes on to suggest something very different and supposedly nobler. Sisyphus can refuse to submerge himself in his task, insist on staying conscious of the absurdity of what he is doing, and thus deprive himself of the happiness of submersion. He can "keep the Absurd alive," in Camus' curious locution. Thus considered, Sisyphus's scorn and defiance, Camus suggests, are our only authentic hope, our only source of genuine human happiness, our only honest passions. This would seem to mean, however, that our best (most heroic?) way of coping with the Absurd is through *resentment*. We should be bitterly scornful about a fate that we cannot change. Whether or not Sisyphus could change or somehow alter his fate is a tough question, of course. Those Greeks took the concept of fate very seriously: they were no existentialists. But their fatalism makes the idea of defiance rather hard to swallow. Sisyphus defies the gods but he does not refuse to go on. He does not drop his rock. He does not attack or challenge the gods. He only curses them, and cursing is not defiance. I suggested earlier, when I argued that the meaning of life was to be found in our passions, that some passions are demeaning. They may give life meaning (as resentment surely does), but there is something pathetic and hardly heroic about such passions. Resentment renders Camus' self-consciously heroic stance less admirable, and it lends itself to all sorts of ad hominem suggestions about Camus' later confrontation with Sartre and his fellow revolutionaries. In the end, when we are told that we must "consider Sisyphus happy," we wonder whether he is supposedly so because he heroically made the best of an awful situation or because he expressed that same resentment that Nietzsche harshly chastised as "slave morality."

If our experiences are repetitive, there need be nothing absurd about them. Indeed, it is the repetition of routines and habits that gives us comfort and familiarity. It is the repeated visits to old friends and cherished places that give us our sense of meaning. Our daily and weekly rituals have meaning just because of their repetitiveness. But reflection can subvert those pleasures as well as enhance them. Camus thinks that stepping back and looking at the repetition as such, as opposed to the pleasures of the experiences themselves, makes the whole thing absurd. Whether one is working in an assembly plant or saving lives in a hospital, the abstract idea of mere repetition (and won't all of those patients eventually die anyway?) poisons one's engagement. Camus' Absurd thus requires a certain leisure in life, a luxury of distance made possible by reflective consciousness. It is thus true that the Absurd must be judged a bourgeois malady; it is a malaise that does not affect the hungry, the threatened, or the desperate. Life is not absurd to a Mexican peasant; it is only cruel, punctuated by moments of relief. It is not absurd to a refugee, only terrifying. It was not during the invasions of Napoleon that the Absurd was born in Europe, but after, during the tedium of "the reaction," when lives were safe but life was pervaded by ennui. (It was during this time that Kierkegaard wrote *The Present Age*, complaining that modern life had become all reflection and devoid of passion.) It was not during the enthusiasm and ambitious hopes of the 1960s that the Absurd was reborn. It was after the enthusiasm and hopes died down. The Absurd is not turbulence but an awkward silence. It appears in moments of reflection when we discover that empty translucency that Camus describes in both *The Stranger* and the *Myth* as the seeming "indifference of the universe."

The Metaphysics of the Absurd

> Gentlemen, you must excuse me for philosophizing.
> —Dostoevsky, *Notes from the Underground*

In addition to these many arguments and images, Camus gives us one spectacular knock-'em-dead analysis of the Absurd, again not an argument nor a mere image but a vision that is hard to ignore. According to Camus, the Absurd is "the confrontation of man and universe": our expectations and our "reason" against the infinite "indifference" and "inhuman silence" of Reality. Here is the breathtaking conclusion of *The Stranger*, as Meursault looks to the "brotherly" universe while awaiting his last morning. Here is the cashing out of the mythological Sisyphus shaking his fist at the bemused gods watching him. Here is the real existential problem lurking behind all of those poor arguments about the infinite and impending death and those disturbing images of momentarily absurd human features and behavior. We are rational creatures, not just in the Russellian sense that we are capable of abstract symbol-mongering ("we can do sums") but also in the much broader sense that we impose our categories on the world. But these are not just the categories of the understanding, as Kant taught us, but, more important, our values, our expectations of how things should turn out, our demands concerning what *should be*. We expect justice, not because we were taught about justice (what Hume therefore called "an artificial virtue") but because certain expectations are in our very bones: "The good should prosper, the evil should suffer," no matter what we might mean by "good and evil."[12]

One might conclude from this that Camus is a modern Manichaean, a dogmatic moralist (as Sartre depicted him in his touching obituary). But the confrontation presented here is not between good and evil, or even between good and bad, but between rationality on the one hand and indifference on the other. We are not, contra Meursault, capable of true indifference. That is what makes Meursault so "strange." Camus was anything but indifferent. He was a passionate moralist. But he was also—as Voltaire once declared himself, unconvincingly—morally confused. Camus frequently admitted as much, and his most impassioned moral essays, against the death penalty and against terrorism, for example, are riddled with that sniff of apologetics and inconsistency that Sartre and his friends came to so despise.

Perhaps calling the image of Camus' confrontation of rational man and indifferent universe his "metaphysics" is a bit overdone. After all, few philosophers (though again mentioning Voltaire) have been less interested in metaphysics and the epistemological problems that normally go along with it than Camus. But the source of the model here is obvious enough. It is that same "rational mind/physical universe" dichotomy that stands at the base of so much French philosophy (including Sartre's), a dichotomy that is inherited (and taught in grade schools) from René Descartes. What is missing, of course, is the third "substance," God, who, in Descartes and in Jesuit philosophy holds the "created" substances, mind and world, together. But in Camus, they are in opposition. The rational expectations of our minds are not met by the supposed rationality of the universe. Here is why that rationality, the discovery of rational laws operating in the universe (or, à la Kant, its receptivity to our Categories) is so irrelevant to Camus. So, too, Hegel assures us, in his philosophy of history, that looking rationally into something evokes a rational response. But it is this that Camus is directly challenging. We look at the universe as rational, but the universe laughs rudely back in our faces. Our expectations are not met. And though Camus is willing to extend this analysis (rather casually) to science, it is clear that what he has most in mind are the moral aspirations of men and women (though the latter receive little voice in his works). We expect the universe to be just and fair, what Kant and Hegel refer to as "the moral order of the universe." But it is not. The universe is indifferent (even if "benignly") to our demands. Thus Meursault, who is without empathy, finds it so "brotherly."

"The inhuman silence of the universe": Is that our experience? Sartre points out (in *Being and Nothingness*) that the world imposes on us every second, issues commands and orders, gives us duties and warnings, arouses us with dangers and desires. What is Camus listening for, that he hears only silence? What is his conception of the universe, as if reality were forced upon us value-free, investment-free, ego-free? (The contrast with Sartre's *Nausea* could not be more evident.) Sisyphus alone, with his rock and his endless chore: Is that what our lives are like? Sometimes, perhaps. But it is surely not the lot of most mortals, for whom tragedy and surprise are at least as significant as unvarying repetition. So where does it come from, this metaphysics of rational consciousness versus the cold, not cruel but indifferent, world? Here, I think, we come back to Nietzsche's "shadow of God," and to Camus' incomplete atheism.

Sisyphus's world is not, as it first appears, his rock, the mountain, and his futile labors. His salvation, Camus tells us, is his "scorn for the gods." Similarly, Camus celebrates the virtue of defiance; but defiance against what? As an atheist, he would have no gods to scorn. Compare Clamence, in *The Fall*, who had committed no major crime (except, perhaps, receiving stolen property); yet he, too, like everyone, is said to be "condemned." But for what? What makes him guilty, "as all men are guilty," the theme of both *The Fall* and *The Stranger?* Camus tells us that we should live "without hope, without appeal"; but why? Hope for what? Appeal to what or whom? Camus (like Clamence) would seem to have every reason to hope—for peace in Algeria and Europe, a mild or sunny day, a new friend, some justice in postcolonial Algeria or in the post–German occupation trials in France. Yet Camus clearly thinks of himself as hopeless, as condemned, as a tragic ("absurd") hero in a meaningless world.

But here the diagnosis emerges, a metaphysician's diagnosis. Whether or not Camus would have had much interest in rationalist metaphysics, he retained his Jesuit education in the subject. It is a metaphysics not only of dualism of the psychical and the physical; it is, more important, the traditional Christian metaphysics of guilt and redemption. Camus, in other words, is still stuck under "the shadow of God." The "appeal" to which Camus refers is the Christian sense of "appeal"; the object of his scorn is indeed a god—or the shadow of a god—who has abandoned us. Or, rather, Camus has abandoned God, but he has retained the whole of the Christian order of the passions, sin and guilt, condemnation and redemption. But now, while guilt and condemnation remain, redemption becomes impossible. Thus "John the Baptist" Clamence guzzles but does not taste Dutch gin in the seedy bars of Amsterdam, having given up a once eminently successful life in justice with the realization that "no one is innocent." He has rejected the judge, but he has taken the judgment upon himself, as a "judge–penitent," defensively projecting his own sense of guilt and resentment upon mankind as a whole. "We all want to appeal against something! Each of us insists on being innocent at all cost, even if he has to accuse the whole human race and Heaven itself." *Ecce Homo*!

Camus (and not only Camus) is a traumatized atheist, taking on his own quixotic shoulders the weight of Divine judgment. We now expect from the "indifferent" universe what we formerly hoped for from God. And given the indifference of the universe, we then demand justice of ourselves. But still there is no justice (or at any rate too little of it), and the testimony of our senses—as opposed to our blind faith in the hereafter—tells us that there is no hope and no appeal to the possibility of justice elsewhere. Camus' absurd hero is a very Christian hero who seeks absolution for unspecified but in some sense "original" sins, much like Kafka's Joseph K, in a world where there is no longer absolution. Christianity, whatever else it has done, has taught us the meaning of objectless and self-demeaning guilt, guilt by virtue of our very existence. Hitherto, it also offered us the hope of salvation. But the basis of the guilt and the hope were one and the same. Having given up the latter, we should give up the former as well. (Meursault somehow manages to do so, and this is the hint of spirituality that becomes so palpable at the very end of *The Stranger*.)

But we have taken the sin upon ourselves and kept the guilt as well. Underlying the metaphysics of the Absurd lies the ghost of a much older metaphysics, and underlying that is a familiar but often undiagnosed malady of passion, a bitter and defensive view of the world in which the passions of self-demeaning guilt and despair play a leading role. The Absurd is but the rationalized façade of resentment, the "passions of Sisyphus" that constitute the Absurd. Camus took this passion, which he ennobled as "defiance," to be a "consequence" of the Absurd. This sleight of hand is not infrequent in philosophy; one "rationalizes" his prejudices, arguing "objectively" and persuasively on neutral ground, drawing the distortions of his biases from this incontrovertible base. But the "objective" arguments presuppose and do not entail the passions of the Absurd that form their support. The absurd hero begins with a victimized and resentful view of himself as inferior, as impotent, as persecuted and unfairly treated by the universe. He then finds an "objective" viewpoint from which to develop and formulate his resentment in a philosophically convincing manner.

It is not that I think that Camus has gotten his phenomenology completely wrong. On the contrary I think that he does capture an important sense of a widespread sensitivity in our (and many other) times. It remains to be said that the new religiosity that has gripped some of the more "advanced" societies in the world neither denies nor overcomes this victimized and resentful view of ourselves. It feeds on it but then holds out some hope, the appeal that Camus denies us. This sense of the enormity of our guilt and the indifference of our world and the sense of our own smallness is as at home in Christianity as in Camus. Kierkegaard, for example, whose piety is beyond doubt, retained a sense of the Absurd at least as keen as Camus', and his wholehearted devotion to God did nothing to reduce, but only made more palpable, that extreme sense of personal absurdity. But Camus' own sense of the heroic must have suggested to him a very different possibility, not so much "keeping the Absurd alive" as overcoming it, rejecting that sense of victimization and, like Nietzsche, endorsing the love of fate, accepting things just as they are. Or, perhaps better, but also like Nietzsche, to give up that victimized and resentful view of ourselves and that metaphysics in favor of a more holistic and Hegelian view of the world. It is not us against the universe. We are one with the universe, whether one then concludes, with the Buddhists, that both we and the universe are "empty" or, more in sympathy with Nietzsche and Meursault, that the universe is indeed benign.

Conclusion: The Passions of Sisyphus

Why does Camus' myth strike such a responsive chord in so many readers? The arguments are not very good. The phenomenology is impressive but dubious. Such mock-heroic notions as "the Absurd" and "without appeal," "defiance," "rebellion," and "condemnation" won't stand even sympathetic scrutiny (much less the harsh examination of a Sartre or a Jeanson). What is it, in Camus and in ourselves, that renders us so receptive to his seduction, where his appeal to "reason" is no more than a forged stamp of authority, and his phenomenology smacks more of the quick appeal of a ten-second television ad than deep analysis?

I think that we are impressed, first of all, by Camus' impassioned world-view. His is not merely a metaphysics—a cold construction of concepts just as well retained in the original Latin or Greek—but the expression of passions that we, too, are likely to share. Sisyphus is ultimately characterized in terms of his passions: "His scorn of the gods, his hatred of death, and his passion for life." He is without hope, without power, "wretched" but "rebellious." Yet he feels a "silent joy," Camus tells us, and "one must consider Sisyphus happy."

But Sisyphus also perversely appeals (as "the absurd hero") because of a defensive syndrome that is all too familiar. It is precisely that syndrome that projects our world in an absurd perspective, a syndrome of great expectations and consequent bitterness, helplessness and consequent resentment, hopelessness and consequent scorn, silent defiance and that consequent "sour grapes" self-satisfaction that tries to pass as "happiness," the spiteful joy of "negating the gods," that desperate last-ditch strategy of accepting and even celebrating a hopeless and futile life. Only one ingredient is missing from this degrading portrait of human existence: the passion of guilt, later supplied by Clamence from his barroom pulpit. Sisyphus has the emotional advantage of being "condemned" by the gods. We, on the other hand, condemn ourselves. Camus' literary genius enables him to paint this ghastly scenario in heroic colors; but we must see it for what it is. It is a degrading, spiteful, and hopeless version of the Christian denigration of man, as petty and helpless, as virtually crushed by the weight of his guilt and his self-punishment, as salvaging his last crumb of self-respect through resentment, scorn, silent defiance. This is humanity at its low ebb, man at his worst, casting himself as an inferior being in a universe that has already defeated him. But we seem to like that vision of ourselves. As a counterweight to the existentialist emphasis on responsibility, it lets us off the hook. We can get away with mere *attitude*.

Camus admits: "I know, to be sure, the dull resonance that vibrates through these days. Yet I have but a word to say: that it is necessary." But I do not think so. Having learned to see through that degrading metaphysics that has defined humanity for so many centuries, we can now learn to see through the more secular self-imposed degradations that get rationalized as "the Absurd." "The point is to live," Camus tells us. But it is not enough to live out of stubborn defiance, like an unwelcome guest in life. Our self-image should not be Camus' scornful Sisyphus but, rather, Camus' Sisyphus engaged, a strictly this-worldly Sisyphus who may, indeed, earn the right to be happy.

3

MEDITATIONS ON *NAUSEA*:

Sartre's Phenomenological Ontology

It came as an illness does, not like an ordinary certainty, not like anything evident. It came cunningly, little by little: I felt a little strange, put out, that's all.
—Jean-Paul Sartre, *Nausea*

Nausea was Sartre's first popular published work. It appeared in 1938, three years before Camus' *The Stranger*. Before that, Sartre had published a number of technical journal articles on phenomenology, and he was preparing a large tome on "the Psyche" which was never published. (He did publish one or two pieces of that book, however, notably a "sketch" of a theory of the emotions, which I will discuss in the next chapter.) But unlike those scholarly studies, *Nausea* was a novel, and in addition to making the young Jean-Paul Sartre famous and setting the stage for what would soon enough become known as "existentialism," it set forth in creative form many of the difficult themes he had been working on in phenomenology. I have not yet said very much about phenomenology, other than to mention its importance to both Sartre and (implicitly) Camus, and to insist that it will become one of the main themes of this book. Phenomenology is a philosophical method (which is to say, the philosophy) invented or at least named by the German—Czech (Moravian) philosopher Edmund Husserl (1859–1938). Husserl originally intended it as a solution to certain specialized problems in logic and the philosophy of arithmetic, but Sartre (following Heidegger) turned it to very different "existential" concerns. Phenomenology serves as a device for self-examination, if not an excuse for self-absorption as one dwells on one's own experience. Thus it is no secret that *Nausea* is somewhat autobiographical and that the rather disturbing experiences of its protagonist, Antoine Roquentin, are not very well disguised (although exaggerated) expressions of Sartre's own anxieties and difficulties in dealing with his life and with other people.

Phenomenology (now it is time to get into the details of this) is *the study of the essential structures of experience*. It involves a Cartesian retreat to "subjectivity," but with the aim of finding objective or at least universal truths. For Sartre, it was a way of examining human consciousness, and thereby human nature, and the essential structures he sought would be the essence of human nature. According to Simone de Beauvoir, Sartre's lifelong companion, Sartre took to phenomenology like the proverbial duck to water. It began in a café conversation with their friend Raymond Aron in which Aron suggested that phenomenology was a method that would allow one to develop an entire philosophy about virtually any mundane object. Pointing to a drink on the table, Aron reputedly said to Sartre, "You see, my dear fellow, you could talk about this cocktail and make a philosophy out of it."[1] *Nausea* is that philosophy. Husserl had been only tangentially interested in the phenomenology of perception and apparently was not interested in questions of value and ethics, much less the Big Questions about the meaning of life and human nature. But Sartre, following Husserl's most prominent student, Martin Heidegger, saw a way to use Husserl's method to ask, and in a way to answer, the Big Questions. I say "in a way" because the answer in *Nausea*, at least, is not at all what we would expect, and it is certainly not uplifting. It certainly is not an answer of the form "Life is meaningful because . . ." or "The meaning of life is . . ."

The usual interpretation of the book is that it shows life to be *meaningless*, but this, I think, is much too quick. *Nausea* does provide us with a grim view of at least one man's diminished world, and at the same time it addresses the same "widespread sensitivity" that Camus would describe just a few years later in *The Myth of Sisyphus*. *Nausea* is a book that raised the question of the meaningfulness of life for the anxious generation of "alienated" young people just before the Second World War. It continues to do so for postwar generations, and that is not the least of its merits. But the question whether this is merely autobiographical, just generational, or inherent in the very nature of human experience is no small issue in phenomenology as well as in existentialism. As one studies the essential structures of (one's own) experience, a nagging question, whether one is considering the nature of mathematics or the meaning of life, is to what extent what one describes is a personal or cultural idiosyncrasy or whether it truly is a transcendent or transcendental truth. This question of scope always was the Achilles' heel of phenomenology.

Thus one might read *Nausea* as Sartre's personal confession, or as a young people's wartime perspective, or (as Camus writes) a "widespread sensitivity of the age," or as an insightful but usually repressed representation of universal human experience. But behind this question of scope is another: whether any such perspective is or can be "objective." On the one hand, one might argue, "objective" only means "referring to the object," and in this sense (Sartre would say) all experience is objective. That is, all experience is of objects of one kind or another. (This is to say, in the jargon he borrows from Husserl, that it is *intentional* or has *intentionality*.) On the other hand, if "objective" means "true apart from any experience whatever," then nothing is objective, for our only handle on the world is by way of experience. Outside of phenomenology, from a third-person point of view, there is no mention of perspective, giving rise to the illusion that what is being described is being described from no perspective at all, but rather from an omniscient point of view. Sartre does not talk much about this, though no doubt he appreciated Nietzsche enough to know that there is no "God's eye" view of the world. But within phenomenology, it is a very real question: Is Roquentin's experience that of a distinctively sick and abnormal consciousness, or is it in some sense a "true" account of what all of us are but dimly aware of?

Nausea, whether or not it is a study in pathology, is first of all an accessible exploration of some of the themes Sartre had been vigorously pursuing in phenomenology. *Nausea* is, one might say, an application, if not a demonstration, of the phenomenological method. The novel gives us two hundred pages of description of a young writer's monotonous, if not downright tedious, experience. Not much happens. The book itself, apart from its philosophical sparks, is pretty thoroughly and intentionally boring. There is no discernible plot. The lead character is an "alienated" and not very nice young would-be scholar who, we would not be unfair in saying, was probably a lot like Sartre—grumpy, somewhat antisocial, but lonely and needy for the company of other people. He is judgmental and, when the opportunity presents itself, perverse and even cruel. At the beginning of the book he has just finished a draft of a historical study, which he fusses about throughout the novel, and it is no closer to completion at the end of it. *Nausea* also includes a number of insightful reflections on the nature of history and the past, but both the history and the character of the study (of a M. Rollebon, who is implicated in the undoing of Paul I in Russia about the time of the French Revolution) are utterly secondary and merely foils for an ongoing description of the experience and reflections of *Nausea*'s protagonist. But neither is *Nausea* a study of the character of Roquentin, whose unpleasant personality becomes evident enough through his ongoing descriptions. It is not as if we get to understand very much of his psychology. Thus I read *Nausea*, as I do Camus' *The Stranger*, as an exploration in phenomenology. But Sartre, unlike Camus, is clearly explicit that that is exactly what he is giving us.

It would be a mistake, however, simply to read back into *Nausea* the philosophical position that Sartre would defend five years later in his monumental *Being and Nothingness*.[2] Roquentin is not Sartre, and the unrelenting bleak outlook of *Nausea* is radically different from the sometimes ebullient spirit of *Being and Nothingness*. For one thing, the central theme of the meaninglessness of life is rarely to be seen in the latter work, and, for another, the pivotal concept of freedom receives only a negative and mostly pathetic treatment in the novel, a grim version of the Kris Kristofferson idea that freedom is just another word for nothing left to lose.[3] For yet another divergence, Sartre's later ontological category of Being-for-Others, as we shall see, plays no role in *Nausea*. Other people, for the most part, are just like things to Roquentin, and he is mostly unconcerned with what they might think of him. But despite these divergences the *practice* of phenomenology is just as well exemplified in the novel as in Sartre's great tome on "phenomenological ontology," and so it will often be expedient to refer some of his early insights to his later ones (and vice versa).[4] *Nausea* is a very particular (and peculiar) exercise in phenomenology, as it concerns the psychology and the experience of a very particular and quite peculiar sort of subject.

The Phenomenology of *Nausea*

The most obvious place to start an account of the phenomenology in *Nausea* is with its titular experience, nausea. But we should take note of the fact that Sartre's original title for the novel was "Melancholia," which his publisher wisely rejected. (Sartre countered with "The Extraordinary Adventures of Antoine Roquentin," which was clearly inappropriate [as Sartre planned to state in a blurb, "There are no adventures, or something like that"]. It was his publisher, Gaston Gallimard, who came up with the winning title.[5]) Nausea is a familiar experience, but few of us have thought of it as a general, much less global, mode of experience. Nausea is, in short, a complex, usually physiologically based, sensation or set of sensations prompting rather violent, sometimes disgusting, and mostly involuntary behavior. It is typically a most unpleasant feeling coupled with a more or less strong urge to expel, to "throw up" (or, more literally, "throw out"), whatever one has ingested. As usually conceived, it has no *intentionality*. It is not "about the world." To be sure, something we perceive in the world can *make* us nauseous, and when we are already nauseated, almost anything (and perhaps everything) can intensify our nausea. But in such cases the perception is usually said to "trigger" the nausea; it does not constitute it. The connection between the perception and the nausea is strictly contingent. Like disgust, its emotional kin, nausea seems to be primarily a physical sensation and reaction, only secondarily an attitude directed toward the world. (For that reason, disgust has sometimes been denied the status of an emotion.[6]) Disgust is almost a reflex—for instance, an almost instant reaction to the taste of spoiled fish in one's mouth—and nausea is what follows. The bite of fish disgusts and then nauseates, but neither the disgust nor the nausea is "about" the bad fish that causes these sensations. Moreover, nausea, unlike disgust, need not be caused by anything at all.

Nevertheless, we recognize that there is a broader notion of disgust—for instance, *moral* disgust—which is clearly intentional and about some behavior (our own or others'). So, too, there is a broader notion of nausea—perhaps we can even call it moral nausea—but in any case it includes a form of nausea that is about the world. One can (and should) feel properly nauseated about the extent of abject poverty and cruelty in the world, or about the greedy behavior of some top executives and politicians. One might argue that, despite such specific objects, nausea is more often a mood than an emotion, where emotions tend to be about more or less specific events, people, or states of affairs, while moods are more global and less determinate. This is often misinterpreted as "lacking an object," but the object of most moods is *the world*—the world as experienced—and the object of nausea is the world (or any particular aspect of it) experienced as nauseating. This need not be in a strictly physical sense, but may be so in an extended sense that loosely shares certain features with its physiological counterpart. For one thing, it finds its object disgusting. For another, its expression tends to mock the expulsive gesture (tightened face, turning away from the object). If one discovers a betrayal of trust, or that another person has been thoroughly hypocritical, this symbolic sense of disgust and nausea may well follow. Or the disgust and consequent nausea may concern an absence or lack rather than an object (for example, when one expects to find something of significance but it turns out to be meaningless, or when we are desperately looking for a friend, think we have found him, but it turns out to be a stranger—or worse, someone merely pretending to be him).

Insofar as Roquentin seeks to find meaning in life, he is first disgusted, then nauseated, by its absence. Insofar as he expects agreement with his pessimism from other people—for instance, from the curious and ultimately tragic character described throughout as "the Self-Taught Man"—he is first disgusted, then nauseated, by those who refuse to agree with him. So he becomes nauseous *toward them* as well. The nausea of the title is, accordingly, a global perception of the absence of meaning, the lack of meaning of his historical project, the lack of meaning in the relationships he observes, the lack of meaning in the Self-Taught Man's oddly ambitious project for self-improvement, the lack of meaning in his own life. But nausea is not just this perception of absence. It is also a sense of being overwhelmed by existence, and it is existence (the world's, other people's, his own) that he finds most nauseating. Roquentin is like Baudelaire: "The depth of the sky dismays me; its purity irritates me; the insensibility of the sea, the immutability of the whole spectacle revolts me. Nature, pitiless sorceress, ever victorious rival, do let me be!"

This is, admittedly, a stretch from ordinary experience. But the whole point is that Sartre draws from perfectly ordinary experience and tries to show us what lies just beneath the surface of appearances for all of us. But perhaps the phrase "beneath the surface of appearances" (which Sartre employs in the novel) is misleading. It is not as if phenomenology goes beneath the surface, as in Freud's psychoanalysis, with its concept of the Unconscious, which Sartre adamantly rejects. Nor is it as if (in classical philosophy) the appearances are a deceptive cover hiding the way things really are. Phenomenology describes the "appearances," that is, experience, but there are, nevertheless, more or less superficial and profound descriptions of experience. Superficial descriptions just point to the obvious, often the most evident facts about the object— for instance, the fact that this hand has five fingers, the fact that it has small hairs on the knuckles, the fact that the fingernails are cut and polished or long and cracked. Profound descriptions point to something else, something not readily seen or attended to—for example, the resemblance of a hand to a creature, or to a piece of meat.[7]

One might object that, at this point, phenomenology starts looking more and more like poetry, relying on metaphor rather than literal description, but I think that this is a mistake. Our vocabulary for talking about experience is not nearly so developed as our vocabulary for talking about things in the world, so naturally we retreat, in describing our experiences, to description of *other* things that they resemble in some revealing way. But this should not be confused with the distinction between the literal and the metaphorical or, worse, with the distinction between the merely apparent and the metaphysically real. Phenomenology asks the question, How do we experience things? And one part of a general answer is that we experience things *as* and *as like* other things. These metaphorical identities and comparisons not only make our speech more "picturesque" and poetic but actually determine the nature of our experiences. One can become nauseated at the sight of his or her own hand, not (presumably) because it has five fingers but because it looks like a crab or a piece of meat. That, rather than the fact of having five fingers, is what determines the nature of the experience.

Or, more philosophically, one might become nauseated at the sight of his or her own hand because its very existence suddenly strikes us as mysterious or superfluous, in a word, *contingent*. Perhaps it is not obvious on reading the book, but Sartre claimed that contingency was the central philosophical notion of the novel, the idea that prompted it, and the concern that sustains it. Here, again, we might have reason to question the author's own view of his work, since Sartre rarely even employs the word. But de Beauvoir reports that Sartre was already obsessed with this notion as early as 1928, and he started the book that would become *Nausea* soon afterward. "Contingency" embodies the idea that things exist without necessity. God, by contrast, is sometimes said to be the only "necessary existent."[8] Our own existence, in particular, is contingent, however necessary it might seem *to us*, even logically, as in Descartes' famous argument or inference, "I think, therefore I am."

The existence of the world is also contingent, and much ink has been spilled over the ages trying to answer the brain-torturing question "Why is there something rather than nothing?" Nausea, as Sartre conceives of it, is the realization—or, rather, the immediate experience—of the fact that the existence of the world and all things in it, including one's own existence, is contingent. The fact that he rarely employs the word (176–177, 213) is no proof that he did not take the idea very seriously. Colin Wilson suggests that it "becomes the cornerstone of his philosophy."[9] But the connection between the contingency of any particular thing (including oneself) and the contingency of everything is by no means obvious. Nor is the connection between the contingency of everything and the idea that it is all meaninglessness. The radical conclusion that Sartre seems to draw (at least in the novel), that life is meaningless, does not follow from the fact that existence is merely contingent and not necessary. The contrast with God is again revealing, for in theological circles God's necessary existence is somehow supposed to ensure His meaningfulness. (That is why Sartre teases, in *Being and Nothingness*, that we essentially want to be God.) But surely we can question this, as many philosophical critics have in the past (Voltaire: "One might as well say that God is blue as that he is good"). And the fact that everything in life (including life itself) may be contingent only makes it more precious, not meaningless.

In *Nausea*, nausea is the experience (not merely the belief) that everything, including our own existence, is contingent. It is therefore without meaning (but this "therefore" can be understood as a subsequent experience, not as the conclusion of an argument). Roquentin oddly interprets this as *freedom*, in particular, freedom from obligation.[10] This negative conception is certainly at odds with Sartre's pervasive emphasis in *Being and Nothingness* on freedom as responsibility. But I do not think that nausea is, for Sartre, a uniform or singular experience. There is nausea as a reaction to emptiness or, to use Sartre's later, more formal notion, Nothingness, and there is nausea as a reaction to contingency. These are not the same. A healthier mind would see life's contingency as its richness, a reason to be cherished and appreciated. One might also experience a life of necessity, even a god's life, as tedious emptiness. Nausea is also a reaction to the meaninglessness of life, but meaning, emptiness, and contingency are different concerns, and meaninglessness, as Camus rightly sensed, is the product of reflection rather than of lived experience as such. Then there is Sartre's peculiar experience of nausea as a reaction to the intrusiveness of sheer existence, something else again.

These ideas are clearly related—a rather ugly family resemblance, perhaps, but they need to be distinguished and defended separately. Nevertheless, there is good reason to take very seriously the idea that nausea in all its forms is a concrete and philosophical experience of the world. It is genuine phenomenology, not a mere physiological disturbance. It is a philosophical disturbance of profound proportions, just like Camus' experience of the Absurd. But it can be understood in far more sophisticated philosophical terms.

Phenomenology, Intentionality, Transparency

Before we get farther into the phenomenology of *Nausea*, we ought to say something more about what phenomenology is and what it does. In discussing *The Stranger*, I suggested that looking at the world through Meursault's eyes is like looking through a colorless piece of glass, and what we see is not Meursault's mind but his world. Phenomenology is the study of experience, and experience is about the world, not about the contents of one's mind. According to Husserl, and then to Sartre, the study of experience involves *intentionality*. Experience (consciousness) is always experience *of* something. This sounds innocent enough, but it represents something of a revolution in philosophy. In the modern tradition, from Descartes to Hume, philosophers interested in "the problem of knowledge" tended to think of experience in terms of "inner" thoughts, sensations, and representations, raising the difficult issue of how these "inner" experiences could be verified as faithful representations of the "external" world. Indeed, it raised the problem, soon to become an obsession in philosophy, of whether the actual existence of the external world could ever be known or not, and if not, how existence could make any difference to us.

Edmund Husserl did not help matters when he promulgated a "phenomenological reduction" (or *epoché*) in which we distinguish the realm of consciousness from the natural world, phenomenology versus ontology. Husserl, accordingly, did not end, but further encouraged, the debate about how experience could represent the existence of the "external" world. It was left to Heidegger and then Sartre to eliminate the very idea that experience (consciousness) is a self-enclosed realm. What one experiences is the world and its actual existence.[11] Doing phenomenology *is* doing ontology. Thus Sartre's book *Being and Nothingness* is "an essay in phenomenological ontology."[12] Thus *Nausea*, as a description of Roquentin's experience, is also and at the same time a description of Roquentin's world. It is not just a description of his "state of mind." Thus a phenomenological description of an empty or meaningless world, presented by an absurdist like Camus or a pessimist like Roquentin, is a description of that world, not just of a state of mind. There need be no mention of the cynicism or pessimism. That may be evident in the description of the object—"meaningless" is a typical adjective here—but it is not something that needs to be said over and above that description of the world. It is not that one's feelings are meaningless. It is the world that is meaningless. In a word, our experience is *transparent*. It is not about itself but about the world.

The great virtue of *Nausea* is also what frustrates philosophers about it. It is virtually a theory-free book, as opposed to *Being and Nothingness*, which is a theory-obsessed book.[13] *Being and Nothingness* has some great examples, of course, and several others that are curiously inadequate to illustrate the point that Sartre is making. But I think we sell Sartre short when we take those anecdotes and examples as mere "illustrations" of a philosophical point. It is not as if the philosophical formulation and the arguments supporting it are the essence of the matter and, just to help us along, an example or two will do. The twentieth century made much too much of formulations and arguments, and in doing so, I think that it indeed lost sight of experience—a lament shared by both the phenomenologists and at least two of the leading American pragmatists, William James and John Dewey. One of the virtues of phenomenology, I want to argue, is that it corrects this overemphasis on argument alone. Husserl famously told his students, "If we ascribe no value to the reply, 'I see that it is so,' we fall into absurdity."[14] Argumentation has its limits.

This is not to say, of course, that Sartre has no "thesis" or "theory," nor that he has no arguments. It is not as if he should be considered, as has often been argued, "just a novelist." It is, rather, to say that the philosophical form that so many philosophers have learned in their graduate training may be a misleading way to understand even *Being and Nothingness*, the most undeniably professional and philosophical of Sartre's works. But *Nausea*, the novel, is just this: an exploration of experiential examples without the distraction of excessive and often obscure theory.

The Role of Reflection in *Nausea*

Nausea, unlike *The Stranger*, makes no effort to describe pure, unreflective experience. Roquentin's experience is reflected on through and through. The book is a kind of self-diagnosis, in diary form. Roquentin's experience does not include just his reflective experience. It also includes his reflections on his reflective experiences. Camus makes experience and reflection seem opposed by giving us a character who is as close as imaginable to being utterly without self-consciousness, without thought, without reflection. Then he throws him into a situation where all he can do is reflect because the lived experience of his life is virtually at an end. Roquentin, by contrast, is a thoughtful, obsessively reflective person, and his future is entirely open. He does not just describe his experiences; he takes notes on them, comments on them, tries to understand them. And all of this, of course, is part of his experience, too. In fact, it defines it, for unlike Meursault, he takes little pleasure in the sensuous delights of life. (In this he resembles Camus' later character Clamence, in *The Fall*.)

What is reflection? In one sense, it refers to any kind of thought or thinking, regardless of its object. Thus one can reflect on the origins of the universe, on the curious fact that there are so few blue flowers, on the once sad fact that the Boston Red Sox could not seem to win a pennant, on the convenience or inconvenience of the fact that a standard public school term has fifteen weeks. But the sense in which we are using "reflection" here is more restricted. It means reflection on (and in) one's own experience. It thus goes hand in hand with self-consciousness (although one should not confuse the two, as Sartre sometimes does). For Camus, reflection interferes with experience. For Sartre, reflection clarifies experience. In particular, reflection describes and makes explicit the perspective from which one has an experience. Because phenomenology describes the world and not the mind of the subject, what is often not described in phenomenological description is the state of the subject or his or her perspective. But reflection on experience does take account—or in any case, *may* take account—of the state of the subject and the perspective from which he or she has that experience. One might reflect, "Now why do I experience him as hateful?" or wonder, "Why do I find her so attractive?" One might wake up and ask, "Now why do I feel so cranky today?" or later in the day reflect, "How can I get out of this bad mood?" Thus one central function of reflection is to question, digest, and deal with one's experiences.

In this light, *Nausea* is a much more complex book than *The Stranger*. In *The Stranger*, part I, Meursault rarely reflects at all. But throughout *Nausea*, Roquentin is always reflecting. We watch Meursault's experiences unfold by way of the words of a narrator who is clearly *not* the same dull fellow as the character Meursault. But in *Nausea*, because of its diary form, what we get are the exact words and thoughts of Roquentin. And he tells us not only how he feels and what he has experienced, but he obsessively reflects on the meaning of what he experiences, even if, for the most part, he finds his experiences (and everything else) meaningless. But in a deeper sense, Roquentin does not adequately reflect on his experience. He never asks why he is so callous or where his nausea comes from. The role of reflection in the book is thus both pervasive and limited. Roquentin's experience consists for the most part of reflective experience and reflections on experience. He describes the nausea rising up in him as a definite experience, but it is clearly an experience born of reflection and made sense of only through reflection. And at the end of the book, when he has more or less digested the experience of nausea (sorry about the somewhat disgusting mix of metaphors), he bizarrely experiences this as a form of self-liberation.

In reflection, one distances oneself in order to get a broader or sharper view of one's experience. But sometimes, that distance is obtained only by looking at oneself "from the outside," taking up the point of view of another or others. This begins to explain why both Camus and Sartre tend to think of reflection as something of a break from and in opposition to lived experience (although Camus' views are much more radical than Sartre's). It is also why Roquentin seems so oddly distanced from the environments he routinely inhabits. His continuing reflection prevents him from ever just "getting into" his situation. Meursault, by contrast, experiences no such distance, only the "indifference" that is so characteristic of his personality. When Roquentin does get into his experience, it is almost always the experience of nausea that so engages him. And this, it seems, is something of a meta-experience, a reflective experience in which what he experiences is his *lack* of engagement with the world or, alternatively, the unwanted *intrusion* of the world and its existence into his resisting but ultimately victimized consciousness.

Life Is (Not) an Adventure

This sense of distance also explains Roquentin's odd obsession with having an *adventure*. (So, too, we can see its effects in his girlfriend Anny's hang-up with "perfect moments.") What is an adventure? One would think that it is a paradigm case of "getting into" an experience, being swept away, or otherwise so absorbed that, at least at the time, nothing else matters. Thus adventures are typically highly emotional and exciting. They involve risk and uncertainty, generating more emotion and excitement. They "unfold," as new challenges or complications present themselves. But this, Roquentin contends, confuses experience and reflection, living and telling about it. An adventure is not the "getting into" it but the narrative, the story that is told after the fact. Of course, one may narrate as one is having the adventure, but insofar as he or she does so, he or she will be that much less engaged in the adventure. The adventure lies in the retrospective story, not in the engagement, and thus the adventure and the story are at odds: "You have to choose: live or tell" (56).

Roquentin tells a story about a woman he met in Hamburg. While she is in the ladies' room, he weaves a tale about their relationship, including his waiting for her and his expectations about what might happen when she returns. Then she comes back (and fulfills his expectations). He reflects: "I hated her without knowing why. I understand now: one had begun to begin living again and the adventure was fading out" (56). Later on, he imagines himself growing old with a woman (whom he has merely observed casually), and describes this as "the feeling of adventure" (79). So longing for an adventure turns out to be a pragmatic contradiction. One does not actually *have* an adventure. One imagines or constructs an adventure, but without ever having one. (We should remember that one of Sartre's suggestions for the title of the book was "The Extraordinary Adventures of Antoine Roquentin," clearly ironic.) Sartre's own view, apparently, was that there are no adventures, at least not in this book, and that adventure is one of those evasive meanings that Roquentin is incapable of grasping.

The logic is interesting if not convincing. Telling a story means giving events a beginning and an end, a meaning. The adventure lies in the linkage, not in the events themselves. In other words, the adventure is due to the story, not the actual events.[15] "Things happen one way and we tell them in the opposite sense. You seem to start at the beginning. . . . And in reality you start at the end" (57). As Roquentin puts it in one of his more philosophical moods, "Structure or formula corrupts an event." Differently stated, the idea of an adventure depends on the notion of a (purely) prereflective engagement. But adventure requires storytelling, which is a form of reflection, so therefore an adventure is impossible.

Nevertheless, *Nausea* has a concern for time that is clearly lacking in *The Stranger*. The idea of history and concepts of the past are frequent topics of Roquentin's reflections and thoughts, despite the fact that, like *The Stranger*, the book is written for the most part in the tenseless present. (This is the inevitable result of the diary format.) There are, however, memories and "flashbacks" indicating that Roquentin's world had not always been as dreary and unexciting as his life in Bouville. In fact, it seems as if only a few years prior he was quite the world traveler, even an adventurer. And so, in the absence of any ongoing adventure, the novel is concerned with the idea of adventure. Sartre's peculiar view that there are no adventures is in stark contrast to Kierkegaard, who thought that existing through time was in itself an adventure. Sartre's character stands in stark contrast to Kierkegaard, too, because life is (for him) devoid of passion and passionate commitment. Roquentin is not, like Meursault in part I, devoid of emotions, but his emotions are embittered and taut. Like Meursault, he seems to have no capacity for empathy, but he does have a sense of history. In fact, in Roquentin's version of the vacuous present, it sometimes seems that all that is left to him is history, and he cannot get a grasp of that either. He even goes so far as to claim *that the past does not exist*.

Nausea is in part a book about a book, a historical study that never gets finished. Early in the novel, Roquentin despairs, "I am cast out, forsaken in the present; I vainly try to rejoin the past: I cannot escape" (33). Thus Roquentin forms a troubled relationship with a minor historical figure, whose story he tries to tell ("M. de Rollebon was my partner; he needed me in order to exist and I needed him so as not to feel my existence" [132]). But there, too, lies a philosophical irony. At first, it seems that Roquentin lives for the Marquis de Rollebon. That is his (rather limited) reason for existing. But he comes to realize that the continued existence of the Marquis now depends entirely on him, that in a sense the life and death of the Marquis are in his hands. And at this point he dismisses him, giving up on the project. In its place, he curiously decides to write a novel "beautiful and hard as steel," in other words, the very antithesis of the ugly viscosity of *Nausea*.

My good friend and guru Sam Keen likes to ask the question, "Whose stories are you passing on?," the idea being that the stories we tell are rarely our own, even when they are stories about ourselves. Roquentin tries, in effect, to make the Marquis de Rollebon's story his own, but then he abandons him in favor of a (never written) story of his own. Because the truth is, he has no story. Moreover, because the diary is for the most part a solipsistic exercise (as opposed, say, to Dr. Rieux's journal in *The Plague*), it, too, fails to be a story. " 'When you live alone you no longer know what it is to tell something,' Roquentin admits" (15). *Nausea* (his diary) offers us a disjointed description of mostly routine experiences and proceeds at an excruciating, plodding pace, and for the most part *nothing happens*. Nor is there any linkage, buildup, or suspense that would make anything significant seem to happen, except, perhaps, for Roquentin's long-awaited rendezvous with Anny at the end of the novel. This turns out, predictably, to be a great bust. Again, he anticipates an adventure (though with misgivings) and emerges empty-handed.

Even if something dramatic were to happen in *Nausea*, it is doubtful that Roquentin would recognize or experience it as an adventure. The failed romance with Anny displays classic tragic-romantic form, with Roquentin's longing and anticipation and then the confused climax with its conflict, frustration, and humiliation. It might not be a happy adventure, but for most people it would at least count as an adventure, even the adventure of their lifetime. Like Anny's "perfect moments," Roquentin's "adventures" are impossible fabrications, requiring both total absorption in the moment and a distancing reflective stance that gives that moment significance. In fact, of course, we narrate our ongoing lives all the time, engaged but not wholly absorbed in the moment while we reflectively endow not just that moment but an extended sequence of moments (defined by anticipations, expectations, and reflections) with meaning. But Sartre is playing off lived experience against reflection in a radical way, much as Camus does, so that a perfectly ordinary part of human experience appears to be impossible.

But if in *Nausea* nothing happens, the contrast with Camus' *The Stranger* would seem to be instructive. In *The Stranger* all sorts of things are happening around, with, and to the docile central character. The Algerian civil war and murderous racial tensions are heating up. He is surrounded by pimps and perverts who are his pals and who frequently get violent. He has an affair with a lovely young woman, gets involved in a knife fight with an Arab, and ultimately kills a man. Then there is the Kafkaesque trial and imprisonment. Through it all, Meursault remains remarkably blasé, but it would be hard to deny that he lives through an adventure. Of course, one might ask whether it is an adventure *for him*, which is the relevant question to ask here. If one (rightly) insists on subjectivizing the concept of adventure such that it is not just what happens but what one reflectively *experiences* that makes a string of events an adventure, then there is considerable room for doubt. Meursault doesn't reflect (until later), and at the time he does not get excited about any of this. Much of the time, he does not even notice. He anticipates very little, and he spends little time trying to put the events of his life in order and give them any meaning. He certainly doesn't *think* in terms of having an adventure. He is pretty clear and (for him) philosophically articulate when he insists that it doesn't much matter how one lives, as it all comes out the same "in the end" anyway. But then, although Meursault is quite bored on Sunday (when, according to him, nothing much happens), he seems quite satisfied with his life on the other days. And in contrast to the grim description of work and repetition in *The Myth of Sisyphus*, we might be willing to admit that Meursault seems to live his life and its routines as something of a subdued adventure, even if not reflectively. In any event, it certainly is not the case that "nothing happens," even *for him*.

But *Nausea* is a narrative, too, however disjointed and devoid of dramatic events. Narratives are not just *telling about*. They are also maps and guidelines, correctives and implicit criticism. Roquentin is wrong about what reflection is, because for him it is mere commentary. We can and do weave narratives as we live, even as we engage in our lives, and we guide and alter our living by way of those narratives. Insofar as reflection is a matter of narrative, it is particularly effective as a corrective to our outlook on the world, including our emotions and those global emotions (moods) of weltschmerz and boredom that Roquentin so obviously displays. (For

Meursault, by contrast, his moods are just transient facts, like the weather.) This is why Roquentin's reflections, though obsessive, are inadequate. He tries to understand himself, but without any impetus to change, no matter how unhappy he is. He misses the adventures of life not just because he denies himself (at present) the experiences, and not just because he insists on reflecting all the time. His reflections are ineffective and uncritical (even if they are loaded *with* criticism). His emotion of boredom and his pervasive contempt thus eclipse the possibility of any adventure. True reflection is not just observation and commentary, but *management* of one's states and feelings, a deep truth later recognized by Sartre in his treatment of "bad faith" in *Being and Nothingness*. Life is an adventure precisely in that one is doing the driving as well as the navigating, not just watching the scenery go by.

In Roquentin's (and Sartre's) case, the tedium of life and the emotions of boredom and contempt are, at least in part, caused by the (external) fact that they both are living in dreary little provincial towns. (Sartre taught grammar school in Le Havre and then in Laon from 1934 to 1937.) An utterly minimal amount of reflection is needed to disclose the fact that an immediate and effective corrective to those unpleasant emotions might be found in moving away. Sartre, accordingly, left the provinces and returned to Paris as quickly as he could. Roquentin, by contrast, decides to leave only when life in Bouville becomes utterly pointless. When one's experience of life is that it is increasingly meaningless and without adventure, then there would seem to be a real need to reflect on the causes, motives, and circumstances of one's experience as a first step to a cure. But Sartre's character (and in many ways Sartre himself) is in no mood to be cured.

Contingency and the Meaning of Existence

Roquentin's malaise is by no means so simple and straightforward as boredom with the place where he lives and contempt for the bourgeoisie that surround him. His is a profound "existential" malaise, suggesting something extremely disturbing about the nature of existence and the meaning of life. But before I get into a discussion of the most famous climactic passage about contingency in *Nausea*, let me say something, briefly, about what I think is at stake. What is most important of all in the phenomenological method, I think, especially in the light of those philosophers in the analytic tradition who now argue that philosophy is all about arguments, is the fact that phenomenology is an alternative to *philosophy-as-argument*. (Robert Nozick has some harsh words for this kind of philosophy in his *Philosophical Explanations*, before he goes on to practice it quite brilliantly himself.[16]) I want to suggest that it is the very point of phenomenology to take us beyond arguments, to the fundamental ("eidetic") experiences that define human existence. The point is that arguments are not the sine qua non of philosophy.

Sometimes, experience trumps reason. Or, at least, it trumps the sorts of reasons that philosophers are so adept at putting forward. Thus the point of Sartre's phenomenology is to show that in philosophy, as in the empirical sciences, experience trumps a priori reasoning (although the experience that phenomenology describes is not supposed to be empirical). Sartre gives us quite a few persuasive examples to make his case. *Nausea* is exemplary in this regard.

The primary example of this phenomenological argument against arguments is Sartre's best-known passage in *Nausea*. It perfectly exemplifies the claim that experience trumps reasoning and eclipses the sophisticated arguments of the philosophers. The scene is Roquentin's discovery of "being as such," the ugly intrusiveness of sheer existence, toward the end of the novel. (We might well wish for a happier example of intrusiveness, for instance, the captivating power of a beautiful piece of sculpture or the sublime power of a mountain looming before us. But it is Roquentin's experience in Bouville, so we can hardly expect aesthetic edification.) The troubling intrusiveness of existence had been anticipated earlier in the novel, for instance, in Roquentin's meditation on the oddities of his hand's existence (134ff.). But the scene I have in mind is the scene in the park, where he sits down beside a spreading chestnut tree root (170ff.).

> I was in the park just now. The roots of the chestnut tree were sunk in the ground just under my bench. I couldn't remember it was a root any more. The words had vanished and with them the significance of things, their methods of use, and the feeble points of reference which men have traced on their surface. I was sitting, stooping forward, head bowed, alone in front of this black, knotty mass, entirely beastly, which frightened me. Then, I had this vision.
>
> It left me breathless. Never, until these last few days, had I understood the meaning of "existence." I was like the others, like the ones walking along the seashore, all dressed in their spring finery. I said, like them, "The ocean *is* green; that white speck up there *is* a seagull," but I didn't feel that it existed or that the seagull was an "existing seagull"; usually existence hides itself. It is there, around us, in us, it is *us*, you can't say two words without mentioning it, but you can never touch it. When I believed that I was thinking about it, I must believe that I was thinking nothing, my head was empty, or there was just one word in my head, the word "to be."... If anyone had asked me what existence was, I would have answered, in good faith, that it was nothing, simply an empty form which was added to external things without changing anything in their nature. And then all of a sudden, there it was, clear as day: existence had suddenly revealed itself...—naked, in a frightful, obscene nakedness. (*Nausea*, 170–171)

One could read this, needless to say, as a self-description of the onset of insanity, as one would read a clinical interview as part of a case history from Sigmund Freud or Oliver Sachs. But this is not how Sartre intends it. This is a strangely liberating experience, a sudden insight into the truth of things. From a philosophical standpoint, it is arguable that "existence is nothing," that it is "added to external things without changing anything in their nature." A unicorn is an animal with a horse's body and head and a large horn in the middle of its forehead. It is merely a contingent fact that no unicorn exists. A platypus is an implausible mammal that lays eggs and has a ducklike bill and ducklike feet, and it exists in Australia. So, too, with all beings, odd or ordinary: This is what they *are*, and Do they exist? is a secondary question. They are contingent. The only exception is God, the "necessary being." According to centuries of "ontological" argument, knowing what God is (e.g., "most perfect being conceivable"), we know that *therefore* He must exist. But everything else is contingent, and its existence or nonexistence is merely something "added on."

This idea of existence is often tied to the notion of "essence," a term invented by Aristotle to characterize the necessary features of a thing. Thus a necessary feature of Socrates, according to an old Aristotelian syllogism, is that he is a man, and thus mortal, and that he thinks. Merely accidental features of Socrates, by contrast, are the facts that he has a beard, and gout, and a wife named Xantippe. Sartre employs a famous formula, in a popular Paris lecture in 1947: "Existence precedes essence."[17] It is a slight misstatement (and with a quite different meaning) borrowed from Heidegger, but as Sartre uses it, it is quite straightforward. We exist before we have essential features, before we know *what* we are and how we are to behave, how we are to be. What he has in mind are not the definitional features of *Homo sapiens* (vertebrate, mammal, walks upright, opposable thumbs, twenty-three pairs of chromosomes, etc.) but such more or less "moral" features, such as being selfish, being loyal, being cruel, being kind—in other words, the virtues and vices. (In *Being and Nothingness*, Sartre seems to argue that *freedom* is an essential feature of human being, but let us not discuss this here.) In the passage from *Nausea*, Sartre is much more concerned with Aristotelian metaphysics than with ethics, and the question is whether something's essence (what it "*is*" essentially—the "is" of predication) is definitive or whether its mere *existence* is what matters (the "existential" use of "is"), regardless of its essence. Thus, "The ocean *is* green; that white speck up there *is* a seagull" suggests that what matters is the essential *whatness* of the ocean or the bird, whereas what Roquentin comes to see is that what matters first of all is their brute existence.

Against "the ontological proof" of God's existence (by Saint Anselm, later by Descartes and Leibniz), Kant argued that existence "is not a predicate," and so not part of the definition or essence of things. Thus Kant also concluded that theoretical reason could not prove that God is a necessary being (although His existence could be defended in other ways). Again, what counts is the definition or essence of a thing, not its existence. In current symbolic logic, students also learn that "existence is not a predicate." It is a "quantifier," so that "the present King of France is not bald" (which is false, as there is presently no King of France) is best transmogrified as the complex false claim "There exists one and only one present King of France, and he is not bald." It is the existence claim that is false. Baldness is a property (that is, "baldness" is a predicate), but existence is not.[18] I would not want to push such examples too far, and I certainly do not want to pretend to squeeze some phenomenological or existentialist significance out of symbolic logic, but the insight that Roquentin gains in this strange passage does point to an elaborate history of phenomenological and ontological debate about the nature of existence that any philosopher would recognize.

For many centuries, philosophers strained to prove the obvious: that there are, undeniably, substantial objects right there in front of our eyes. Problems concerning the contingent existence of things permeated medieval philosophy and reached a crisis stage with Descartes, who insisted that their existence could be philosophically doubted. Other philosophers followed with more extreme conclusions, for instance, David Hume in his skepticism, which insisted that there was no rational alternative to doubt: The existence of the world could not be rationally proven. Husserl, in response, insisted, "If we ascribe no value to the reply, 'I see that it is so,' we fall into absurdity."[19] But with Husserl, quite frankly, I often have trouble seeing exactly what *it* is that I'm supposed to see that is so. In Sartre, by contrast, the illustrations are graphic, well-placed, and well-crafted, especially in *Nausea*. On the one hand, there is that history over the centuries of philosophical arguments that would reduce any *this* to an idea, a word, a theory, a function. Hegel's famous argument in "Sense Certainty," at the opening of the *Phenomenology*, is exemplary. A mere "this" refers to nothing at all. To refer, even to point, requires a concept. But Sartre is challenging this. A "this" refers to *something* first of all. A subsequent question might be "What is it?," but it is the existence that intrudes on consciousness, not the concept.

In this passage, Sartre also expresses a surprising ambivalence toward "words." Words protect our fragile ordering of the world, and for this it is necessary to have categories. We could not even perceive, much less think or talk, without them. In *Nausea*, the Self-Taught Man struggles to figure out whether Roquentin is a "misanthrope" or a "pessimist," and he labels himself a "humanist" and a "socialist." What we call things makes an enormous difference, whether a bomb thrower is a "terrorist" or a "freedom fighter," for example. (In Chinese [Confucian] philosophy, this essential philosophical concern is called "the rectification of names.") In his autobiography *The Words*, Sartre makes the even stronger claim that we get to "own" things and we take possession of them by naming them, a sensibility that is familiar to us in such routine activities as naming a new pet or, more seriously, naming a new baby. (Naming a toy poodle "Poodiful" is clever; naming a boy baby "Sue" sets him up for life.) Many of us even name our cars ("Little Blue," "Ralph," "Rachel," "Harald"). Naming and the right to name connote true ownership and a kind of ontological control. But in *Nausea*, "Things are divorced from their names. They are grotesque, headstrong, gigantic, and it seems ridiculous to call them 'x' or say anything about them. I am in the midst of things, nameless things, they surround me" (Thus). Roquentin is, "without words, defenseless" (169). How fragile is our little conceptual scheme. This is not a problem of relativism or the incommensurability with alternative conceptual schemes, but the very fragility of talking about conceptual schemes at all. What is not at all fragile, only contingent, is *being*. And that transcends all language and reference, all concepts and categories.

After describing the ugly intrusiveness of the chestnut tree root—not the fact that it is a root but the sheer fact of its existence—Roquentin goes on to describe his own existence and the existence of others as

> a heap of living creatures, irritated, embarrassed at ourselves, we hadn't the slightest reason to be there, none of us, each one, confused, vaguely alarmed, felt in the way in relation to the others. *In the way*: it was the only relationship between these trees, these gates, these stones. . . . *In the way*, the chestnut tree there, . . . And I—soft, weak, obscene, digesting, juggling with dismal thoughts—I, too, was *in the way*. . . . I dreamed vaguely of killing myself to wipe out at least one of these superfluous lives. But even my death would have been *in the way*. . . . I was *in the way* for eternity.

The suggestion here is that we are not only contingent—it just happens that we exist— we are somehow inappropriate, intrusive, and therefore we ought to be embarrassed or ashamed at our existence. So, too, at the end of the book Roquentin aspires to write a novel that will "make people ashamed of their existence" (237). Thus the experience Roquentin describes is not meaningless. It does have a meaning, and that meaning is utterly demeaning. The meaning of our existence is that we ought to be ashamed of ourselves.

The chestnut root, by contrast, has no reason to feel ashamed, though it, too, is "in the way," intrusive, out of place. This perceived aggressiveness on the part of things by virtue of their sheer existence, over and above its being a symptom of the subject's incipient psychosis, is a witty turnaround of the traditional phenomenological notion of intentionality, which Husserl described as consciousness *directed at* various objects which themselves were essentially passive. But here Sartre is giving us a disturbing description of various objects not only directed *back at* consciousness but downright invasive. Existence is not neutral. It is offensive. And so even his own existence comes to seem to him as offensive both to himself and to other people.

This relationship between contingency and offensiveness is by no means all that clear. Just because something is contingent (or exists only contingently), that would not seem to indicate its unwelcomeness, much less such offensiveness. The rarity of precious stones does not make them unwelcome, nor does the rarity of true friends. Of course, Sartre will defend this strange idea of the world as a "plenum," that is, as completely *full* (excepting only consciousness, which is "nothing"). But the fact that the world is full of contingent things (or that the world is itself contingent) would not seem to indicate anything about its status in our experience. The connection seems to be the lack of meaningfulness of existence as such, since meaningfulness would seem to depend on *what* something is and how it fits into one's world. Thus a root would be meaningful to the gardener who takes care of the park, but as a chestnut root (etc.) and not just as an existing thing. One's life might be meaningful if he or she has projects and purposes and these are going well, especially if one has a passion for these projects and purposes and these passions are (more or less) satisfied or satisfying. But one's sheer existence is not meaningful at all. And neither is existence as such.

Paradoxes of Contingency

There is a curious but very familiar logical paradox built into the recognition of one's own existence. Descartes, looking for the one necessary and certain truth with which to launch his *Meditations* (and his *Discourse*), stumbled on his own existence. (In the *Discourse*, "I think, therefore I am.") He thought that he could not be wrong about his own existence, which thus took on the apparent status of a necessary truth. But it is a strange necessary truth that depends on the existence of the thinker. At the same time that one realizes the peculiar logical status of the proposition "I exist," one becomes instantly and painfully aware that it is in no way impossible that one might not have existed.[20] Thus those many poor philosophical jokes and cartoons about not thinking and therefore not existing (most of which embody the logical fallacy of "If A, then B; not A, therefore not B"). The obvious truth that emerges from Descartes' reflections is not the necessity of either the self or (by a curious deduction) the world but the contingency of both. One's own existence is contingent and the existence of one's world, that is, the world of one's experience, is contingent. There might well have been no such experience.

It does not take much of a psychoanalytic leap of imagination, however, to see that what bothers Sartre about contingency is not contingency at all, the thought that he or anything in the world or, for that matter, the world itself, might not exist. What bothers him is his own peculiar existence. He is (in his own opinion) short, unhealthy, and ugly. And when one is so afflicted, it is natural to ask, "Why? Why could I not be otherwise than I am? Why do I have to be here at all?" And here, too, there is an interesting paradox that every novice philosopher has encountered. Once one starts down the road to "if only...," there is no logical limit to the number of changes or possibilities that might be waiting. "If only I were not so ugly, I would have been popular in school, in which case I would not have studied anything so strange as philosophy, in which case I would not have become a philosopher, in which case I would not have gone back to Paris, in which case I would not have gotten together with Simone and the gang," and so on. After a few long trains of such thinking, the conclusion often seems to be that nothing could be other than it is, since if it were even a little bit different, it might be altogether different. Thus contingency gets interestingly wedged between sheer happenstance and a bizarre kind of necessity.

What also bothers Sartre, those psychoanalytically inclined are sure to suggest, is his own mortality. It is not so much that he might not exist, but rather that he will someday no longer exist. And this is not only possible but necessary. Thus a man's desire to be "indispensable" (as Sartre puts it in *The Age of Reason*) is just so much vanity. He (like everyone) is utterly dispensable. The rest is philosophical puzzles and games. This concern with one's own mortality becomes problematic and even obsessive when one is particularly unhappy. In the throes of depression, one might actively want to end one's life. But living as Roquentin is living—not depressed but merely bitter and cynical, without passion, his historical project having collapsed beneath him, his adventurous life behind him, and his romance with Anny already over—the thought that he is mortal prompts only ambivalence and confusion: "Why should I not be relieved or even glad to leave this meaningless life?" But then again, what's the point of doing so? Many normal people in such states have "dreamed vaguely of killing" themselves, but it is no more than this, a passing thought. Life has no meaning, yet killing oneself seems to have no point either. Here we see Sartre anticipating Camus and his dramatic opening to *The Myth of Sisyphus*, though in much more subdued and (one might argue) evasive language. Recognizing the contingency of existence is not so much a phenomenological insight as it is an existential trauma.

Anticipating Camus, Sartre writes:

> The word absurdity is coming to life under my pen; a little while ago, in the garden, I couldn't find it, but neither was I looking for it, I didn't need it. . . Absurdity was not an idea in my head, . . . only this long serpent dead at my feet, this wooden serpent. . . . And without formulating anything clearly, I understood that I had found the key to existence, the key to my nausea, to my own life. In fact, all that I could grasp beyond that returns to this fundamental absurdity. (173)

In an earlier description of his own hand as if it were a dead crab, and then in his revelation about his own sheer existence (134), Roquentin goes on to toy with Descartes: " 'I exist, I am the one who keeps it up [the thinking] . . . not to think . . . don't want to think . . . I think I don't want to think. I mustn't think that I don't want to think. Because that's still a thought.' Will there never be an end to it?" Then "My thought is *me*: that's why I can't stop. I exist because I think . . . and I can't stop myself from thinking." Two pages later, "I have the right to exist, therefore I have the right not to think." I do not pretend that this is very profound, or that its points have not been made many times before (including by Descartes' contemporaries), but I quote it here to confirm the claim that *Nausea* is a quite conscious and quite knowledgeable contribution to phenomenology more than a mere novel or narrative, and that it is the curious confusion of contingency and necessity in the first-person standpoint that Sartre is highlighting. On the one hand, the existence of the self (or consciousness) is clearly contingent. It could just as well not be. One might not exist or have existed at all. But from the first-person standpoint non-existence is unintelligible, and in this sense seems necessary. One can imagine oneself never having existed, but it is one's self (or one's consciousness) that is doing the imagining.

The experience of nausea is a very peculiar reaction to the contingency of things, to be sure, but it displays much more than an odd psychosomatic neurosis suffered by Sartre and his narrator/character Roquentin. It is, I maintain, a dramatic presentation of an admittedly rare philosophical experience, which may take years of preparation. It does not so much make an "obvious" philosophical point as it cuts through a dozen anything but obvious philosophical arguments and sophistries. It is, in one sense, the phenomenological equivalent of Dr. Johnson's kicking of the stone, except that in this case the kicker clearly knows what is at stake in the demonstration. It is, from another perspective, a skillful undoing of the power of language by a master of language, giving us a vivid reminder of what we all in some sense already ("pre-analytically") know but in recent philosophy too easily tend to forget: that the world is not a text and not merely interpretation, and it is not composed of or even defined by ideas. There is no necessity to it, in the sense so long pursued by philosophers, no *logos* or reason for its being, no answer to the question "Why is there something rather than nothing?" Is Sartre's phenomenology going to be persuasive to every reader? No, of course not. I find it extremely odd myself. But do we really need all of those twisted arguments about the "phenomenon of being" and "the being of the phenomenon" at the beginning of *Being and Nothingness,* or are they something of a philosophical afterthought to a point already well made in *Nausea?* Argument is often beside the point in philosophy, and the ontological quibbles that are so obsessively rendered by philosophers but never settled by arguments may not be the true stuff of philosophy, but a kind of distraction from it.

The Origins of Angst
and Nothingness

In the preceding sections I focused on Jean-Paul Sartre's odd obsession with the notions of contingency and existence, and I argued that Sartre's phenomenology was in part an attempt to counter some skeptical philosophical arguments with exemplary and undeniable experience. There is another example I want to present (of experience trumping argument) that also has a good deal to do with contingency and with Sartre's concept of *Nothingness.* (I momentarily retain the capital "N" to emphasize the Teutonic style of Sartre's ontology.) Nothingness is a central motif in *Nausea,* particularly in Roquentin's continuing experiences of meaninglessness. It plays a larger and more explicit role in *Being and Nothingness*, where it becomes definitive (as *freedom*) of consciousness itself. In his pursuit of nothingness, Sartre follows in the footsteps of Heidegger, to whom he is obviously heavily indebted, but he is again pursuing his own agenda of coming to grips with his reputedly lifelong obsession with contingency. One might say, somewhat glibly, that the other side of contingency is nothingness. It is its constant companion, its essential horizon. For if contingency is the permanent possibility of non-being, then nothingness as Hegel and before him, Parmenides had argued, might be something of a condition of being. And if existence is as aggressive as Sartre seems to suggest it is, at least in *Nausea*, then one might well say, with Heidegger, that nothingness is active as well, so that "nothing nothings" or "nothing nots." It is no mere absence. But all of this philosophical cuteness aside, nothingness has an essential phenomenological role to play, first in a general account of experienced absences, second in the very particular account of anxiety, *angoisse*, or good German *angst*.

The experience of absences permeates and to some extent defines *Nausea*. Most of Roquentin's descriptions of his experience are descriptions of disappointments, disillusionments, dissatisfactions, and regrets. A general account of experienced absences is this: one cannot explain the perception of an absence—for example, the absence of Anny, who was expected to be in the café—by enumerating all of the things that *are* in the café, and then, with an additional effort of reflection, take note that Anny is not among them.[21] One simply *sees*, assuming that one is looking for her, that Anny is not in the café. In fact, insofar as the meeting is desperately desired, that may well be *all* that Roquentin sees or notices in the café. Bertrand Russell, in the analytic tradition, raised quite a howl when he suggested that there must be "negative facts." Whether this makes ontological sense or not, in the realm of phenomenological description it seems to make perfectly good sense. We perceive absences because what we bring to experience are expectations (and, more specifically, hopes, fears, and anticipations). And it is in light of these that we are disappointed (or delighted, as the case may be). In any case, it is against the active ingredient of anticipation in our experience that we experience what Husserl, showing a rare flare for the dramatic, called "the explosion of the noema," when the horizon of our expectations is not fulfilled. But it is not *reflection* on this lack of fulfillment that constitutes the perception of nothingness. It is in the prereflective or unreflected upon experience itself.

Sartre adds to this familiar account an extensive general theory of the activities of consciousness, which are not just receptive but, as above, anticipatory and reactive as well. One does not just perceive an empty café. One perceives, on the basis of prior expectations, the absence of Anny. Furthermore, particularly if one is disappointed, one can react toward this perception with a number of different *negatités*, ranging from irritation to outright denial. A *negatité* is a judgment or an experience that contains an essential negativity, but it often seems that this includes virtually all judgments and experiences insofar as an always available alternative is the negation of that judgment or some other experience. Sartre's basic insight is that consciousness is thoroughly active, and this activity consists in part of negative acts of consciousness, summarized in our ability to respond, think, or say "no!" to any experience, not necessarily in a word or in words, obviously, but in the way that we have that experience.

An experience can repulse us, disgust us, alienate us, and it is this alienation from or, rather, *in* experience that characterizes Roquentin's life throughout the book. Virtually our every experience consists of fulfillment or frustration of any number of expectations, what Husserl calls the "horizon" of experience or "noemata," its meanings. Thus our every experience is shot through with the possibility of fulfillment, disappointment, or surprise. Sartre and Heidegger no doubt overdramatize this possibility of nothingness and the pervasiveness of contingency, but the point is a good, solid, phenomenological point. We perceive absences against a background of expectations. What Roquentin mainly perceives in his drab experience in Bouville are absences, disappointments, frustrations, counterfactuals, as-ifs, a present rendered boring in the light of memories of the past and rendered hopeless in the face of unrealistic anticipations of the future. It is not hard to imagine Sartre, during his year or so stuck in the provinces, having many similar experiences. So, too, it is not hard to read Camus' later novel, *The Fall*, as an elaborate description of a similar world overshadowed by a once bright shining past and by continuing disappointments and other *"negatités."*

Anxiety, angst, or *angoisse* is a phenomenon of nothingness.[22] As I said, Sartre's account of nothingness and anxiety is heavily indebted to Heidegger. In fact, it is virtually lifted from the pages of *Sein und Zeit*, part I, sections 40 and 41. But Sartre, much more than Heidegger, gives us a full phenomenological description of this peculiar emotion (or mood, as the case may be). Anxiety is peculiar in that, one could argue, it is more or less unique to human beings, as opposed to fear, which we clearly share with a good part of the animal kingdom. Fear is a reaction to danger. Sometimes it is unthinking, merely reactive, even instinctual, as in the sudden fear of a very large shadow crossing one's path, even in circumstances that one considers safe and nonthreatening. Sometimes it is a learned, largely reflective response, such as fear of being audited by the income tax people after having knowingly taken excessive deductions or not including substantial income. But in any case, fear is the fear of something in the world (where threats to one's health and injuries to one's body, as well as damage to one's bank account, clearly count as "things in the world"). We might debate about dread, which Kierkegaard described as the fear of the unknown, and ask whether "the unknown" counts as a "thing" (an intentional object) or not. Or we might assimilate dread to anxiety and sharply distinguish it from fear. But in any case, there is an emotion or a mood that is to be sharply distinguished from fear, and that is what Sartre is talking about in *Being and Nothingness* and anticipating in *Nausea*.

Anxiety might seem to be irrational. Freud certainly believed it to be so. But it is not at all irrational in the sense that phobias and irrational fears are irrational, where there seems to be a "split level" of both belief and emotion ("On the one hand, I know that spiders are not dangerous, but on the other hand I freak out whenever I see one"). There is also a distinction between fear and panic, where it is a mistake, I would argue, to simply assume the latter as an extreme or extremely irrational form of the former. Panic sometimes seems to be more or less objectless, and in any case it quickly leaves the object (phenomenologically as well as spatially) behind. But, without grappling with these interesting issues, we can summarize Sartre's plausible claim as the claim that fear is always fear *of something*, and this is what distinguishes it from anxiety.

Anxiety, by contrast, is not a fear of anything, and it is, in an important sense, not "about" anything, or at least any "thing" in the world.[23] Anxiety strikes us when we become aware of our own possible actions and their consequences. Of course, one could insist that anxiety is "about" our own actions, and thus is a special kind of fear, but this loses the important contrast that Sartre is trying to make. There is a difference, we would agree, between fear of something happening to us and being afraid of *what we might do*. Sartre draws us a convincing picture of anxiety and its difference from fear in *Being and Nothingness*. It is a scene along a precipice—although I usually suggest the window ledge of a tall building for my urban students. Walking along the precipice, or leaning out of the window, we face a very likely lethal fall. We might find much to be afraid of—falling, for one thing; being pushed, for another; slipping, which is somewhat different from either falling or being pushed; and, in certain circumstances, having the edge or the ledge collapse under one's weight, which is something quite different again. The objects of one's fear, in other words, can be quite varied, although all presumably come down to one thing, which is that involuntary plunge through empty space and the prospect of a gruesome landing. Of course, this fear can be embellished in any number of ways: a fear for the well-being of unfortunate hikers or pedestrians underneath, a fear for the effects on one's dependents and loved ones, the fear of missing an important upcoming meeting, the shame or embarrassment of screaming uncontrollably, the horror of imagining one's body contorted and broken on the rocks or the sidewalk below. But the essential fear, in this case, is the fear of falling. Anxiety, by contrast, is the awful realization that one could simply, spontaneously, *jump*.

Anxiety, in short, is the awful realization of one's freedom. (Heidegger, we should note, takes *angst* to prompt much more than this, and also arguably less, since freedom is not a major consideration in his philosophy.) For Sartre, anxiety is the experience that there is *nothing* that stands between that fatal decision and me. One need not ontologize nothingness to appreciate the force of this.[24] The walk along the precipice (or leaning out the window) illustrates, in one particularly powerful experience, the over-

whelming "fact" of our freedom. Anxiety is the direct experience of nothingness, but it is not *about* nothingness, considered as a peculiar phenomenological object. (It is not, in other words, the experience of an absence,
such as Anny missing from the café.) It is "about" our own actions, which
(as Kant said) we cannot consider as other than free. It might be objected, by
philosophers interested in defending the integrity of the scientific worldview—at least the scientific worldview of prequantum science—that such a
"fact" could in fact be an illusion, and thus not a fact at all. If scientific
determinism is true, they would say, then there is no room for freedom,
however powerful our merely apparent experience of it. But between the
overwhelming experience and the merely convincing arguments, the latter
are no match for the former.

Science, of course, is an "objective" or third-person discipline. And Kant
was right, at least in his still Newtonian context, to insist that causality was
essential to the scientific viewpoint. But Kant, long before Husserl or Sartre,
realized that there was a standpoint other than the natural standpoint. (One
need not get confused that, for Kant, the natural standpoint was also the
phenomenological standpoint, but from the point of view of science.) Kant's
other standpoint was what he called "noumenal" or "intelligible," both
terms designed to intimidate and confuse. But more to our purposes here,
this other standpoint was the "practical" standpoint, the way we view
ourselves and the world when we consider ourselves as agents who have to
make decisions, employing what Kant referred to as "Will." Whenever we
act, we *have to* take up this standpoint, according to Kant. And within it,
"We cannot but conceive of ourselves as free."

This, I propose, is exactly what Sartre has in mind. Walking along the
precipice, we have to see ourselves as agents, and we cannot but conceive
of ourselves as free. For Sartre, this simply follows from the phenomenological perspective. And as for the scientific perspective, Sartre makes no
commitment about that whatsoever.[25] It is enough that, from the phenomenological perspective, especially in urgent situations, anything other
than freedom (and the responsibility that goes along with it) simply becomes
unthinkable.

In *Nausea*, too, freedom is a mere absence, but it is an absence of
meaning: "I am free: there is absolutely no more reason for living. . . . Alone
and free. But this freedom is rather like death" (209). Indeed, one might
wonder if nausea itself is the experience of freedom, an oddly perverted form
of anxiety, or the very opposite, an experience of unfreedom, the experience
of there being *nothing* to do. In *Nausea*, it seems to be both, but in the mature
Sartre, there is no doubt that it is the experience of freedom and the responsibility that goes with it that defines his philosophy.

We Americans, of course, may be put off by Sartre's examples. We like to
think that freedom is a happy phenomenon, an occasion for joy and celebration, fireworks and vacuous political speeches, one of the wonders of
American life—our many choices in the supermarket and in the mall, the

seemingly limitless choice of cable stations, hi-tech gadgets, and weighty vehicle options, the fact that we can say what we want (the Attorney General permitting), go where we want (travel advisories and visa restrictions notwithstanding), and vote as we want (no information or education required or encouraged). But I think that this is our mistake rather than Sartre's. Freedom is indeed anxiety-producing—not, perhaps, the choice between two brands of detergent or two competing airlines, but the really serious "existential" choices that we all face from time to time. Our luxurious menu of choices is misleading, and it is indeed in the anxiety of choosing rather than in the number of options available that our freedom is to be found. Most of us would admit that the little choices we make every day are for the most part better explained by determinism—attractive packaging and exploitative advertising, for instance—than by our freedom. But in the face of life-and-death examples, the arguments defending determinism seem so empty, and those defending free will, so irrelevant. The important thing is to choose. Nevertheless, the freedom that is so undeniable is a burden, not a blessing. And Sartre never lets us think otherwise.

The last part of *Being and Nothingness* is filled with such examples, and it is not coincidental, in my view, that most of these involve emotionally charged or highly dangerous situations and cases in which our "Being-for-Others" is very much a consideration. Sartre's personal example of refusing to stop and rest on a hike with his friends, although he is thoroughly exhausted, is a case in point. Given the risk of humiliation, most of us exercise remarkable "willpower" and go against what science and medicine would probably predict of us. Science ultimately deals in probabilities, and we know from experience that if someone is sufficiently self-determined, he or she can sometimes "beat the odds." Such experiences can be so powerful that all of those arguments for scientific determinism that seemed so plausible in the seminar room fade into nothing in the face of an existential crisis. The *experience* of free choice is much more convincing than the mere arguments for determinism, no matter how persuasive. (Of course, a stubborn determinist would then gladly heap the sociological pressure onto the list of "antecedent conditions" and continue to deny any role for choice. But, again, the experience of choice overwhelms any such increasingly ad hoc arguments.)

Contrary to some of Sartre's less sympathetic (and less informed) critics, it does not matter that we often fail to do what we want and try to do.[26] The experience of freedom lies in the choice, in the trying, not necessarily in the doing. When someone says, whether on the basis of supposed science or by appeal to New Age fatalism, "Whatever will happen, has to happen," as a way of not choosing, I think we can agree with Sartre that he or she is thereby "choosing not to choose" and is acting in "bad faith." Our experience of freedom trumps the many rationalizations we devise in order to deny it. We have become expert at manufacturing excuses why we could not do this or could not choose that, but Sartre puts the kibosh on all such rationalizations to return our attention to the undeniable experience of freedom, the realization that *nothing* stands in our way. And here it is obvious that Roquentin is anything but a Sartrean hero. His malaise is a lush garden of rationalizations, paralyzing his desires and his will. The fact that he equates freedom with nothingness (that is, with meaninglessness) is no more than a curious play on words. The nothingness that Roquentin intends is the total absence of both meaning and responsibility. The nothingness that Sartre defends is both the "positive" freedom to make choices and the total responsibility that follows from this.

Again, phenomenology takes us beyond arguments to the "eidetic" experiences that define human existence. And these experiences trump the supposedly irrefutable arguments that philosophers have put forward. Sartre's description of the walk along the precipice, as a palpable description of what our sense of freedom ultimately comes to, struck me at the age of nineteen (when I was steeped in the lore of science), as it still does today, as the quintessential experience of what it means to be free. It remains the definitive reply to all of my friends who are still publishing books and articles trying to define that minuscule "gap" in determinism or the nuances of meaning between "reasons" and "causes" of action. Freedom is our reality; it does not need proof, but only a moment's experience.

What Roquentin Is Missing: Shame and "Being-for-Others"

An Ethiopian proverb says, "A man without shame is a man without honor." Aristotle, in the *Nicomachean Ethics*, argues much the same thing at length. He calls shame a "quasi virtue," in the sense that while it is not good to feel shame (as that indicates that one has done something wrong), it is even worse if one does not feel shame when one ought to.[27] What is wrong with Roquentin, among his other character faults and flaws, is his lack of shame, or what Sartre more generally calls a sense of "Being-for-Others." Roquentin minutely describes the behavior, dress, and foibles of other people (like Meursault at his mother's funeral, though without the cool neutrality). He also (unlike Meursault) neurotically assesses his own body, behavior, and activity. But there is hardly any suggestion that he is aware of other people's awareness of him, nor does he seems to care about his effect on other people. Roquentin lacks not only shame but any semblance of empathy and all of those emotions having to do with being with other people that give life so much of its meaning (both positive and negative). It is this that makes him so callous. (Meursault, by contrast, expresses mere Rousseauesque "indifference.") But it is also what makes Roquentin's life seem so meaningless. Aristotle famously insists, "No one would choose to live without friends." Roquentin's virtually global contempt (at least in the situations we find him in) makes anything resembling friendship impossible. And even

Sartre can be called as a grudging witness here. If "Hell is other people" (as his characters come to realize in *No Exit*), then perhaps Heaven is other people, too. What makes life meaningful is, at least in part, the fact that we share it with others. The possibility of shame and being shamed is part of the price we pay.

Shame provides us with a third example of an experience that overwhelms all arguments, although I will save most of my discussion of "Being-for-Others" in any detail for a later chapter on *No Exit*. Briefly, the philosophical history is a series of modern arguments trying to tackle the problem of *solipsism*, the absurd dilemma in which the philosopher is unable to prove the existence of anyone other than himself, including, presumably, his audience and readers. In *Being and Nothingness*, Sartre refers to this (with typical literary flair) as "the reef of solipsism," and he focuses his account on Husserl, Hegel, and Heidegger. In fact, the problem goes back to Descartes and the empiricists and infects virtually every philosopher, including Kant, who takes his own subjectivity as his starting point. Sartre even points out that he himself thought (about the time he was writing *Nausea*) that rejecting Husserl's conception of the "transcendental ego" would resolve the problem of solipsism, but five years later, in *Being and Nothingness*, he admits that this will not do.[28] He then comes to see that the problem of solipsism can be solved only by giving up "the affirmation that my fundamental connection with the Other is realized through *knowledge*."[29] He thinks Hegel made a major improvement by making the Other indispensable to the constitution of *self*-consciousness through reciprocity.[30] Heidegger, finally, in his "barbaric fashion of cutting Gordian knots rather than trying to untie them," simply defines his *Dasein* as "being-in-the-world," but thereby (according to Sartre) loses any chance of establishing *concrete* relations with others (as opposed to some a priori relationship with other people in general).[31]

Probably without having read Hegel, John Stuart Mill tackled the problem in the nineteenth century and developed what has since been called "the argument from analogy."[32] The argument is that we observe other beings behaving much as we do, so we then infer that their behavior is caused by the same kinds of mental states as our own. The argument has often and easily been refuted, on largely empiricist and inductive grounds. Since we can never check whether another being's behavior is in fact motivated or caused by mental states, such states by definition (in that tradition) being accessible only to one person, it is an inference which cannot ever be confirmed. It is possible, at least "logically," that I am in fact the only conscious being in the world.

Roquentin is not so very different from such a solipsist, but of course there is nothing by way of argument for this position in *Nausea*. Sartre simply has his character assume a more or less solipsistic role. But such a position is not only an intellectual embarrassment, it is morally unacceptable as well. What the philosopher cannot prove is what Roquentin refuses to see: that he shares the world with other people who are as deserving of respect as he is.

The fact that he has no self-respect, however, goes a long way in explaining the fact that he has no respect for others. So, too, his sense of his own contingency might be taken as a curious explanation of the fact that he treats other people as if they might just as well not exist. The philosophers of the twentieth century needed to go beyond solipsism, which they recognized as an absurd position, but they also struggled to make *respect* the common currency of our social relations. Yet the reef of solipsism remains, insofar as it has survived all arguments against it, and mutual respect remains an evasive ideal.[33]

Then there is the experience of shame. On Mill's argument, we infer that another person has a consciousness from his or her behavior. For Husserl, the existence of the other is necessary for us to know the world. For Hegel and Heidegger, it has something to do with reciprocity or being-in-the-world. In any case, we do not experience the other person's consciousness as such. But in shame we do not observe or "know" other people so much as we are observed, we are judged negatively, we are *looked at*. So Meursault, in *The Stranger*, for one "absurd" moment thinks that the old folks in the funeral home are looking at him, judging him, and this makes him feel extremely uncomfortable. Later, in court, they are indeed both looking at him and judging him. In shame, Sartre says, we are immediately aware of the other person's consciousness. No philosophical argument to the contrary could convince us otherwise. And so it is on the basis of shame and other such experiences that the reef is phenomenologically dissolved. It is on the basis of being judged by others that Meursault is prompted to become a social self. In *Nausea*, Roquentin is not put on trial, however, and he remains essentially shameless. No one really looks at him.[34] Nevertheless, there are two "relationships" worth exploring briefly, not because they throw much light on Being-for-Others as such but because they reveal something of Roquentin's jaded and pathetic personality. I will discuss them in the next section.

But to sum up one argument of this chapter, I have given three examples of Sartre's phenomenology, two of which are central to the themes of *Nausea*, the third conspicuous in its absence, which are intended to trump certain familiar philosophical arguments. Let me reiterate what I take these three examples to signify. What makes Sartre a great philosopher and *Being and Nothingness* a great book is not the confused and confusing ontology but the insightful phenomenology. What is of the most value is not the book's arguments, which admittedly often border on sophistry, but its best examples, which bring home in a moment the undeniability of a conclusion that has long evaded definitive argumentation. This is not to say, of course, that the arguments in *Being and Nothingness* should be systematically ignored or that Sartre's arguments (some of them quite good) are not themselves part of the reflective fabric that is itself inescapably part of our experience. Nor is it to insist, as I teasingly suggested, that ontological matters do not matter. But I have tried to shift the emphasis to what is, I think, best about Sartre, the place where he strikes us and our students not as a disputatious ontologist nor even as a Phenomenologist (with that same capital "P" that Richard Rorty uses to excoriate pretentious Philosophers), but as a sensitive, reflective human being who shares our experiences and the very real living concerns that motivate our inquiries.

Being-for-Others? Roquentin's Callousness, Roquentin's Love?

It would be odd, too dismissively philosophical, to discuss an entire novel while hardly mentioning the plot or the characters, even though *Nausea* is essentially without a plot and almost devoid of characters. People come and go routinely in Roquentin's little world, but he isn't much interested in them, so we don't find out much of anything about them. But there are two characters, besides the not very likable protagonist, who do permeate the novel: Roquentin's former girlfriend Anny, and an oddly tragic-comic character whose name, we are told (in an early footnote) is "Ogier P . . ." but who is referred to rather sarcastically throughout the text as the Self-Taught Man. Through them, and Roquentin's interaction with them, we learn a good deal about him that we might not discern through the medium of the bitter but dry phenomenological reporting of the novel itself. Indeed, this is an important lesson in phenomenology: the fact that our experience is not only affected but dominated by our exchanges with other people.[35] Our experience is not just "for-itself" but for others, too. With these two characters, we see Roquentin as he is "to Others" and "with Others," though hardly "for Others," because in neither interaction is there much indication of either sensitivity or reciprocity on his part. With the Self-Taught Man, Roquentin displays his contempt and lack of empathy, and even suggests a bit of cruelty. With Anny, in some sense his "beloved," we come to appreciate not only his poor taste in women but also his utter inability to handle a situation in which he is actually engaged. He has no control in his meeting with her, as she displays her contempt, lack of empathy, and even cruelty *toward him*. As we noted in Meursault in Camus' novel, it is not so much *in* as *through* Roquentin's phenomenological self-descriptions that his character is revealed.

The Self-Taught Man is introduced on the first pages of the novel, and he serves as a foil for Roquentin's cynicism throughout the novel. Even the label Roquentin gives him drips with sarcasm, and Roquentin talks to and treats him contemptuously. He contemplates gratuitous murder: "I feel as though I could do anything. For example, stab this cheese knife in the Self-Taught Man's eye. . . . A taste of blood in the mouth instead of this taste of cheese makes no difference to me" (166). But the Self-Taught Man's fate is in some ways crueler than being stabbed in the eye. His reputation and his life are ruined. His ambition had been to better himself by reading through the library alphabetically from A to Z (already marking him as something of a nitwit). But about halfway through the alphabet, he is caught in an act of blatant pederasty in the library, and he is effectively humiliated and banned for good. [36] This puts an end to his ambition to become a good humanist (which he seems to conflate with reading all of the books). Sartre, of course, had similar aspirations (though presumably not alphabetical) as a child. Roquentin consequently despises the Self-Taught Man and his humanism. But he is sufficiently moved by the Self-Taught Man's plight, or enraged by the crude Corsican's assault on him, to respond with his one act of aggression in the novel (again inviting comparison with *The Stranger*, which also climaxes in an act of rage). One might argue that Roquentin behaves somewhat sympathetically *after* the row, but it is more out of condescension and contempt for the Corsican than sympathy for the Self-Taught Man. It is clear that he does not feel anything like an echo of responsibility or fellow feeling, much less shame, as most of us would surely feel for an acquaintance or even a stranger in such a situation.

To appreciate how pathetic, if not tragic, this is, I would say that the Self-Taught Man is almost a paradigm of "a decent guy." He is earnest. He is honest. He thinks of himself and acts as a good citizen, a humanist, a Socialist. He is a war veteran and was once a prisoner of war (143, 153). He thinks that love overcomes hate. He wishes no one ill. He urges Roquentin to spare the life of a fly. He wants to better himself. He wants to learn. He is passionate about his ordinary life. So of course he does not understand Roquentin's cynicism and contemptuousness. The Self-Taught Man is not the sort of person whom we should admire, perhaps, but he is surely someone we should accept and respect. It is no doubt one of the blacker marks against Sartre's own character, to be considered in conjunction with his off-the-wall and sometimes despicable political sympathies, that he so despised the "bourgeoisie" that he was willing to countenance virtually any violence against them. [37] Not that the Self-Taught Man is a typical bourgeois. He is more of an ordinary good citizen. (We are told—in that same early note—that he was a bailiff's clerk.) He has none of the arrogance and sense of self-importance of the bourgeoisie. But Sartre despises him nonetheless, and he has his narrator Roquentin assassinate him in his descriptions.

Virtually every mention of the Self-Taught Man is condescending and makes some unflattering reference: his hand is "like a fat white worm," his arm fell back "flabbily" (11, again on 175). He is compared to "a dog who has found a bone" (44); again to a dog (140) and to a rat (216); he is described as a child ("as if he were going to cry"; 51); he cannot express himself (152); his love for people is "naïve and barbaric, a provincial humanism" (153). "He can go to Hell" (49). He becomes the target of a "terrible rage" (155). He embodies all of the weaknesses and hypocrisies of humanism, and keeps them all "locked up inside himself like cats in a bag and they are tearing each other in pieces without his noticing it (x). [38] By the time Roquentin comes to avenge and comfort him after the humiliating incident in the library, Sartre has already established the Self-Taught Man as foolish and pathetic rather than a tragic character. And although they spend many hours together, it is clear that the two men create no sort of relationship, much less friendship, and so they both end up lonely and alone.

Anny, by contrast, is the "romantic interest" of the novel. She has the longest section of the book (182–206) and Roquentin thinks of her frequently, although he has casual sex and engages in several flirtations with other women, waitresses and matrons mostly.[39] Toward the end of the book, just after his long meditation on existence, he hears from Anny that she will come to visit. He anticipates seeing her with remarkable longing and enthusiasm, quite out of kilter with the indifference, distance, and callousness with which he treats virtually everyone else in the novel. It is the only time that he admits "a strong feeling of adventure." But here, too, a bit of a character sketch is in order. If Roquentin's contempt for the Self-Taught Man is proportional to the poor man's virtues, his fascination for Anny seems to be proportional to her vices. She is as callous as he is. She is completely self-absorbed, another solipsist. She is flighty and utterly irresponsible. (In college, didn't we all know someone like Anny?) She is utterly indifferent to Roquentin's feelings, and with that indifference, she provokes the sole example of Being-for-Others in the book. (Note her sarcasm: "Poor boy! . . . The first time he plays his part well, he gets no thanks for it" [206].) We should note that in *Being and Nothingness*, indifference is one of the attitudes consequent to love, a manipulative ploy in our ongoing struggle with other people for respect and recognition. In her indifference, she makes *him* a matter of indifference, a pure contingency. She thus reinforces his worst thoughts about himself.

Rejected by Anny, disgusted with his history project, abandoned by the Self-Taught Man, Roquentin finally prepares to leave Bouville. He is emptily alone. Toward the end of the novel, he takes refuge in a song, "Some of These Days." It plays an odd role in the novel, as a sort of leitmotif, comparable to a similar song a few years later, "As Time Goes By" in the movie *Casablanca*, which pointed to the travails of the French in those terrible years. Songs are like narratives; they move in time and link events that otherwise might have nothing in common. But by the end of *Nausea*, "Some of These Days" plays an almost mystical role. Unlike Roquentin and the rest of his world, the song transcends contingency. It also finishes off the book, and in a sense, it continues to exist when the book itself is over. Early on, when one playing of the song ends, Roquentin has the unusual feeling that "*something has happened*. The nausea has disappeared." He describes an existential experience, an actual "getting into" something: he tells us that the music "filled the room with its metallic transparency, . . . I am in the music" (34). At the end of the novel, sour still, he self-righteously pours contempt on the bourgeoisie who "imagine that the sounds [of Chopin] flow into them, sweet, nourishing, and that their sufferings become music, like Werther [Goethe's tragic young hero]. They think that beauty is compassionate to them. Mugs" (232). It might be that the music engages him, but it does not make him any less mean-spirited or contemptuous, and instead of "letting himself go" with the music he spends his listening time raging against the philistines.

The song, however, makes him *ashamed*. "A glorious little suffering has been born." But his shame and his suffering are again not at all compassionate, "not even ironic." This shame has nothing to do with the shame that exists because of other people. It is, rather, a self-absorbed solipsistic shame at one's own contingency. "Like a scythe it cuts through the drab intimacy of the world" (233). This is because the music, unlike the world, does not exist. It transcends our reach. Unlike the horrifying chestnut root, with its obscene existence, the music "does not exist because it has nothing superfluous; it is all the rest which in relation to it is superfluous." And in language anticipating Being-in-Itself in *Being and Nothingness*, Roquentin simply declares, "It *is*." And anticipating the later account of bad faith, Roquentin declares, "I, too, wanted to *be*." It is the music that comes to justify his existence, "at least a little." And it is at this point that Roquentin ecstatically daydreams about transcending himself with his intended novel, "beautiful and hard as steel, to make people ashamed of their existence" (237). Perhaps by so shaming others, this would allow him to accept himself (238). But the intended novel is little more than another mean-spirited daydream, and one gets the sense that it has no more chance of realization than Meursault's imaginary one-in-a-million chance for escape in *The Stranger*. Thus the ultimate phenomenology of *Nausea* is the phenomenology of despair. And it is *against* this bleak vision that Sartre's philosophy will flourish as a phenomenology of hope and engagement.

4

SARTRE ON EMOTIONS

A Reading of His "Sketch" of 1939

The existentialist does not believe in the power of passion. He will never regard a grand passion as a destructive torrent upon which a man is swept into uncertain actions as by fate, and which, therefore, is an excuse for them.
—Sartre, "Existentialism Is a Humanism"

Emotions are . . . magical transformations of the world.
—Sartre, *The Emotions*

What are emotions? Ancient poets described them in terms of insanity and brute forces. ("Love is a kind of madness," wrote Sappho; "Anger is like riding a wild horse," wrote Horace.) Medieval and modern poets alike have talked of the emotions in terms of physiological disruptions and outages—the breaking of hearts; the outpouring of bile, spleen, and gall; the paralysis of reason. Our present-day language of the emotions is riddled with metaphors of passivity: "falling" in love, "struck by" jealousy, "overwhelmed by" grief, "paralyzed by" fear, "haunted by" guilt, "plagued by" remorse. The classic modern psychophysiological theory of the emotions, the so-called James–Lange theory (simultaneously formulated by William James in America and by C. G. Lange in Denmark), was a scientific canonization of these metaphors: the emotions are physiological disturbances with certain epiphenomenal "affects" (feelings or sensations) in consciousness. Simultaneously, Sigmund Freud described the "affects" as we might speak of hydraulics, in terms of various pressures and their outlets: filling up (cathexis) and discharge (catharsis), channeling (sublimation), and bottling up (repression). Like James and Lange, Freud links this "hydraulic model" to scientific, but at that time merely hypothesized, operations of the central nervous system.[1] James, Lange, and Freud viewed the emotions as untoward and disruptive forces or pressures, erupting in "outbursts" or manifesting themselves in behavior that is aimless and "ir-rational," degrading and often embarrassing, inimical to our best interests and beyond our control. They are not our responsibility (except in their expression, which we are told we ought to control).

Jean-Paul Sartre was among the first twentieth-century writers on the subject to break with this tradition. He did so incompletely, but I shall argue that he must nonetheless be credited with a persuasive alternative to the ancient model of invasion by alien physiological and "animal spirits" assailing our normal patterns of behavior and thought. In his *Esquisse d'une théorie des émotions*,[2] Sartre defends a view of the emotions as conscious *acts*, as purposive and "meaningful" ways of "constituting" our world, for which we must accept responsibility. The *Esquisse* is the only published portion of a projected four-hundred-page manuscript that was to be titled "The Psyche."[3] It is worth noting that it was written in 1939, about the same time as *Nausea,* Sartre's first "existentialist" novel, and only a short time after "La Transcendance de l'égo," his best-known phenomenological essay.[4] The "sketch" on the emotions not only anticipates but also actually argues many of the familiar themes of *Being and Nothingness*,[5] mapping out its phenomenological presuppositions with a simplicity that is lacking in the larger work. (In fact, I suggest to my students that they read the "Sketch" and/or *Transcendence* as an introduction to *Being and Nothingness* in place of the opaque so-called introduction to that work, in which the paradoxes of phenomenological ontology obscure more than they clarify the existential themes that occupy Sartre for the rest of the book.)

After the "Sketch," Sartre did not attempt to develop his theory of the emotions as such. Its basic structures, however, are prominent throughout *Being and Nothingness* and in his later "psychoanalytic" studies. In his brilliant analysis of the career of Jean Genet,[6] for example, the conception of an emotional "transformation of the world," the key to the theory of his early piece, is also the key to Genet's "word magic" and his "poetic use of language." Sartre's gargantuan study of Flaubert also demonstrates that no matter how his interests shifted over the years, he continued to hold and to employ something of the theory he sketched for us some seven decades ago.[7]

Sartre's Method: Phenomenology
(The Introduction)

In the preceding chapter, I tried to give a fairly simple description of Sartre's basic method, phenomenology. But in the introduction to *The Emotions*, he gives us his own none-too-clear characterization of his technique. The introduction to Sartre's "Sketch" tells us that the key to his approach to the emotions lies in an appreciation of the fact that "the consciousness which must be interrogated and what gives value to its responses is precisely that *it is mine"* (11, my italics). He contrasts this precept with what he characterizes as "the methods of the psychologist," in which "our knowledge of the emotion will be added *from without* to other knowledge about the physical being" (6:7). What difference will appreciation of this fact make? It will allow us, according to Sartre, to investigate "the very structure of human reality," the possible conditions of emotion, arrived at by the same phenomenological inquiry that will be central to *Being and Nothingness.* The psychologist reports the "objective" and "empirical" physiological facts of human behavior and, if he allows himself, examines certain "states of consciousness" through introspection (which Sartre insists is equally "objective" and "empirical"). What is missing in the psychologist's method, Sartre complains, is a consideration of consciousness as a *meaningful activity* in and for itself, a consideration that "cannot come to human reality *from the outside*" (17). This is what phenomenology will provide. Note Sartre's attempt, from the very outset, to oppose and distinguish his phenomenology from any kind of psychology.

From the outset Sartre rejects the notion of the emotions as sporadic and inessential disruptions of behavior with conscious "affects." Rather, he says, the emotions are "essential" and "indispensable structures of consciousness" (15). Moreover, emotion should not be considered as a set of empirical facts gained through introspection or as a "corporeal phenomenon" (19), but rather as "an organized form of human existence" (18). Phenomenology goes "beyond the psychic, beyond man's situation in the world, to the very source of man, the world, and the psychic." This idea was essential to Husserl's "transcendental phenomenology," that phenomenology is not just a kind of psychology. The phenomenologist, according to Sartre, attempts "to describe and fix by concepts precisely the essences which preside as the transcendental field unrolls" (11). Again anticipating the central theme of *Being and Nothingness,* Sartre argues that it is "just as impossible to get to essence by accumulating accidents as to reach 1 by adding figures to the right of 0.99" (5). Sartre's "phenomenology of emotion" would, following Husserl, "put the world in parentheses" in order to study "emotion as a pure transcendental phenomenon," "to attain and elucidate the transcendental essence of emotion as an organized type of consciousness" (12). But this strategy compromises Sartre's analysis from the very beginning, I think, because, like Husserl, he begins by separating consciousness from the world. (*Nausea*, by contrast, gets this right: the idea that reality imposes itself and cannot be "bracketed.")

In this essay, therefore, Sartre seems to accept what he would soon reject in Husserl, not only the idea of the *epoché*, or "putting in parentheses," but also the very idea of a "transcendental phenomenology" as Husserl conceived it. What is more, it is interesting to note that in these same passages of the introduction Sartre expounds and endorses the views of Heidegger, whom he refers to simply as "another phenomenologist" (12) who adds to Husserl's transcendental method the need to "assume" human reality (what Heidegger calls *Dasein*). He also attributes to Heidegger the idea that to be human is "to be responsible for it [one's emotion] instead of receiving it from the outside like a stone" and "to 'choose' itself in its being" (12, quoting

Heidegger's *Sein und Zeit*). These are, of course, the theses that will become the centerpieces of Sartre's philosophy. (Their centrality is rather doubtful in Heidegger's philosophy, even in his "existential" period in *Being and Time*.) Sartre does not seem to understand the radical disagreements between Husserl and Heidegger, as if he believed that Husserl's transcendental phenomenology and Heidegger's existential phenomenological ontology could embrace one another without conflict. Thus he talks about Heidegger's *Dasein* or "being-in-the-world" side by side with Husserl's *epoché*, apparently without noticing that the one is a radical rejection of the other.

Sartre's analysis is peppered with phenomenological jargon, not always employed accurately and often superfluous. Its use is more an expression of novice enthusiasm than a conceptual need (previewing a "borrowing" tendency that Sartre will display throughout his career). Throughout the introduction to the "Sketch," we find mentions of "neomatic correlate" (58, 65), "noesis" (79), "hyle" (60, 73), "thetic consciousness," and "non-thetic consciousness" (51, 57, 77)—all Husserlian jargon—but it is clear that then, as later, Sartre adopted the language of other theorists only insofar as it suited his own creative intentions. It should not surprise us that all that will remain of his Husserlian enthusiasm in *Being and Nothingness* is its basic Cartesianism, its emphasis on the "first-person standpoint" and its stress on "subjectivity." The more striking "existential" perspective, on the other hand, would be drawn more from Heidegger than from Husserl, anticipating Sartre's well-known view that "man makes himself" (46, 49), that he has no "essence" and "assumes" or "chooses" himself and takes responsibility even for his feelings. "It is senseless to think of complaining since nothing foreign has decided what we feel, what we live, or what we are" (B&N, 708).

Sartre insists that the emotions are to be viewed as "essentially" acts of consciousness, and therefore as intentional and as purposive. I think that it is too easy to read this with an easy acceptance today, as if these are two humdrum theses that everyone will accept, the first as obvious, the second as one of the evident implications of the Darwinism that has properly come to dominate biological and psychological thinking. But the first thesis, intentionality, signals a radical break from the hydraulic and sensation models of emotion that dominated modern psychology and traditional empiricism. And the second thesis, the purposiveness of emotion, is much more radical than Darwinism alone would suggest, for it posits *personal* purposes rather than inheritance and survival through the rigors of natural selection. An emotion, we might say, is *an organized strategy for dealing with the world*. We should also note Sartre's incipient holism with regard to emotions. He says that an emotion is a mode of consciousness that "by its synthetic activity, can break and reconstitute forms," "transforming an aspect of the world" (40). Again, he puts the emphasis on the *meaning* of emotion. "One can understand emotion only if he looks for *signification*" (41). This means, within the phenomenological framework Sartre is presupposing, that we must ask what its "intentions" are, in a double sense: what it has to do with the world (its "intentionality"), and what *purposes* it serves (its "finality"). As opposed to merely reporting "the facts" of our emotions—their manifestations in behavior, physiology, and "states of consciousness"—Sartre intends to tell us what we are *doing* when we have an emotion.

Sartre's Critique of James and Freud (Chapters 1 and 2)

Given his phenomenological approach, the thrust of Sartre's criticism of traditional psychological theories of emotion is that such theories pay attention only to "the facts," not to the essence of emotion: they regard an emotion as passive, that which afflicts us or, in Freud, "invades us" (49). Traditional theorists regard an emotion as disruptive, purposeless, and meaningless. And most important, they do not see an emotion as a structure *of* consciousness, as a conscious *act*, but rather as a state or occurrence with manifestations *in* consciousness (as "affect"), as well as in behavior and physiology. Sartre refers to William James's theory in particular as "peripheric," both because it treats consciousness "as a secondary phenomenon" and because what James mainly refers to as the primary bodily response is the "peripheral" manifestations of the autonomic nervous system and the effects of hormones (flushed face, faster heart and pulse rates, skin sensitivity, etc.) not (as today) processes in the central nervous system.[8] These are manifested in what James ambiguously calls the "expression" of emotion, by which he means both these more or less automatic manifestations in the body and actual behavior. Thus the confusion in his famous observation, "A mother is sad because she weeps." Weeping (crying, sobbing) is in fact a very complex bit of physiology and behavior.

In chapter 1 of the "Sketch," Sartre singles out two theories for attack: that of James, which holds that the conscious "affects" of emotion are mere "epiphenomena" of certain physiological (particularly visceral) disturbances, and that of Pierre Janet (1859–1947), an important contemporary of Sartre's whose theory places far greater stress on behavior and "organization" than on physiology. Yet the target of Sartre's attack is far larger, including all the variations on physiological ("peripheric") theory (e.g., those of Cannon and Sherrington: 24–25, 41–42), all versions of early "behaviorism" (e.g., of James Watson) that attempt to do away with "consciousness" and conscious purposiveness, and all the later varieties of "philosophical behaviorism" that have sprung up (since Sartre wrote his "Sketch") in the wake of the later Wittgenstein and Gilbert Ryle's *Concept of Mind*, in which emotion is reduced to "agitations," behavioral dispositions, or else a breakdown in normal, "rational" behavior patterns.[9] These theories may, as in Janet (and subsequently in Freud), involve a "hydraulic" model of accumulated tension and nervous energy, or they may confine themselves to the operational definitions and pure behavioral descriptions of latter-day behaviorism. What they all have in common is a radically deemphasized conception of consciousness. It is only an "epiphenomenon" (James) or a "secondary phenomenon" (Janet), or it is no phenomenon at all (as in behaviorism).

Against them all, Sartre argues, as anticipated in his introduction, that there can be no accounting for emotions in a model that does not take consciousness seriously and does not treat emotions as purposive. He refers to the German Gestalt psychologists Wolfgang Köhler, Kurt Lewin, and Tamara Dembo, although he quotes only the Frenchman Paul Guillaume at considerable length (33–36) in order to show, by way of a single example, that our emotions *must* be interpreted "functionally"; as purposeful and meaningful, yet neither explicit nor deliberate. Anger, his example, "is neither an instinct nor a habit nor a reasoned calculation. It is an abrupt solution of a conflict, a way of cutting the Gordian knot" (36–37). It is "an escape" (37). Thus Sartre insists that reference to "finality" is unavoidable and that we must "return to consciousness, with which we should have begun" (40).

I think that Sartre's attack on James regarding emotion is the important beginning of a long and persuasive rebellion in psychology as well as philosophy, despite the fact that at this point in his career Sartre insists, in his allegiance to Husserl, that phenomenology and psychology must be kept wholly separated, as the one has to do with "essences" and the other with "facts." I think that this is a huge mistake, although quite a few contemporary philosophers and psychologists would insist on the same distinction, that philosophers work with conceptual analysis and psychologists do empirical research. But James was quite comfortable being both a philosopher and a psychologist, as were many of the empiricists before him (not to mention Aristotle *well* before them). Knowledge of human nature and consciousness requires both the understanding and analysis of concepts and empirical knowledge of the facts, including the troublesome facts one discovers (or constitutes) immediately in one's own consciousness or through mediation by being aware of one's own behavior. But as I said, Sartre's attack and his alternative analysis of emotion began an important rebellion in both philosophy and psychology, which begins with the insistence that emotions have intentionality.[10] James, accordingly, remains the main target and the antithetical model of emotion as an essentially physiological state or process.[11]

Actually, James is a more interesting figure regarding emotions than Sartre would suggest. True, his "official" theory is that "*the perception causes a bodily disturbance and the resulting sensation IS the emotion*" (James's italics). But it has been argued that a great deal more goes on in that "perception" than is acknowledged by critics of the theory. James has a behavioral theory of emotion that is arguably distinct from his "peripheric" theory, and then there is the elaborate phenomenology of a few select emotions that we find, for example, in his *The Varieties of Religious Experience*. But, focusing just on the "official" theory, it was soon pointed out that the known peripheral physiology was too impoverished to explain the great variety of emotions, and that the "sensation" James cited was far too simple to explain the elaborate structure of emotions and their variable behavioral tendencies. Some of this was Janet's criticism as well, but the full concept of intentionality waited for Sartre and phenomenology.

The second chapter of the "Sketch" is aimed at Freud, who would remain Sartre's (apparent) nemesis throughout his career.[12] Of particular interest is Sartre's interpretation and critique of Freud's psychoanalytic theory of the emotions (41–49). He credits this theory with being "the first to put the emphasis on the signification of psychic facts, that is, the fact that every state of consciousness is the equivalent of something other than itself" (43). (Freud, who had studied with Brentano, also referred to this equivalence as the "meaning" of a psychic act.) According to psychoanalysis, an emotion is "a symbolic realization of a desire repressed by censorship" (44). As in *Being and Nothingness* (pt. I, ch. 2; pt. IV, chs. 1, 2), Sartre's interpretation in the "Sketch" of Freud's complex and evolving theories is oversimplified and highly critical, aiming doubly at (1) the problem of self-deception, anticipating his analysis of "bad faith" in *Being and Nothingness* as needing both "to know and not to know," and (2) causal or "psychic" determinism.

Regarding causal (or "psychic") determinism, on the one hand, Sartre acknowledges that the psychoanalytic theory recognizes the emotion as meaningful and purposive, but as *symbolically so.* On the other hand, "one *undergoes* it: it takes one by surprise: it develops in accordance with its own laws and without our conscious spontaneity's being able to modify its course appreciably" (42). Thus it "invades us in spite of ourselves" (49). But this is "a flagrant contradiction" (46), Sartre complains, and in support of this assertion he cites reasons similar to those he will marshal to attack the Freudian notion of "the Unconscious" in *Being and Nothingness*: "It cuts off consciousness from itself": in once fashionable Saussurian language, "The thing signified is entirely cut off from the thing signifying" (45). One must be conscious of one's own symbolism, but at the same time one cannot be. The argument, as in *Being and Nothingness*, turns on the Cartesian conception of the *cogito* and its Kantian conditions of possibility: "If the cogito is to be possible, consciousness is itself the *fact*, the *signification* and the *thing signified*" (46; Sartre's italics).

Sartre contrasts sharply, as he will in *Being and Nothingness*, the intentional model of emotions as meaningful and the mechanical model of emotions as merely caused. These are, he assumes, mutually exclusive. "The profound contradiction of all psychoanalysis is to introduce *both* a bond of causality and a bond of comprehension between the phenomena it studies" (48). Similarly, he accuses Janet (from whom Freud borrowed heavily in his early years) of wavering between "a spontaneous finalism and a fundamental mechanism" (32–33). A decade or so later, Wittgenstein set the stage for a similarly sharp distinction in Anglo–American analytic philosophy, between "reasons and causes." That debate went on for more than another decade, as philosophers like Donald Davidson rejected the distinction and argued that reasons were a kind of cause.[13] I mention this here because I think that Sartre's separation of the two explanatory modes is debatable, at least, and in the light of contemporary neurophysiological theories of emotions, untenable. It now seems obvious that emotions do involve causal mechanisms in the brain. But it is also obvious that emotions provide us with reasons for what we do. I also doubt very much that one mode of explanation can be reduced to the other, but I do not doubt that they are both appropriate and applicable, depending on what one wants to know or explain.

The Sartrean position emerges from the rubble of a tradition that downplays the role and meaning of an emotion in consciousness in favor of an emphasis on the body and physiology. Sartre instead insists that the fundamental emphasis must be on consciousness, its purposiveness and its signification, only secondarily on the "expression" of emotion in behavior and its physiological correlations. Against Freud, he insists that there can be no "unconscious purposes," and therefore no "unconscious emotions," although we may well find ourselves in a position of *refusing* to recognize our own emotions and their purposes. Freud tried to finesse this question by insisting that there could not be unconscious affects (feelings) but that there could be, and evidently were, unconscious emotions and unconscious purposes. But if an unacknowledged emotion is a matter of "refusal" rather than repression, this leads us to suspect that this behavior is motivated as a way of "saving face." Accordingly, the phenomenological sketch that follows is of paramount importance in unmasking a kind of deception we have about ourselves that Sartre would explore four years later in *Being and Nothingness*.

Sartre's "Sketch" of a Theory of the Emotions (Chapter 3)

I have said that Sartre's theory is based on the idea that an emotion has meaning ("signification") and purpose ("finality"). It is not merely a "state of consciousness" but an *intentional act*, something we *do*, a mode of behavior *(conduite)* that has distinctive purposes and characteristics. Moreover, the act is inseparable from its object ("the affective subject [*le sujet ému*] and the affective object [*l'objet émouvant*] are bound in an indissoluble synthesis" [52]). This is another borrowed Husserlian thesis. The emotion is "not absorbed in itself" but "returns to the object at every moment" (51). In other words, it is *nothing but* intentionality, nothing "in itself." Nor is an emotion an isolated disturbance of consciousness. An emotion is "a certain way of apprehending the world" (52), a "transformation of the world" (58), a "mode of existence of consciousness" (91), an "existential [*existentielle*] structure of the world" (83). "There is," Sartre tells us, "a world of emotion" (80), just as there is a world of dreams and there are worlds of madness. Or, as Wittgenstein insisted several years later, "the depressed man lives in a depressed world." Like Heidegger, Sartre takes a position (contrary to his seeming endorsement of Husserl) that there is no opposition of self or consciousness and the world. There is just emotional being-in-the-world.

Although Sartre's *esquisse* is only a "sketch" of a theory that has yet to be filled in, the phenomenological structures of the theory are spelled out with a clarity that is sometimes missing from *Being and Nothingness*. For example, a defining characteristic of the emotions in the "Sketch" is that they are "unreflective" (*irréfléchive*), and Sartre here gives us (52ff.) the explication of that conception which is so painfully opaque in the introduction (sec. III) of *Being and Nothingness*, defining "unreflective behavior" as behavior without consciousness of self. He writes, "In order to act it is not necessary to be conscious of the self as acting" (56). The absence of consciousness of self, lack of self-consciousness, is also Sartre's characterization of the prereflective in *Transcendence*. But it is hard to see how many emotions (notably those necessarily self-referring emotions, pride, shame, and embarrassment) could *not* be self-conscious, whether or not they are acknowledged or recognized, whether or not they are objects of reflection. But Sartre's essential point is that emotions involve purposive and meaningful acts that are not themselves objects of consciousness. This is not to say that they are "unconscious," Sartre insists, but only that they are "non-thetic" (57) or "non-positional" (51), thus anticipating a long and familiar phenomenological tangle that emerges in the opening pages of *Being and Nothingness* (see my discussion in chapter 6, pp. 140–42). Briefly, and without the tangle, Sartre claims that emotions are conscious but not reflective. And, contra James, he insists that they have conscious *significance*, not just conscious manifestation in sensations.

An emotion is "significant." But wherein lies its significance? It certainly does not lie in pure "intentionality," much less mere "information," which Sartre, like Husserl, takes to be purely cognitive, a mere knowing. But the objects of our emotions are not merely "things to be known." They are objects of personal concern. What Sartre wants to say, but doesn't say precisely, is that intentionality is also a matter of *caring*, of evaluating, of appraising, even of bestowing values. What he says encourages confusion, for he often uses "intentionality" to mean significance, that is, having meaning, which may just mean "having an object." (Later on, Maurice Merleau-Ponty will avoid the term "intentionality" as a purely cognitive term by replacing Husserl's term with his own conception of motivated "motility.")[14] But Sartre clearly means more than this, and borrows from the German Gestaltists the concept of the *Umwelt*—the world of our desires, our needs, and our acts (57), making a clear reference to caring and concern. Thus, from the Gestaltists (but possibly also from Husserl's most recent and last work), Sartre gets the idea of a "life-world," a value-laden world, the kind of world most people mean when they employ the philosophical term "subjectivity." Such a world is not, contra (early) Wittgenstein, "everything that is the case." The world is shot through with meanings and values, personal and cultural significance. Emotions are significant and have meaning because they involve the things that we care about, including, of course, the things we hate or despise or want to attack or to avoid.

The meaning or significance of an emotion must be referred to its purpose. And what is this purpose? According to Sartre, it is not one we would readily acknowledge. The purpose of our emotions is to allow us to cope with a world that we find difficult, frustrating, "indifferent" (in Camus' terms), if not downright "hostile" (in Sartre's almost paranoid view). When the paths traced out by our intentions and desires become too difficult, or when we see no path at all, we can no longer live in so frustrating and difficult a world. All the ways are barred. But we have to do something! So we try to change the world, that is, to live "as if the connection between things and their potentialities were not ruled by deterministic processes, but by magic" (58). This is Sartre's singularly bold thesis: that emotions are "magical transformations of the world." What he means by "magic" may be a bit misleading and (for some New Age or occult-minded readers) a bit too exciting. It also betrays a phenomenological inconsistency, to be corrected in *Being and Nothingness:* the Husserlian separation of consciousness as a self-enclosed realm from the world it intends.

What Sartre means by "magic" is in contrast to what we might better call "*really* changing the world." Sartre claims that although we cannot change the world itself, we can nevertheless change "the direction of consciousness" (59) and our "intentions and behavior" (60). It is thus that our emotions "transform the world." That is to say, by shifting our attention, changing our expectations and/or our intentions, taking on a different worldview, we can alter the world we experience, even though we cannot change the world as such. This is the "magical" compensation Sartre refers to. Choosing a familiar example from Aesop, he analyzes the emotional structure of the "sour grapes" attitude of resentment. In the fable, the fox spies a bunch of grapes "having to be picked," but he cannot reach them. In order to save face, and by way of compensation, he comes to see them as "too green." Sartre notes that "this is not a change in the chemistry of the grapes" but rather a change in attitude. So it is, he suggests, with all emotions. In order to cope with frustration, "a difficult world," through our emotions we change our view of a world we cannot change.

Such behavior is not "effective" (60), if what we mean by that term is "effective in changing the world." It surely is effective, however, in allowing us to cope and live with our own impotence. But neither is it merely "symbolic." We do not believe our emotional behavior is a satisfactory substitute. So we do not—cannot—admit to ourselves what we are doing: substituting an ineffective way of saving face for effective action that would in fact get us what we want. Thus the need for emotions to be unreflective.

According to Sartre in the early essay, every emotion has the purpose of allowing us to live with our own "unbearable" conflicts and tensions without explicitly recognizing them. Sartre calls such behavior "magical" because of this ineffective yet psychologically effective change, not in *the* world, but in *our* world. In one sense, we fail to do anything, that is, anything effective; but in another sense, we are very decidedly "doing something," namely, transforming the world to suit ourselves, through our "magical comedy of impotence" (*comédie magique d'impuissance*; 67). This, I think, is poetic and ingenious. It is also a mistake. Sartre is right to think that emotions are purposive, but he is certainly wrong to think that all emotions have the same "escapist" purpose.

Furthermore, Sartre tells us, every emotion "sets up a magical world by using the body as a means of incantation" (70). Here is his way of accounting for James's observation that an emotion is essentially a bodily disturbance. We *feel* an emotion (a sensation) because of our physiology. That puts the emotions squarely in the category of passivity, which is exactly what Sartre wants to deny. Nevertheless, Sartre is not about to dismiss such bodily disturbances and feelings. They are obvious data to be taken into account. What he does is to turn upside down James's famous formula (which was in turn a reversal of the usual "folk psychology"). James had challenged the common idea that an emotion causes bodily activity ("A woman weeps because she is sad") and suggested, instead, that the bodily activity causes the emotion ("A woman is sad because she weeps"). Sartre goes back to the earlier, commonsense formula, but with an existential twist. We *actively produce* the disturbances in our bodies (and with them, the consequent sensations) by using our bodies "as a means of incantation" (70).

In other words, when we decide to be angry or sad, we play out a role we have chosen that includes distinctive bodily activities, gestures, and postures. Of course, many current psychophysiologists would challenge the idea that a person is capable of choosing or causing the kinds of bodily changes that James suggests. But a sympathetic interpretation is that, at the very least, Sartre is pointing out that, sometimes, we *work* our way into an emotional state, we *make* ourselves depressed or angry, we *cultivate* sadness— and we bolster this by altering our physical state. The radical move in Sartre's treatment of the emotions is moving them from the category of things that we suffer into the category of things that we *do*. And this is so even of those aspects of the phenomena that would seem to make James's case, the bodily dimensions of emotion.

Thus we can understand how it is that an emotion is not to be taken as a mere "disruption," as "a trivial episode of everyday life" (89). It is a "total alteration of the world" (87), even (pretentiously) "an intuition of the absolute" (81). It is not a disorder, but a response to an emergency. We must not allow ourselves to be stunned or turned off by this Hegelian terminology; what Sartre means is something quite intelligible: an emotion is not a distraction in our lives, like an itch on the calf or an arthritic shoulder. It is not an isolated interruption of consciousness but a "mode" of consciousness, an attitude that defines our consciousness of the world with its singular concerns. When we are angry, we do not think or see much other than the object of our anger. When one is in love, he or she does not think or see much other than his or her beloved. An emotion is thus an "existential structure of the world" (83), even a world unto itself (80). An emotion is not a disruption or an intrusion, but a full act of consciousness creating a structure in which we can live.

Sartre adds that an emotion is often an obsessive structure, extending forward into the indefinite future (81). I think that this is often correct: when one is depressed, it seems that the depression will last forever, and when one is in love, it is not just a cliché but part of the experience that it will be "forever," and one cannot imagine it otherwise. Thus Sartre is making another important point against the Jamesian view (though one fully compatible with Freud), and that is that emotions are not just momentary phenomena, lasting only as long as a hormonal rush or one's increased pulse rate. An emotion may establish a durable view of the world and the structure of one's personality. (It would be wrong, for Sartre, to say that it would provide a durable structure of consciousness, because, as he so forcefully reminds us in *Being and Nothingness*, consciousness as "nothing" cannot have a structure.) But in many emotions, notably the "poisonous emotions" (a.k.a. the "deadly sins"), the sense of the future duration of the emotion may be a self-fulfilling prophecy. It is because envy and anger (also hatred) perceive the future in terms of the structures they have created that they tend to continue into the future, feeding on themselves. On a happier note, this is also true of love. But it also casts doubt on the idea of any "durable" structure of personality. In *Being and Nothingness*, Sartre makes it very clear that personality structures are no more than the tentative results of decisions made and acts undertaken.

Sartre further elaborates on the peculiar nature of "magical" behavior. Borrowing from Heidegger, he analyzes the difference between the "magical," ineffective behavior of our emotions and our effectively doing something in terms of "instrumentality" (compare *Sein und Zeit*, pt. I, div. I, sec. 3: "Die Weltlichkeit der Welt"). In action, the world appears as a "complex of instruments," in which "each instrument refers to other instruments and to the totality of instruments: there is no absolute action or radical change that one can immediately introduce into this world" (89). In other words, we do something *in order to* do something else (for example, one pulls the trigger to shoot a rifle to propel a bullet to kill the dictator to open up the way for democracy so that . . .). In the "magical" world of emotion, however, this "world of instruments abruptly vanishes" (90), and we act *as if* to transform the world in one "magical act." So instead of pulling the trigger, one comes to terms with the regime, perhaps even coming to love the dictator. Or one collaborates, not through newfound love but through greed and ambition, "magically" transforming the world into new opportunities instead of oppression. It is as if one wanted to produce a house not brick by brick and board by board, but by a simple magical wish, as if in a fairy tale. But, Sartre reminds us, this is "not a game" (59) or a joke (61). Quite the contrary: our emotions are typified by their "seriousness" (74), by the fact that they require *belief* (73), even to the point where we "cannot abandon [the emotion] at will" (73).

Here Sartre begins to back off from his strong voluntarism regarding emotions. Emotions are not just choices that we can do or undo at will. Seen one way, this is perfectly plausible. Some emotions involve a commitment or an investment that cannot easily be retracted, and others surprise us and come upon us suddenly. But Sartre sees a deeper problem here, and thus he distinguishes two forms of emotion, one in which "we constitute the magic of the world," the other in which "it is the world which abruptly reveals itself as being magical." His example of the latter is "a face appears at the window" (85). This may well evoke emotion (surprise, fear, terror, outrage), but it is clearly not "chosen" and not a strategy for anything. Thus Sartre introduces a distinction *within* the emotions between active and passive, a distinction that betrays a weakness of will in his theory, which I want to examine. But to sum up Sartre's theory in this "sketch," an emotion is a "magical transformation" of an "unbearable" world, a compensating and necessarily unreflective (and thus easily but not necessarily self-deceptive) strategy for changing our intentions and behavior toward the world when the world itself will not satisfy us.

Sartre's Theory: Appreciation and Critique

Many contemporary psychologists and neuropsychologists ("neo–Jamesians") will respond, naturally, that Sartre has too glibly downplayed the physiological correlates of emotion and that he has attributed too much to consciousness and too little to simple behavior, that he has made far too voluntary what is demonstrably involuntary,[15] and that he has obscured a fairly simple set of "primitive" reactions by his use of phenomenological, Hegelian, and occultist terminology. My complaint, however, is the very opposite, and it explains my enthusiasm for Sartre's work on emotions. Although Sartre's "sketch" of a theory needs to be supplemented with more detailed arguments against traditional physiological, behaviorist, and "emotions-are-simply-feelings" theorists, his theory is a major step in the right direction, that is, away from the view of emotions as passive disruptions, invasions from a Freudian "id," disorders in our physiology which are registered as "states of consciousness," or mere feelings that are no more our doing than are headaches, itches, and pains in the groin. From my point of view, the problem is that Sartre has *not gone far enough* in this early work, and he has retained *too much* of the traditional view of emotions as involuntary patterns of behavior and reaction, as irrational, disruptive, passive, and degrading—granting, of course, that some but not all emotions are indeed like this. Adopting the radically voluntarist philosophy of *Being and Nothingness* as my basis (although my arguments have been expanded elsewhere[16]), I want to argue that Sartre's early theory of emotion must be further radicalized and the notion of strategy taken more seriously, according to the very principles he himself has been so instrumental in formulating.

My first objection is one that I have already expressed and that Sartre clearly accepted, for he changed his conception of phenomenology, and with it his conception of emotions, by the time he wrote *Being and Nothingness*. In the "Sketch," he accepts the Husserlian separation of consciousness as a realm self-enclosed from the world it intends. Sartre interprets the emotions, accordingly, as alterations of consciousness that have no effect in the world, and his key phrase "magical transformation of the world" must be interpreted as a change only in the way we experience the world and not in the world itself. But once he has eliminated Husserl's transcendental ego and the "realm" of consciousness, and made intentionality the sole structure (or, better, activity) of consciousness, this separation is no more. An emotion is a magical transformation *of the world* and not just of consciousness. Whether or not it is also *effective*, as Sartre says, depends on the emotion and its expression. Anger is often a very effective way of changing the world, intimidating other people, and motivating oneself to do what must be done.

My second objection turns on a similarly problematic distinction, though one that has long been central to most theories concerning the emotions. The distinction between an emotion and its *expression* has often been considered absolute, with the emotion as some "inner" mental occurrence or state, and its expression the "outer" behavioral manifestation of that occurrence. This concept of "expression" has been expanded by some theorists (by James, for example) to include various physiological manifestations as well. Thus the emotion becomes "the emotion felt," while expression includes "vigorous action" as well as ineffective gestures, physiological flushing and grimaces, and "faces" and facial "expressions."[17] Sartre, anxious to reject these Cartesian distinctions between "mind" and "body," "inner" and "outer" (even as he firmly retains a related dualism at the very core of his phenomenological ontology), denies these distinctions and characterizes the emotions in terms of behavior, in terms of "our body lived." I now think that this move was the right one, but it is compromised by Sartre's unyielding Cartesianism. In *Being and Nothingness*, he vigorously animates "the body" to make room for the idea that an emotion may be both bodily and conscious without employing any mysterious Cartesian connectionism. Here, however, he criticizes Janet for asserting that emotions are behavior only, and "behavior pure and simple is not emotion" (71). But matters become more complicated, though more promising, once Sartre has made his Heideggerian shift. Then there is no such thing as "behavior pure and simple."

Because of his lifelong interest in the theater (a love he shared with Camus that led to their becoming friends) Sartre took a special interest in feigning emotion. In pretense, he says, we feign emotional behavior without having the emotion. Such behavior "is not sustained by anything" (72). But modern research (and our basic "instincts") tells us that it is not so easy to fake or feign an emotion. Paul Ekman argues, for instance, that "the eyes" almost always betray us. And the best way to "fake" an emotion, we often find, is to actually get ourselves into that emotion. For Sartre, the definitive element is our belief and the "seriousness" of the emotion (73, 74). Yet the emotion, according to Sartre, is a mode of behavior, an employment of the body to change one's relations with the world (61). Here, again, Sartre's Cartesianism causes him problems. What he really wants and needs is an integrated "unitary phenomenon" (Heidegger's phrase) of mind and body, emotion and behavior, emotion and expression. Thus he moves here immediately from his discussion of unreflective consciousness to a discussion of "unreflective behavior" (52). (But see *Being and Nothingness*, pt. IV, ch. 1, sec. I, 559ff.) In his examples it is always behavior that attracts his emphasis, although it is "change of intention" that best describes his thesis. For example, he singles out "acting disgusted" in his description of the "sour grapes" phenomenon, when it is the "magical conferring of a quality" ("too green") that is the point of the example. Yet Sartre concludes, "An emotion is not a matter of pure demeanor [*comportement*]. It is the demeanor of a body which is in a certain state" (74). But to make sense of this, we would have to either give up Cartesianism or describe the relevant "state" in question-begging terms.

My third objection is also a familiar one, and it points to an error that is often repeated or uncritically accepted by a great many phenomenologists. It concerns the confusion of *reflection* with *self-consciousness*. These must be distinguished, although the reason they often are not is that the usual contrasts between prereflective chores or mechanical skills and the clearly reflective self-consciousness of philosophy give us no reason to suspect that there are at least *two* sets of distinctions at work here. We can be reflective without being self-conscious (for example, in thinking about a problem, even a problem concerning ourselves), and we can be self-conscious without being reflective (as in the experience of embarrassment or pride). Sartre long struggled with these two distinctions, between reflective and prereflective, and self-conscious and unself-conscious, and developed a convoluted but demonstrably unsatisfactory conception of the *prereflective cogito* in response. In a theory of the emotions this is a particularly serious problem, for it is not plausible, nor does it follow that because the emotions are prereflective, they are therefore without self-consciousness. In fact, I would argue that every emotion, as part of its essential structure, involves consciousness of oneself. This is not to disagree with Sartre's contention that emotions are prereflective (although I would strongly disagree that they are essentially so).[18] It is, rather, to say that his oft-cited example of "my writing but not being aware of *my* writing" (see, for instance, 54, and *Transcendence of the Ego*, ch. 2) has confused many readers because Sartre seems to be claiming too much. It would be sufficient for him to say, simply, that such acts are unreflective. It does not follow, nor is it plausible, that they are not self-conscious.

My fourth objection has to do with Sartre's need for a "second form of emotion," in which "the world reveals itself as magical," such as the case of the face appearing at the window. Here, Sartre complains, "there is no behavior [*conduite*] to take hold of" (82), and so "the emotion has no finality [purpose] at all" (83). But for Sartre, who insists that emotions and emotional behavior must be purposive and significant, this is a disaster. It also ignores the development of emotional habits and the background of emotions (prior expectations, standing hopes and fears). My diagnosis, very briefly, is that Sartre has not made an important distinction. There are many emotions—the ones most prone to Jamesian analysis—that happen suddenly because something suddenly happens to us. But we can and should distinguish between what suddenly happens to us and what we do in response. What suddenly happens to us is by the nature of the case beyond our control, not within the bounds of our plans or expectations, and therefore involves no strategy on our part. But what we do in response may be practiced and cultivated, may be anticipated and prepared for. Even "spontaneous" emotion and behavior involve a context and a background. Here is an old point of Aristotle's that fits well into Sartre's mature thesis about responsibility. We are responsible for our characters, says Aristotle, because we cultivate them in everything that we do. We are responsible for our emotions, therefore, not because we take responsibility for everything that happens to us but because we are responsible for how we train ourselves to respond to emergency situations as well as temptations and difficult situations. Soldiers train for battle; they learn not to panic under fire or facing a Spartan with a sword. Young lovers condition themselves for love, helped along by the media, by movies, by watching older couples. They do not just "fall" in love, even when the person of their dreams happens to walk into their lives. So whether it is a face at the window or the face in one's dreams, it does not follow that the form of emotional consciousness is different because it is unexpected. It is just more *spontaneous* (Sartre's favorite term later on), which does not mean that it is beyond the bounds of responsibility.

I also think that Sartre puts *too* much emphasis on behavior in his theory. Perhaps he has not taken seriously enough the phenomenological perspective and the Husserlian conception of "constitution" with its Kantian overtones, the conception of an "act of consciousness" that need not be exhibited in terms of any resultant behavior. Our "setting up of a world that is magical" need have no behavioral manifestations. Sartre is surely right that, through our emotions, we "constitute" and "transform the world." But the notion of "ineffective" which he adds to this idea of transformation only betrays his thinking that an emotion *ought* to be physically and socially effective, and if its behavior is ineffective, it is therefore "inferior." But not all emotions involve behavior, effective or otherwise. It is the very essence of certain emotions—for example, guilt, resentment, or envy—that they refrain from any expression no matter how "ineffective," even from facial expression, for they find it much more to their interest either to hide from view entirely or to show the world a bland and superficial smile, a pretense of hearty handclasps, and an "expression" of self-confidence. One can feel even love or fear and yet express nothing in word or stance, in gesture or grimace. Psychologists like Paul Ekman might argue that even so, there are subtle and quick facial cues to the "hidden" emotion. Probably, but that is not the behavior that Sartre has in mind. It is not essential to an emotion that it be overtly expressed. We do not need to *act* disgusted in our "sour grapes" attitude, nor do we need to break down in tears in our sadness or shout insults in our anger. In resentment, we may well mutter curses, but we need not thereby *behave* in any distinctive way. This point is crucial to our understanding of the emotions: they are transformations of our world through "acts" of consciousness, but they need not involve our behavior and they need not entail either effective or ineffective expression.

My most serious objection follows from the idea that emotions represent ineffective behavior or, to use the term Sartre borrowed directly from Janet, "inferior behavior." Despite his persuasive rejection of the traditional theories in which the emotions are viewed as disruptions, as irrational and degrading, Sartre has retained many of these attitudes in his own theory. Toward the end of his essay, he offers us many examples. He says, "In order to believe in magical behavior, it is necessary to be highly disturbed" (75). And an emotion is "an irrational synthesis of spontaneity and passivity" and a "collapse of the superstructures laboriously built by reason" (84). Emotions "obscure" consciousness (76) and fail to see "the event in its proper proportions" (87).[19] In language reminiscent of Freud, Sartre tells us that emotions lead to "*captivity*" (79), that they are "undergone," and a "trap" in which we are "caught" (78). Sartre tells us that "when, with all paths blocked, consciousness precipitates itself into the magical world of emotion, it does so by *degrading* itself" (75–76; my italics), and again, "the origin of emotion is a spontaneous and lived degradation of consciousness in the face of the world" (77), and yet again, "consciousness is degraded" (83).

In short, Sartre has fallen prey to the very attitudes he seeks to refute. Despite his contributions to our thinking, he evidently believes that our emotions are "inferior," "irrational," and "degrading." They are meaningful, but their meanings are de-meaning: they have purposes, but their purposes serve only to betray and ineffectively compensate for impotence. They may be our own conscious "acts," but they are nevertheless beyond our control, "traps" in which we are "caught," "a consciousness rendered passive" (84). What Sartre had yet to realize is the effectiveness and even the revolutionary relevance of our emotions, the variability of their purposes, and the fact that they are as important in sustaining our effective behavior as in rationalizing our failures and our impotence.[20]

The Emotions: Strategy, Ideology, and Magic

If emotions are "transformations of the world," those transformations are not always or even usually "magical." For Sartre in his "Sketch," the concept of magic serves to underscore the *ineffectiveness* of emotional behavior, the fact that our emotions merely change the direction of consciousness without really changing the world at all. Like Janet, and like the Gestaltists from whom he borrows his most extensive example, Sartre treats the emotions in general as isolated modes of frustration behavior, as ways of *coping* or "escaping" from a world that is "too difficult." In short, in his "Sketch" Sartre seems to treat all emotions as forms of escapist denial and delusion. But our emotions are much more than this. Using the doctrines of *Being and Nothingness* and the examples of his more recent works, I think that I can offer a far more vital and existentially inspiring account of the emotions.

Sartre insists that our emotions are "meaningful," but in his "Sketch" this meaning is minimal, capturing the rudiments of Husserl's thesis of "intentionality" but surely giving us much less than the "meaningfulness" which Sartre (and so many other philosophers) have sought and demanded in other contexts (for example, in the sense of "the meaning of life" or the concept of "meaningful action"). The problem is that Sartre continues, in the fashion of those psychologists whom he castigates, to treat the emotions as "isolated" and to insist on a separate "world of emotions," as a world that is distinct from the "real" world of effective action and commitment. But it is our emotions that motivate our actions and sustain our commitments. The "fundamental project" that later dominates so much of Sartre's writings is by its very nature an emotional project, one in which we heavily invest ourselves, transforming or reorganizing our entire world around its demands. Thus Nietzsche, following both Kant and Hegel, proclaimed, "Nothing ever succeeds which exuberant spirits have not helped to produce."[21] It is through our emotions that we constitute not only the magical world of frustration and escape but also the living and often radical ideologies of action and commitment that Sartre spent his life defending and amending.[22]

In *Being and Nothingness*, Sartre tells us: "A Jew is not a Jew *first* in order to be subsequently ashamed or proud. It is his pride of being a Jew, his shame, or his indifference which will reveal to him his being-a-Jew, and this being-a-Jew is nothing outside the free manner of adopting it" (677). On the same page, Sartre speaks of "my own choice of inferiority or pride," which appears "only with the meaning that my freedom confers upon them." In other words, an emotion, such as pride, is not an isolated conscious transformation, restricted to those cases of reaction and frustration to which Sartre limits his view in his early "Sketch." The emotions are the constitutive structures of our world. It is through them that we give our lives meaning. Thus the emotions become, in Sartre's philosophy, elevated from their status as "degradations" and "disruptions" to the level of those "existential structures" (or, better, essential existential choices) of our existence which Sartre tried to define throughout his career.

In view of Sartre's more recent emphasis on "the power of circumstances" and the demands of politics, it is necessary to go beyond the view of emotions as frustration reactions and to stress the idea that every emotion has as part of its essential structure an *ideology*, a set of passionate demands regarding how the world *ought* to be changed. Some of these—for example, moral indignation and anger, love of mankind and Rousseauesque "sympathy"— may have straightforward political ramifications. Others—notably guilt, envy, and resentment—may betray precisely that self-indulgent ineffectual "sour-grapes" attitude that Sartre discusses in his "Sketch." But the point is to recognize *both* kinds of ideology, effective radicalism as well as ineffective, reactionary frustration, to appreciate the revolutionary power of the former as well as to reject the reactionary weight of the latter. Resentment and conservative ideologies, on this view, might well be understood as "degradations of consciousness," but certainly not because they are ineffective.

Regarding the *expression* of emotion, it is similarly an error to restrict our attention to "emotional outbursts" and frustration and emergency reactions. Our emotions may also be solid and durable structures of our lives— dedicated love of a spouse, a friend, or a child; "wholehearted commitment" to a cause or a project; or passionate involvement in a movement, a faith, or a relationship. Most such emotions are not even plausible candidates for "degradation" or "irrationality." Although *some* emotions are irrational, it is obvious that not all are. Nor can such emotions—which may not only last for but also give meaning to a lifetime—be plausibly classified as "disruptions." Quite to the contrary, they are precisely those constitutive structures in which we prove ourselves to be most human, of which we are rightly most proud, and in which we justifiably feel ourselves to be most "uplifted" rather than "degraded."

This conception of emotional ideologies merits a brief examination, though this is not the place to work it out in detail. In anger and indignation, we demand rectification, vindication, the righting of a wrong, whether it is a minor personal affront or a social injustice embedded in the political structures of the contemporary world. In sadness and grief we desire the redress or return of a loss. In shame and remorse we seek to redeem ourselves. In love and hate we work toward the welfare of our lover or the destruction of our enemy. This conception of ideology allows us to clarify the abused notion of emotional "expression." The expression of an emotion (the "natural expression," if you like) is precisely that action or set of actions that will most effectively and directly satisfy its ideological demands.[23] This is, of course, not what is usually implied by that term. The "expression" of an emotion is often taken to be the least effective, the least voluntary, and the least "meaningful" of gestures and movements, the grimace of the face and the gnashing of teeth. But focusing on such expressions only underscores the fallacious view of the emotions as "disruptions" and as "ineffective," a view which is all too evident even in Sartre's "Sketch." Joining the revolution or writing an angry letter to one's congressman can be a very effective expression.

Turning to the concept of the "fundamental project" of *Being and Nothingness* and the ideological language of Sartre's later writings, we can revise his thesis and take direct and effective expression as our paradigm: Mathieu's grabbing the machine gun (in the Roads to Liberty series) or Hugo's finally resolute (if ambiguous) assassination of Hoerderer (in "Dirty Hands"), or Sartre's own lifetime of "engaged" literature. The expression of an emotion is, first of all, *the realization of an ideological demand.* What is so often called the "expression" of emotion is such only by way of derivation, a suppressed or inhibited action that might otherwise be effective, a gesture instead of an act, a grimace instead of a battle, the gnashing of teeth in place of an articulated threat, the knotted fists held rigid at one's side rather than a well-thrown and much-deserved punch to the jaw.

But if expression is the realization of an ideological demand, we must now turn back to Sartre's conception of the "magic" of emotions in order to understand the nature of ineffective expression. Sartre is correct, of course, when he suggests that sometimes such ineffective expressions are a means of coping or escaping, but they may not be so much the expression of the emotion as expressions of frustration, namely, the frustration of the emotion—as, for example, when I beat my cane against a tree in anger whose true target is a person (not the tree).[24] Even if this answer is correct, however, it is not illuminating. Why this mode of frustration behavior rather than another? And why any behavior at all, given its evident ineffectiveness? The traditional idea that we thereby "vent" our emotion is not only metaphorical—a return to the "hydraulic model" of the psyche as a quasi-bodily pressure cooker. It is also false. Such ineffective modes of expression have precisely the opposite result: they do not satisfy the emotion but *intensify* it. Consider yourself reviewing a minor offense—perhaps a slighting comment by a friend—and grimacing, gesturing, cursing, perhaps even stamping and kicking and literally "working yourself into a rage." It is often suggested that such behavior is "symbolic," that you are acting *as if* the curses you mutter would be "magically" effective (like the "incantations" Sartre mentions), as if your stamping and kicking register some mysterious pain to the shins of your malefactor (as if by voodoo). The "symbolic" analysis only underscores the question, Why should we indulge in such useless practices, knowing all the while that they will be without effect and consequently will only increase our demands for satisfaction?

The very idea that such so-called expressions intensify rather than satisfy our emotions provides us with our answer. It is an answer that has so long been overlooked precisely because of a general uncritical acceptance of the "hydraulic model" of the emotions, which posits a need to "get them out" and "discharge" them, a need that seems evident even in the etymology of the word "ex-press," to "force out." But though we demand satisfaction of our emotions, we demand something more as well. The emotions, we have already argued, sustain the "fundamental projects" of our lives, "give our lives meaning," and provide the constitutive structures within which we live. If this is so, we can see that we have good reason for *not* satisfying them—in order to keep them alive and, in a great many cases, to intensify them and their demands. Artistic passions seek the perfect expression even while knowing full well that such is impossible. Goethe has his Faust lust for the moment that will endure, knowing full well that such satisfaction is impossible. Lovers take delight in histrionic responses to small infidelities, "expressions" of love, perhaps, but more literally *impressions* which intensify (and surely do not "relieve" or "discharge") the emotion. Dostoevsky's man of spite acts (or rather *does not* act) in order to intensify the bitterness and resentment through which he constitutes his dubious conception of "freedom."[25]

Sartre engaged his life in the pursuit of an ever intensified sense of injustice and indignation, sometimes at great personal cost: in his own words, "to move history forward by recommending it, as well as by prefiguring within himself new beginnings yet to come." If there is "magic" in the emotions, surely that magic is there, in these *chosen* ideologies through which we dramatize our lives in struggle against an unsatisfactory if not indifferent world, *against* the "power of circumstances," making that world, if not better, then at least less "indifferent" through these very choices. And foremost among these choices are—our emotions.

5

FACING DEATH TOGETHER

Camus' The Plague

> There's no question of heroism in all of this. It's a matter of common decency.
> That's an idea which might make some people smile, but the only means of
> fighting a plague is—common decency.
> —Camus, *The Plague*

There are two themes of great importance in Camus' novel *The Plague*.[1] The
first, immediately suggested by the title, is the high probability of imminent,
horrible death. But it is collective death as well as personal death, and so the
second theme, at least as important as the first, is our "being with Others,"
our collective, interpersonal, and social existence. The theme of imminent
death also came to the fore toward the end of *The Stranger*, but there it was
only a matter of individual death, presented as "absurd." Collective death
may also be absurd, but it involves a dimension only hinted at by the abstract
metaphor in *The Stranger*, "the brotherhood of men." (The sexism is for the
most part confirmed by Camus, as virtually all of his characters are men.) But
this social dimension remains wholly abstract in *The Stranger* (and in *The
Fall*). *The Plague* is, accordingly, the best and most moving presentation of
Camus' social philosophy or, rather, the social dimension of his philosophy.
Several years later, in 1955, Camus would attempt another, much less
moving and much less heroic (indeed, mock heroic) statement of social solidarity in *The Rebel*, where he proclaimed, in yet another parody of Descartes'
cogito, "I rebel, therefore we exist." But in *The Plague*, our existence is both
given to start with and collectively threatened. It is in such circumstances,
Camus more wisely tells us, that we learn to live—or to perish—together.

An interpretation of *The Plague* largely depends on one's attitude toward
Camus, on his or her perspective, and on what ideological ax he or she
wants to grind. *The Plague* is, straightforwardly, based on an earlier text
about a then recent epidemic, Daniel Defoe's *Journal of the Plague Year*

(1722).[2] It is, also straightforwardly, an account of the progress and retreat of an epidemic not unlike the bubonic plague that devastated Europe in the fourteenth century, now set in Camus' romantically remembered, semifictional Algeria. But after that, the subject of the novel—and the identity of the plague—is open to interpretation. Camus, as he did with his retrospective comments on *The Stranger*, confuses the issue enormously with his own statement of his intentions in this book. In a much-quoted conversation with Roland Barthes, he claims there is no doubt that *The Plague* is a metaphor for the very different sort of pestilence represented by the Nazi invasion and occupation of Europe. And, indeed, Camus wrote the novel in Provence during the occupation.[3] But the analogy between plague and occupation is vague at best, ignoring from the outset the distinction between natural disaster and willful human evil that lies at the heart of Camus' sense of justice. One can, of course, treat willful human evil as just another force of nature, on a par with earthquakes, volcanic eruptions, and floods, but so much is lost by doing so that we find ourselves virtually incapable of thinking that way. We need not get totally caught up in "the blame game" in order to insist that this is the critical distinction in any discussion of evil. With regard to the plague, all are victims and almost all are blameless.

So why did Camus insist that the novel was about the Nazi occupation, a very particular episode of distinctively human evil in the recent history of Europe, rather than a very general allegory about human experience in the face of imminent threat? It may be that, as in his later comments on *The Stranger*, he was trying to embellish his own novel and the characters he created with more meaning and a more politically relevant social agenda than he intended at the time of writing. It is true that he started thinking about and writing *The Plague* during and just after the Nazi occupation of France, but that, I think, would have been good reason *not* to belabor the present situation but to meditate on the human condition. In his retrospective comments, he may well have been anticipating the building criticism from Sartre and his friends that he was not sufficiently politically *engagé* (despite the fact that Camus, as much as Sartre, employed his literary talents in direct resistance to the Nazi threat).[4] Or he may just have been pulling our collective leg, as authors are often prone to do when annoyed with the question of what their writing *means*. It has often been said that an author is in no better position than anyone else to know what his or her work means. But whatever *The Plague* means, it cannot be the reduction of all calamity to blameless catastrophe. Indeed, the point of the novel is precisely to focus on a truly blameless catastrophe (with an eye to an even more pervasive and universal catastrophe—death). Even so, it is human responsibility that emerges as its major theme. Thus *The Plague* is properly treated as an "existentialist" social novel. Quite the antithesis of a perverse reduction of human behavior to blameless nature, it is a portrait of how even the most ordinary human actions in times of great peril can be heroic and embody an implicit social philosophy.

Facing Death

"We are all condemned. We live under a death sentence." This bit of pop shock philosophy is neither profound nor terrifying. It is trite and obvious. And yet, we live most of our lives as if it were not obvious at all, as if we will never die, or as if that day of death is so far off that it could not possibly make any difference to us, at least for now. But then, on a few morbid days, we do have this sense that our whole lives are overshadowed by the brute fact of our mortality, and the question then is, What do we do with this? The realization of our impending death can be paralyzing. Every aim, every pleasure, and every good deed seems to be rendered pointless. Or this realization can be invigorating, impressing on us the limited amount of time available. Indeed, the realization of one's impending death can be a goad to philosophizing. The German thinker Martin Heidegger did not hesitate to remind us that we are both "being-unto-death" and ontologically "inauthentic," meaning that although death is our "most necessary possibility," we tend to deny this and "fall" back into the forgetfulness of everyday life. But most of us have moments of personally profound reflection, whether or not these count as "authentic," in which the realization of our own impending death prompts neither panic nor frenzied activity, but serious thought and a sincere search for perspective. What has my life amounted to, thus far? What will or could my life amount to, given what time I have left? Have I lived up to my promise? And regarding promises to other people, what promises have I made? Which have I fulfilled? Which have I betrayed? Did those promises make any sense, in terms of whom I really want or wanted to be? Have I possibly missed *the way* of my life, perhaps altogether? Who am I, really? What does the rambling tale of my life tell me about where I stand in the larger scheme of things, or even in just my own narrative?

These are heavy questions, and asking them is the philosopher's business. They are also are annoying questions, which is why philosophers are considered "gadflies," like those noxious insects that disturb honest citizens' mundane tranquillity (or worse). The novelist has an easier time of it. By creating fictional characters (or by hijacking real life stories), the novelist can create confrontations with death that are both personal and, thankfully, impersonal, in the sense that it is not our person and not our death. We can take up the plight of the fictional character (or not) as our own, but that is our choice, an option, not what Heidegger called our "most necessary possibility." We do not have an "option" with regard to our own mortality. The novelist, by contrast, can offer us any number of possibilities, and we as readers can take them to heart or distance ourselves. It is our choice. Thus, unlike the philosopher, the novelist can ask the heavy questions without being too direct or vexatious. And he or she can explore any number of possibilities without hectoring us, as a philosopher would, "and this is what will happen to you, too."

When the novelist is also a philosopher, the result is, not surprisingly, more philosophical. The questions can still be profound and personal, but they can be asked, as it were, obliquely, and answered indirectly as well. Thus Camus, in several of his novels, asks the question, How will you face death?, but in a crypto-fictional mode. And he gives us an answer so unusual that it is jarring. It is summarized in the odd expression "a happy death," the title of his first novel; in the climactic theme of his famous and still most popular novel, *The Stranger*; as well as in his most morbid novel, *The Plague*, where it is mentioned in the final sentence (in French, the final word) of the book. To be sure, there are other fictional (and quasi-fictional) deaths in Camus' work that are not so happy (*Caligula*, *The Misunderstanding*), and the occasional novel that is not about death at all (*The Fall*), but it is a theme that runs through both his fictional and his philosophical works (insofar as these can be distinguished at all). Camus had read Heidegger, of course, but he had also confronted death as a child when he contracted tuberculosis and when he lost his father in the First World War. More recently, he had lived through the horrors of the Second World War, the occupation of most of France, and the deportation and murder of the local Jews, so death was no doubt on his mind. As was the innocent happiness that he sought and fantasized about, which he may on occasion have experienced. But as a philosopher it was the odd pairing of death and happiness that intrigued him, not just as fiction but as a real-life "possibility."

In *The Stranger*, Camus has his main character convicted of a serious but pointless crime in order to force him to confront his imminent death. Meursault is to be executed by guillotine, and although in his final hours he muses on the desirability of a "loophole," he is quite clear that death could not be more certain. But Meursault, "strange" character that he is, faces this certain death more or less philosophically, asking the crucial questions ("Did I live right?" "Was my life meaningful?") and giving shockingly glib answers ("Yes, because it does not matter how one lives" and "Yes, because life itself is life's only meaning"). But if the second answer is straight from Camus, the first emphatically is not. Does it matter how one lives? Yes, and *nothing else* matters. Camus broke with Sartre and the Left because they condoned a violence he could not abide. In a famous essay, he urged us to be "neither victims nor executioners," to live in such a way that we condone neither violence nor resignation in the face of violence.[5] He wrote eloquently against the death penalty because he found in it the ultimate crime in which we are all complicit.[6] Thus, while Camus may or may not identify with his character Tarrou, in *The Plague* he clearly uses him as a spokesman for some of his most heartfelt moral opinions. Death is the worst thing, and complicity in killing is the worst crime of all.

Of course, one can question this, and I will suggest that Camus gives us a good reason for doubting that death is the worst thing of all. What is so terrifying about the plague is not just death but the manner of death. Death by plague is disfiguring, humiliating, disgusting—it is nothing so clean and clinical as the guillotine. And is killing (or complicity) the worst crime? It is with good reason that the most vindictive murderers in history have preferred slow and mortifying means of killing, which is why torture has become so reviled throughout the civilized world. But for Camus, with his desperate affirmation of life, it is life itself that is meaningful, however awful it may be, so death is the ultimate enemy. Nothing other than life is worth our attention.

It is often said that death is "part of life," but it is not. It is simply life's cessation. So, too, death is to life not life's "opposite" but its end. It is therefore the enemy of all enemies. So Camus perversely insists (in *Myth*) that the "quality" of life is no substitute for "quantity" of life. There is no compensation for loss of life or wrongful death. It is not clear how this view is compatible with the "happy death" that he touts, but he suggests it again here at the end of the book. Camus is concerned with happiness *in* life, which would seem to me to be just what "quality of life" is all about. Or, perhaps, what concerns him is the happiness we ought to have about just being alive. (Caligula screams, in his final seconds of life, "I'm alive!") But insofar as happiness is an issue about life, then one might argue that it must be an issue about death as well.

Characters and Destinies

The plotline of *The Plague* is not about happiness. It is about death. Plague breaks out. And then it passes, or seems to, as quickly as it came. Against this background narrative, however, individual happiness is what the novel is about. The story traces the interweaving fates (and occasional fortune) of Dr. Bernard Rieux, who is the dominant figure in the novel (and, we eventually find out, its narrator); Jean Tarrou, an endearing smart-ass moralist and an occasional spokesman for Camus; Raymond Rambert, a journalist in love with a woman in Paris who got trapped in Oran when the city gates closed; a quite ordinary but ridiculous man ironically named Joseph Grand; a priest/preacher named Father Paneloux; and a scoundrel named Cottard. All of them struggle to come to terms not so much with imminent death as with their own happiness in conflict with their sense of obligation. Rieux, for example, throws himself into his work, in part to distract himself from the absence of his wife, who is suffering from tuberculosis. Rambert, who is also painfully separated from his beloved, spends most of the novel trying to get out of the city, but finally joins the cause. Cottard, by contrast, uses the plague for all it is worth, making a small fortune by taking advantage of the situation and engaging in smuggling. For each of them, too, there is something like a resolution to "start over again," just as Meursault, facing death at the end of *The Stranger*, reflects on his mother, ready to "start life all over again." We are reminded again of Nietzsche's fantastic "test" of life affirmation, the "eternal recurrence of the same." But one is also reminded (as suggested by Stephen Kellman[7]) of Sisyphus in his endless toil, starting (with each roll of the rock) all over again. But in *The Plague*, at least, the "starting over" is in every case a resolution to be happy, to "get it right" this time around.

The most troublesome example is the scoundrel Cottard, who, before the start of the plague (at the beginning of the novel), attempts suicide, fails, and survives. By the time the plague arrives, he has already "started over again," and in many ways has a much clearer sense of how to live with the plague than others. He also has the benefit of a somewhat lessened sense of vulnerability, having already escaped one encounter with the Grim Reaper. So he, more than anyone else (any other major character, that is), tries to live his life to the fullest, which for him means enjoying the luxuries and extravagances still available in Oran. It is said that "it is an ill wind that blows no one good," suggesting that some will benefit from even the worst tragedy. The plague allows Cottard, first of all, to avoid arrest, and then it provides him with the means to profit from the burgeoning black market. He shows no inclination to join the others in their efforts to halt the plague, for it "suits him quite well," and he sees "no reason to stop it" (145). But it also allows him to join in the feeling of solidarity, because the reprieve from his fear of arrest allows him to live as part of society, even soliciting the good opinion of others.

Cottard may be a scoundrel, a crook, and a criminal, but he has a charm that captivates even the moralists around him (even Camus). Grand, not surprisingly, seems attracted to his glamour. Tarrou at one point insists that "the plague has done him proud" (176). This raises a serious question for Camus about how much "happiness" is a moral concept or to what extent it is amoral. Happiness as hedonism, a view to which Camus is obviously attracted, is distinctively devoid of a moral dimension. But *The Plague* is nothing if not a moral tale. Accordingly, Camus gives a somewhat mixed account of the citizens' general sense of indulgence, suggesting at one point that they all become short-term hedonists, and at another that they give up on pleasure altogether, which is probably indicative of not only their schizoid reaction to the plague but also moral confusion and a narrative insight on Camus' part. Cottard takes advantage of the horror all around him, and though he is despicable, he does not come off as a villain, at least not until the end of the novel, when the end of the plague signals the end of his advantages as well, and he goes berserk and starts shooting people. But until his breakdown, there is no suggestion of condemnation or criticism from Camus or Rieux, the narrator.

There are minor characters who are defined only by their absence (Rieux's wife, Rambert's girlfriend, Grand's ex-wife). But another is Dr. Rieux's mother. She is a ghostly presence, a specter that hovers on the margins of the story, but she is a surprisingly poignant presence even though she hardly says a word. If one did not know anything about Camus' personal life, she might not make any sense in the novel at all. But Camus' own mother was deaf and had a speech deficiency. She was a powerful presence in the author's life and also plays a central role in his posthumous, candidly autobiographical novel *The First Man*. So we should not be surprised to see that she is treated respectfully, even reverentially, here by Rieux in the novel but also by the author, despite the fact that she is at most a marginal and mysterious figure in the story. But this, I think, represents a crack in the façade of what Dr. Rieux wants to present as a coldly "objective" and not at all personal clinical report. There is no such thing as a merely "truthful" report, if by that we mean a report without a personal perspective and personal concerns, even a personal agenda.

Camus writes, "There's no question of heroism," but nevertheless he asks through Rieux, "Who is the hero of the novel?" But it is a dumb question, and it is also self-serving. Dr. Rieux is clearly the central character of the novel, the one who seems to make the greatest sacrifices, the dynamic engine that maintains the "resistance"—however ineffective—and therefore, one would think, is the hero. But because Rieux asks the question (to which the answer would seem obvious), he also feels compelled to answer it, in a disingenuous way that is meant to hide its self-aggrandizing nature. So he comments that if anyone is the hero of the story, it is the most unlikely character Grand, who is, one might say, "a hero of everyday life," a phrase that Camus borrows from Lermentov in his opening epigraph to *The Fall*. But Grand is a joke (or as close as anything in *The Plague* ever comes to being a joke). Even his name is obviously ironic, and his job title is ludicrous. He is assistant temporary clerk, a job he has held (without a promotion) for thirty years. Yet his wife left him, he tells us, because he was so caught up in his career. His project throughout Camus' novel, however, is the most ludicrous bit of all. Throughout, Grand struggles to write a novel, despite the fact that he is, almost always (in his own words), incapable of coming up with the words. So after years of writing, he is still working on the first sentence, which he rewrites and rewrites and rewrites. (Speaking of futile Sisyphisian labors!) Some hero! Dr. Rieux is obviously trying to put one over on us (a point that several commentators seem not to notice). But, given his intentions for his journal, this, too, represents a failure of objectivity, trying to shift the focus to his own heroism even after both rejecting the idea of heroism and shifting the focus to the least likely "hero" of the story.

For this reason and others I found myself quite put off by the heroic Dr. Rieux. I found him to be something of a cold fish and a moral prig. He hardly ever thinks of his wife. (By contrast, Rambert cannot think of anything but his woman, so one would think that he would be a constant reminder of Rieux's own deprivation.) Rieux also has no evident sense of humor, a fact thrown into ironic relief by his name, which more or less means "one who laughs." Although he is devoted to the immediate task of building solidarity in his community, he is portrayed as a self-righteous, isolated man. He treats the other characters as if they are at "arm's length"—even Tarrou, who comes as close as anyone to being Rieux's friend, even in the most lighthearted scene in the narrative, when the two of them slip off and enjoy an illicit swim in the sea. Even there, Rieux comes off as stuffy and officious.

Doctors, perhaps, have a better claim than most of us to insist on truthfulness, in contrast to the prevarications and evasions regarding illness and disease that are so prevalent among their patients and public figures (who have the unwelcome task of announcing epidemics). It is Rieux who first dares to pronounce the word "plague," to the horror and objections of his medical and political colleagues—although his elderly colleague Castell beats him to the diagnosis. But Rieux's insistence on the truth, too, readily strikes the reader as overly cold and clinical, a common fault among physicians to be sure, but not usually a desirable trait in narrators. What is missing from Rieux's journal is real feeling, and what makes reading Camus' novel so alienating is not just the gruesomeness of the plot. It is its detached and unfeeling descriptions, which Rieux (but I doubt Camus) confuses for the truth. If he unifies the story and gets credit for the solidarity that emerges by part IV of the novel, Rieux nevertheless provides us with an odd and uncomfortable "hero," whose dedication to fighting the plague is compromised by his own self-righteousness.

I think that we can detect here some of Camus' own defensive self-righteousness as a writer, perhaps thus expressing his discomfort in the presence of such self-righteous and sophisticated pundits as Sartre and his friends (as Rousseau no doubt felt in the presence of the Parisian courtiers two centuries before). In Camus' other work, too, his characters, for instance Clamence in *The Fall*, proclaim themselves champions of the truth, and this, of course, was how Camus retrospectively interpreted his character Meursault in *The Stranger*. But the truth is by no means easy to tell, if by that we mean "the whole truth and nothing but the truth." Every truth is told from a particular perspective, and the very nature of perspectives is such that there can be no capturing "the whole truth," and it is highly unlikely that one will be able to discern the peculiarities of one's perspective in order to guarantee "nothing but the truth." The doctor's perspective is just that, a doctor's perspective, and one might argue that ultimately it may be no more appropriate to the situation than the very different moralistic "fire and brimstone" sermons of Father Paneloux.

Rieux, like Sisyphus (and debatably like Sisyphus), may be "the absurd hero," fighting against an unbeatable foe, whether this is conceived to be death or the meaninglessness of the universe. And, indeed, interpreting the plague as either death or the Absurd is a far more philosophical account of the novel than Camus' own retrospective claims that it is a metaphor for the Nazi occupation. I think that in *The Plague* Camus was trying for something much larger than either political confrontation or an individual confrontation with the indifferent universe. What is important about Rieux's quixotic mission is not its futility but the zeal itself, the "resistance" he displays despite its lack of effectiveness, and the solidarity he forges among the citizens, at the very least a way of giving them the all-important feeling of *doing something* as opposed to just waiting as victims for fate to make its decisions. True, one might well interpret this as just a continuation of the Absurdist philosophy captured in *Myth*, but I think Camus was already well on his way toward the themes in *The Rebel* (still several years off) of rebellion and resistance. And if I think *The Rebel* is a seriously flawed book, even a mistake, it is because of the pathos of Camus' defensiveness against Sartre and his friends, not because I find fault with the themes or the psychological insight that motivates the themes. That is what makes Camus an "existentialist" (despite his denial). It is this emphasis on *doing* something, on *making* one's life meaningful.

Jean Tarrou, in contrast to Rieux, is full of personality and humor, although his jocularity never seems to help the humorlessness of the novel. Tarrou can be annoyingly solicitous, but he can be profound as well. As I suggested earlier, he is more of a spokesman for Camus than any of the other characters, including Dr. Rieux, not least because he makes no attempt to hide or disguise his eccentric subjectivity. Nevertheless, he has an erratic presence in the story, appearing from time to time, often with just a bon mot, and we do not really get to know him at all until toward the end of the novel, when he is dying of the plague. He says that he aspires to be "a saint without God," a pretentious aspiration, to be sure, but one loaded with philosophy. Steven Kellman suggests that the philosophy is distinctively post–Nietzschean, but if that is so, it must be said that Tarrou (perhaps like Camus) is still very much caught up in "the shadows of God," not least in his conception of sainthood. In many ways, he anticipates Clamence in *The Fall*, although with none of the cynicism and resentment. He is a profound moralist, and although he is dedicated to one particular cause (the abolition of the death penalty), it is clear that he has larger quasi-theological issues in mind: innocence, guilt, and redemption. He keeps his own journal of the plague, which (we gather) is far less matter of fact and far more subjective and whimsical than the one we read by Rieux. (I have sometimes wondered what the effect of this alternative *Plague* might have been.) He also throws himself into the project of fighting the plague, second in dedication only to Rieux, although he manages to maintain a sense of humor and an Absurdist perspective that always seems to be out of reach for the doctor. It is another irony that he falls victim to the plague, but his death is anything but the gruesome and tragic scene that we have seen in so many other characters. His, perhaps alone, is a "happy death," and the reason seems to be that he takes it—and the plague—not all that seriously. Is this, possibly, the real lesson of the book? If so, did Camus himself ever manage to take it to heart?

Raymond Rambert, by contrast again, is a Parisian journalist assigned by his newspaper to look at health conditions in Oran. Another irony. The assignment obviously turns into something else. He isn't much of a character, but he provides a different kind of poignancy to the story. Whereas for most of the characters death and plague are the immediate issues, for

Rambert the only issue is love and separation. He is desperate to get back to his woman in Paris but is prevented from doing so by the quarantine, and so he exhausts himself consorting with various shady characters, trying to get smuggled, one way or another, out of the country. The plague, in short, is not his problem, just the cause of his problem. For this reason he is never a candidate for the authorship of the journal (that non-mystery with which Rieux teases us), despite his writing and reporting abilities. But here we might note that it is a curious subtheme of *The Plague* that so many folks seem to be writers, an unlikely avocation for people in such dire circumstances. Rieux is the coy journal author/narrator, Grand is slaving away at his novel, Tarrou has his journal, and even Father Paneloux is working on an essay when he dies. But Rambert, the journalist, never seems to get around to writing anything.

Rambert also illustrates a problem that obsessed Camus, the idea of "exile," even though Rambert is caught in the city rather than exiled from home. But one might rightly argue that these are just two ways of viewing the same dilemma, the idea of being trapped away from "home." Camus makes his own "exile" from Algeria one of the repetitive themes of his work, although one might ask not only to what extent exile in Camus' case is self-chosen but also, more profoundly, whether we are all in "exile" and not "at home," whether we know it or not. Might it not be the "modern condition," emphasized famously by Heidegger in his early work? (Although it should be pointed out that actual homelessness in Germany after the First World War was the highest it had ever been.) All of us are in a society that is not "our own," although, again, we should note that Camus describes Algeria here, as in *the Stranger,* as if it is nothing but a European colony. In *The Stranger* the Arabs who make up most of the population don't have names, and in *The Plague* they don't seem to have deaths either, except, perhaps, in the larger statistics, although the death toll among the native population must have been much worse than what we see among the Europeans. So the "exile" problem may in fact be much more serious than Camus lets on. It is not just a question of being caught away from home. It is a matter of refusing to see and acknowledge the people with whom one actually shares one's existence.

Rambert illustrates yet another point that obsessed both Camus and Sartre, the idea that one is an "exception." Taking oneself as an exception, we might note, is a central concern of Immanuel Kant's moral philosophy. One is, to keep it short, not supposed to make an exception of oneself. The "categorical imperative" is defined to be universal; to make reference to any particular persons or reference to self is, of course, the most egregious violation of morality. But considering oneself as an exception will play a curious role in Camus' later novel, *The Fall.* There, Clamence tells a story about a Jewish prisoner in a German death camp who complains, "But my case is different. I am innocent." Thus it is of particular significance that Rambert, in the end, declines to escape from the city and joins Rieux and the others in their heroic but futile effort to blunt the tide of the plague. In the end, in other words, he realizes that no one is an exception after all.

Finally, there is Father Paneloux. His role in *The Plague* is rather straightforward and is already familiar to us from the figure of the prison chaplain in *The Stranger*. He is the reminder that wherever there is tragedy, the theology of the "problem of evil" is never far away. "Why is this happening to us?" The unpleasant answer is "because of something you have done." This is the central theme of the Hebrew Bible, and it is the subject of Father Paneloux's first sermon. "Calamity has come on you, my brethren, and you deserved it" (86–87). Camus, of course, does not put much stock in this. His atheism and his philosophy of the Absurd preclude it. If there is no divine, there can be no divine retribution. But, nevertheless, there is still guilt and, one might argue, if we acknowledge Nietzsche's "shadows of God," sin. Tarrou, who aspires to be a saint without God, makes this point expressly. In Camus' terms, Paneloux is guilty of "philosophical suicide," but so, too, are we all guilty: of complicity in injustice and murder (according to Tarrou), of indifference to life (according to Camus himself). But there is a change in Paneloux toward the end of the novel, when he gives a second sermon, this one admitting the incomprehensibility of the tragedy, in fact even echoing Camus on the Absurd. But of particular significance here, as pointed out by Kellman, is the shift from the second-person "you" in the first sermon to the first-person-plural "we" in the second, suggesting a transformation in the priest, too, from righteous accuser to a participant in the emerging solidarity of the community. And yet, when Camus has him die of a fever that is not clearly that of the plague, his place in that doomed community is ironically thrown open to question.

Rats! A Short Interlude on Plague

What is plague?[8] Camus learned a good deal from Defoe and from accounts of earlier plagues in England and Europe, in particular the bubonic plague of 1347 (called "the Black Death" in England, because of the black spots that were one of the symptoms of the disease). Surprisingly, Camus evidently did not spend much time reading about or discussing the deadliest plague in history, the worldwide flu epidemic of 1918, which occurred in his lifetime (when he was five). As a sometime enthusiast of the classics, he may have done some reading on the Great Plague of Athens, in 400 B.C.E., recently dubbed the "Thucydides Syndrome," which was probably a flu with secondary bacterial infections.[9] He may not have known that bubonic plague was imported into Europe via Italian merchant ships from China, where there had been a deadly outbreak in the early 1330s. This knowledge might have provided Camus with an alternative exotic setting, but it is worth noting, as in *The Stranger*, that although the setting of *The Plague* is Algeria, there are no named Arab characters, no one speaks Arabic, and the novel could actually have been set just about anywhere. (It is thus disingenuous that Camus said, in his Nobel acceptance speech, that he had "never written anything that was not connected, in one way or another, to the land where I was born.")

In the fourteenth century, the devastation in China, and then in Europe, was horrendous. Twenty-five million Europeans died between 1347 and 1352. An anonymous eyewitness from Sicily in those terrible years reported: "Fathers abandoned their sick sons. Lawyers refused to come and make out wills for the dying. Friars and nuns were left to care for the sick, and monasteries and convents were soon deserted, as they were stricken, too. Bodies were left in empty houses, and there was no one to give them a Christian burial." The Italian writer Boccaccio, who referred to the plague in his *Decameron*, wrote that its victims "ate lunch with their friends and dinner with their ancestors in paradise," so quick was the death that struck many people. After the most horrible years, smaller outbreaks continued for years, indeed for centuries. Medieval society never recovered. Europe lived in constant fear of the plague's return, for it tends to "go underground" for periods of time (when the fleas from the rats go into hibernation) and then returns. It is not hard to imagine that the characters in Camus' fictional Oran continued to be traumatized for many years as well. But it is also easy to imagine, as in Europe six centuries before, a second-order epidemic of denial and distraction. We do not live easily with the possibility of death.

The "problem of evil," made famous by the Enlightenment philosophers of the seventeenth century (not all of them very religious), was but a burp of evil compared with the plague. The devastation of the Lisbon earthquake is not to be dismissed, of course, but that was sudden, communal, unanticipated death and destruction. The plague, by contrast, was ongoing, brutally present, but unpredictable, demanding not retrospective philosophical commentaries but ongoing coping strategies, whether Dr. Rieux's commitment to keep busy or Paneloux's accusatory then kindly sermons. It is Paneloux who raises these classic issues in *The Plague:* how a good God could wreak such havoc on an innocent people. His answer was the answer that had dominated since the tales of the Old Testament: that the people must not have been so "innocent" after all. It is worth noting that Camus is not at all sympathetic to Paneloux, even though in his novels *The Stranger* and *The Fall* he makes innocence and guilt a dominant theme. But in this novel that would so seem to invite some theological speculation, or at any rate some serious consideration of the justice of the situation, Camus is remarkably silent. Dr. Rieux simply reports the deaths of children and scoundrels alike, with no suggestion of desert at all.

The plague is both invisible and grotesquely visible. Camus makes much of this, and the contrast with the very visible hands-on violence of the Nazis is worth noting. But the theme of invisibility and visibility serves Camus' literary purposes very well. Transmission is invisible, but once people are infected, their symptoms are anything but invisible. Plague causes high fever and a painful swelling of the lymph glands called buboes (from which the bubonic plague got its name). Red spots appear on the skin and then turn horrifying black. There is vomiting and all sorts of other gruesome signs of the disintegration of the body, so even if death comes quickly, it is not a pretty, much less a "happy," death. And unlike Meursault's very public execution, greeted with "howls of execration," a death by plague combines public hideousness with the humiliation of anonymity. With so many dying, one's own death would seem to count for nothing at all.

The Plague as Horror

In *The Plague*, in contrast to *The Stranger*, we all face death—or, rather, everyone in the novel faces death together. *The Stranger* forces us to confront the idea of imminent death, but *The Plague* is, by contrast, a horror novel, a novel designed to evoke horror in its readers. People die horribly, and Camus, like Defoe, details their death agonies for us. And people do not just die together, as they might in an earthquake or a flood, nor just as individuals; the citizens of Oran die collectively as individuals, each at his or her own time, no matter how many at a time and no matter how untimely their deaths may be. They all know that they could take ill at any moment, regardless of their age, their health, their habits, their virtues, their vices. So their anxiety is as awful as the death itself, but it is what individuates them, as their deaths do not. And they do not die quietly or with dignity either—again, as a victim of the guillotine might manage to do. They writhe in agony. They vomit and defecate violently. They turn all sorts of gruesome colors. And people do not just die together *as people*, either. Their demise is prefigured and accompanied by the death of the most despised of all mammalian creatures, the rats. Their conjoined demise is a source of special horror, depriving death of the human dignity it might want to claim.

Horror is a special kind of emotion. Horror is not fear or anxiety. Fear provokes action, no matter how aimless, useless, or incompetent. Anxiety creates confusion, insofar as one does not know what threat to protect oneself against. But horror is fully aware of what it sees and what threatens; it just cannot do anything about it. Moreover, horror fascinates. Drivers slow down and gawk at a dismembered body on the highway, despite their knowing how much this will upset them and despite their utter inability to help the victim in any way. We are fascinated by what horrifies us. And plague therefore fascinates. That fascination is what stokes our persistence through the gruesome monotony of Camus' novel. It is not the plot that drives the novel. It is the horror.

Camus has a number of devices, as did Defoe, for distancing us from the characters and their plight. Not least of these distancing mechanisms is the fact that *The Plague* is a novel and thus, unlike Defoe's *Journal*, a piece of fiction. (This may be why Camus avoided the specifics of the 1918 epidemic.) It presupposes our willing sense of disbelief, which, given the gruesome subject matter, may require some persistence. Another distancing device is the quasi-journalistic style, which, like *The Plague* itself, plods on at a dreary and increasingly gruesome pace with only anxious anticipations of what is to come. We become accustomed to the slowly building horror. Moreover, there is no character with whom we get so involved, or with whom we could easily get involved, to draw us into the novel. Rieux, I commented, is standoffish and unsympathetic. Grand is a joke, as is Paneloux. Tarrou is withheld from us for most of the novel. But this makes *The Plague* the least phenomenological of all of Camus' novels. We read the characters only through their behavior, not through their experience. This is true even of Dr. Rieux, who is something of a phenomenological dud. His uncritical insistence on telling the objective truth, however important that may be in a journalist, further removes us from his perspective on the situation. Thus the danger is that the many deaths in the novel remain merely "objective" to us, in the sense dismissed by Kierkegaard and Heidegger as utterly "inauthentic," and not indicative of "our own" deaths at all.

But Camus also keeps us engaged. Some of this engagement is the pure horror of watching the plague manifest itself and take over the town. As readers, there is nothing we can do but watch. That is the nature of horror, and in that sense it already presupposes a built-in distancing mechanism.[10] But for the citizens of Oran, too, there is little they can do. They feel horror rather than fear. They feel helpless. And that, of course, is the point of the novel. With regard to impending death, there is little that one can do. One can try to slow it down for a while. One can hope and even try for a cure or a palliative. One can make the dying more comfortable. One can keep a journal. Or one can simply allow oneself to be horrified (an emotion that Dr. Rieux never seems to display). Thus the plight of the characters in the novel is not so different from the situation of the reader: one of horror and helplessness, except for the all-important fact that we, at the moment, are not facing the plague.

Just a few decades ago, however, many Americans found themselves confronting a real but equally mysterious epidemic, first referred to as "gay cancer" but then identified as HIV/AIDS, which turned out to be indiscriminate as to sexual orientation or gender, or for that matter indiscriminate as to age, as more and more babies were born with the disease. In the late 1980s, as the number of infections and deaths increased exponentially, the panic in America approached epidemic proportions. A few physicians and social scolds recommended that people stop having sex altogether, even within monogamous marriage and despite their use of protection. But so did an accompanying sense of recklessness escalate, displaying just the desperate polarity described by Camus. Here was young America, confronted with death. Hysterics advised abstaining from sex altogether, while rock bands like Nirvana celebrated and even invited the Grim Reaper to their parties. Hoping desperately for some sort of vaccine or cure, whether they were more careful or more careless in their sexual behavior, young Americans watched with horror and a sense of utter helplessness. But both care and carelessness were responses to the epidemic, and we do not understand the psychology of *The Plague* if we do not appreciate both reactions.

The analogy has its limitations. Except for the babies and recipients of contaminated blood transfusions, the victims of HIV/AIDS were at least a little bit complicit in their infection (although suggestions of complicity have almost always accompanied epidemics, as the preacher Paneloux makes quite clear in *The Plague*). And, as in Camus' novel, modern medicine kept alive some hope that human intervention might actually succeed where it had not in the plagues of earlier centuries. Of course, the HIV/AIDS epidemic did not fade away, and it continues to ravage Africa and many populations in Asia. Even in the United States, young people, especially, continue to be infected and to die at an alarming rate. But even more than in Camus' fictional Oran, and over a longer period of time (now more than twenty years), Americans have lost focus and interest. They find it easier to convince themselves that the threat is past, or that it can no longer affect them, or that modern medicine—which has indeed made serious advances in treatment—will take care of it if they should ever get sick. But, at least for a few years, younger American readers had no difficulty at all identifying with the characters in Camus' novel. The horror was all very real to them.

The combination of identification and distancing is what makes *The Plague* so effective. This is the key to horror, from Camus' most gruesome novel to the trash 1950s "horror films" that can still be seen on late-night television. If there were no identification with the victims, horror would become no more than abstract sadism, pity, or indifference. If there were no distancing oneself from the horror, then one would become a victim, and the horror would be pushed aside by the more exigent emotions of fear and anxiety. There is no doubt that, for Camus, the inhabitants of Oran were like people he knew, which made the identification even more poignant. And, for us, the specific names, descriptions, and conversations of the characters help us to identify with them, as we could not, for example, with the nameless Arabs in *The Stranger*. But the fact that *The Plague* is a piece of fiction that Camus wrote while he was in France and in the face of a very different horror provides him with the necessary distancing for his work to remain philosophical rather than, as for Dr. Rieux, a matter of "truthful" reporting. Both the fiction and the exotic location provide the distancing for us. This is not a story of any particular plague or an allegorical history of the Nazi invasion and occupation of France. The horror that Camus describes is nothing less than the human condition. No matter how happy our lives may be, there is an awful fate that lies at the end of them, for all and for each and every one of us.

Facing Death Together:
Being-with-Others

In *The Plague*, the people of Oran do not face death alone. Nor, insofar as we identify with their fate, do we. It is true, as Heidegger reminds us (with more profundity than the point is worth) that each of us must die his (or her) own death. But in plague we face a collective death, or at least we all face a similar cause of death that threatens us all at more or less the same time in more or less the same horrible way. This changes everything.

What is the difference between individual death and collective death? Robert Jay Lifton describes the horrific phenomenon of the "second death" experienced by the victims of the atomic bombs dropped on Nagasaki and Hiroshima, in which their individual deaths were evidently accompanied by the death of their entire world, making individual death all the more horrible. It is one thing to face your own death. It is something quite different to face at the same time the deaths of your loved ones, the deaths of your friends, the deaths of your neighbors, the deaths of your entire community, and the death of your society and your culture. In such circumstances, one could, of course, continue to focus only on one's own death and hope only that oneself might be saved, whatever happens to the others. But such a person would be an ass, a cad, something inhuman. Most of us, social and caring creatures that we are, would care as much (or more) about the deaths of at least some others. Whether or not we were to die at exactly the same time, our deaths would no longer be individual, and we would *not* each die only our own individual death. And if it were the entire community, the entire populace of a substantial city that was so threatened, the possible death of all around us would not be a mere abstraction, despite the small number of people we actually know. It would be very much like a "second death," the death of our world.

But death in *The Plague* is yet more complicated and confusing. It is not just individual death, although there are a great many individual deaths. The plague of Oran is not the sudden death of an entire world, all at once, as in nuclear holocaust. Death in *The Plague* is collective but not simultaneous, not everyone at once; and some people will surely survive, as in just about every other known plague in history. (Some people, remarkably, have immunity.) As unimaginable as the loss of one's whole world is—and as uncomfortable as the idea of the continuation of the world *without me* might be to some people—the uncertainty of death by plague further increases the anxiety and adds to collective death a curiously competitive element. To understand the dynamics of plague, we have to understand a peculiar form of irrationality.

Added to the desperate irrationalism that often defines thoughts and behavior regarding impending death, there is an additional ingredient: the idea of *either you or me*, an idea that may not be warranted by our knowledge of epidemics, but seems to be almost unavoidable anyway. Knowing, for example, that 30 percent of the population is likely to die of a sufficiently lethal plague, it is hard not to think about whether or not one is included in that 30 percent, and if one is not, who is. Thus the thought *maybe me, maybe not*, is oddly competitive and empathetic at the same time. Thus the importance of Dr. Rieux's constant insistence that "we fight the plague together," whether or not there is anything effective that we can really do. Forging solidarity, and with it empathy, is an essential part of the battle. Death is the ultimate enemy but, in *The Plague*, at least, the fragmentation of society emerges as a close second. Facing death in *The Plague*, Being-with-Others turns out to be one of the ultimate values.

A more familiar form of irrationality is to be found in the accusations of complicity and other sorts of blame often accompany the threat of death, as when long-term smokers are blamed for their cancers and, appallingly, gay men were originally blamed for AIDS. This is one more manifestation of the "blaming perspective," which pervades the whole of Judeo—Christian thinking. (Talk of forgiveness presupposes the blaming perspective.) In a competitive situation, or in a situation that is, however irrationally, thought to be competitive, the blaming perspective will be all the more pronounced. It serves as rationalization ("Well, yes, so-and-so died, but he drank the water," or "He didn't say his prayers," and so on). As I will argue in my account of *The Fall*, this form of rationalization is surprisingly effective, and therefore also quite widespread. It is not about blame for the sake of blame. It is about blame as a source of hoped-for immunity, exception, or salvation. ("I did not drink the water." "I do pray.") It obviously contributes to the competitiveness and to the fragmentation of the community, and therefore has to be countered.

The blaming perspective is not the whole story, of course, although people like Paneloux struggle to keep it alive (allowing Camus one of his few bouts of black humor in a grim novel). But the very idea that whether or not one comes down with the plague has anything to do with either luck or blame encourages the divisiveness that is the second mortal enemy of the novel. The struggle in *The Plague*, as opposed to the supposedly heroic struggle to "keep the Absurd alive" that defined Camus' philosophy just a few years earlier, is a social struggle. It is not so much a struggle against death as a struggle for solidarity. It is only by sticking together, Camus suggests, that we can make any headway against our common, ultimate enemy, death. But even if there is no avoiding death, we can, by appreciating our common fate, transcend the isolation that can make "strangers" of us all.

6

TRUE TO ONESELF

Sartre's Bad Faith and Freedom

The true hypocrite is the one who ceases to perceive his deception, the one who
lies with sincerity.
—André Gide, *Counterfeiters*

Sartre's philosophy is best known for its harsh, uncompromising claim, his
insistence that we are free and responsible for virtually everything we do, for
what we are, and for the way our world is. He is also known for a concept,
"bad faith" (*mauvaise foi*), that has much to do with freedom and responsibility: the *denial* of one's freedom and, thus, his or her responsibility. But the
linkage is not entirely clear, Sartre's famous examples are less than fully
persuasive, and there are deep ambiguities and conflicts in both his defense of
freedom and his explication of bad faith. Indeed, I will suggest that one well-
founded concern regarding his defense of freedom would seem to undermine
utterly his defense of responsibility. His treatment of bad faith also seems to
undermine his defense of freedom. Since I accept, for the most part, Sartre's
insistence that we are free and responsible, and I also applaud his notion of
bad faith, these are issues that must be sorted out. But, as you will see, this is
by no means a simple and straightforward matter.

I: Bad Faith in *Being*
and Nothingness

Being and Nothingness is the best known if not the most widely read of Sartre's
straightforwardly philosophical writings, and the chapter "Bad Faith" (chapter 2 of part I) is by far the most widely read section of that huge tome. Thus
it is often assumed, uncritically and even in the absence of familiarity with
the rest of the book, to be central to *Being and Nothingness* and to Sartre's

philosophy more generally. Many "existentialism" courses restrict their reading of Sartre to that chapter alone, or perhaps combine it with his early essay, *Existentialism and Humanism*.[1] Yet it is for the most part an isolated and brief chapter. It is barely anticipated in what precedes it, and the topic is rarely taken up or even mentioned much again. Thus the centrality and importance of bad faith cannot simply be assumed, and it must be shown how what might be considered a merely interesting digression can and should be understood as something of a key to Sartre's thinking. How is the problem or paradox of "self-deception," with which Sartre begins, related to bad faith? Why is bad faith so central to Sartre's freedom-centered philosophy? There is good reason for treating it so, but to complicate matters enormously, Sartre seriously misstates and misrepresents what bad faith is, what it signifies, and how it might be understood.

"Bad Faith" is a lucid chapter, compared with much else in *Being and Nothingness*. It introduces several key ingredients of Sartre's "ontology," provides at least some preliminary considerations regarding what Sartre famously but problematically applauds as "authenticity" (Heideggerian "ownness"), and it encapsulates his running battle with Freud. Most important, it anticipates (if it also somewhat obscures) Sartre's central thesis about freedom and human nature, namely, that we are always responsible for what we make of ourselves. A good part of that responsibility is located in how we think of and identify ourselves. It more or less follows, therefore, that a good deal of *irresponsibility* can be traced to false or deceptive ideas about ourselves, and this is the subject matter of bad faith. Bad faith represents a betrayal, an abuse, a willful misunderstanding of our freedom and ourselves.

Mauvaise foi—the phrase comes from Jean-Jacques Rousseau[2]—is initially treated by Sartre as "a lie to oneself." But it is not just any sort of lie. Walter Kaufmann somewhat questionably translates *mauvaise foi* as "self-deception," but even insofar as this is a defensible interpretation, bad faith is a very particular kind of self-deception, namely, self-deception *about oneself*, about who or what one is. Thus many standard examples of self-deception would not fall under the rubric of bad faith—for instance, the mother who refuses to believe (against all evidence) that her son is guilty of a heinous crime, the smoker who refuses to believe that tobacco products really cause cancer and other deadly ailments, or the partisan who refuses to believe that his habitually lying party candidate is a liar. The question in each is not just what the facts are but *why* they are not acknowledged. A particularly interesting case is Amelie Rorty's example of a doctor who refuses to acknowledge her own evident symptoms of cancer in order to keep on paying full attention to her patients.[3] Insofar as this is only a flat denial of the facts about her health and well-being because she does not want to think of herself as sick or mortal, it would seem to be bad faith. But if it is a strategy to allow her to keep focused on her life's work, it might not be. As these examples illustrate, self-deception and bad faith often go together and may be hard to disentangle, but it is nevertheless important to insist that they are distinct phenomena. As we shall see, the interpretation of *mauvaise foi* as "self-deception" further suggests an unfortunate analysis of bad faith as a lie to oneself, and this model leads to paradox and tends to disguise the real issues.

Furthermore, we should note that the negative pall of "bad" and the quasi-religious hint of "faith" are highly significant, even though Sartre routinely (and implausibly) denies that he is doing any "ethics" and despite his vehement atheism. There is no doubt, in spite of Sartre's demurring, that bad faith is *bad*, a matter for moral condemnation (although the above example of the doctor may make us wonder about this). When Sartre talks about bad faith, nevertheless, he is unquestionably critical and even damning, even though he raises a serious question of whether bad faith is avoidable at all. But, especially if it is unavoidable, we need to know what it is and what is so bad about it.

Sartre also insists that "bad faith is *faith*," first in the usual sense that bad faith involves *belief* (as opposed to knowledge), but more important (and with Kierkegaard in mind), it involves an act, a commitment, a practical project, and not merely belief (B&N, 112). Thus, according to many people (Kierkegaard among them), we can have no knowledge of God, but *belief* in God requires faith. But also, faith in God requires a motivated ("passionate") commitment, a "*leap* of faith." It is a practical and very personal phenomenon, not a theoretical curiosity. Sartre's notion of faith is not intended to be at all religious, of course, but I think that there is a plausible suggestion that bad faith is Sartre's secular and "ontological" version of Christian "original sin," that is, an intrinsic flaw in the human character, something that, no matter how one acts or what one does, cannot be transcended or resolved. Like human sin in Christian theology, it is both blameworthy and unavoidable.

At the end of his discussion, Sartre insists that there is "no way out," that we are stuck in bad faith by our very natures. (This despite the fact that he insists, at least in his popular writings, that human beings have no "natures.") I find his insistence on the inevitability of bad faith more unconvincing than disturbing, but in order to understand why, it is necessary first to go back to the basics: the question of what bad faith is and why it is so important in Sartre's philosophy.

Facticity and Transcendence:
The Fundamental Tension

Sartre's official theory, the one that is most easily promulgated with the aid of two of his more famous pieces of jargon, is this: we (as consciousness or "Being-for-Itself") are essentially, phenomenologically–ontologically, free. That is to say, we have *transcendence*, the ability to intend and reach *beyond* any factual situation in which we find ourselves. We have desires. We hope.

We fear. We have ambitions. We make plans and resolutions. The factual situation Sartre calls our *facticity* (a term borrowed directly from Heidegger). So, on the one hand (again from Heidegger), we find ourselves "abandoned" or "thrown" into a world not of our choosing—born into a violent century, an unjust society, a troubled family, a religious tradition; stuck with a sickly body, a homely face, or a troubled personality. This is our facticity, the facts that are true of us. But because we also have transcendence, we can always imagine "possibilities," alternative ways that the world and we might be and devices by which we might try to bring these about. Thus human reality has two very different aspects: the facts that are true of us, the "given," if you like, and our ability to choose, to aspire, to "transcend" ourselves. For instance, Johnny Weissmuller, the Olympic swimming champion who became the best-known movie Tarzan, suffered from polio as a child and was given a bleak prognosis. But instead of accepting his facticity as a "cripple" (a word that was not "politically incorrect" at the time), Weissmuller took up swimming, practiced doggedly, became a champion, and then spent the best years of his adulthood on camera in a meager loincloth, swinging on vines between trees. He refused to accept his facticity and used his transcendence to make something very different of himself. It is against some such heroic story that the phenomenon of bad faith presents itself.

Johnny Weissmuller might well, as a child, have cursed his bad luck and resigned himself to life as a cripple. Sartre's cruel judgment would have been that he was thus in bad faith. But suppose Weissmuller lived a fantasy life in which he just imagined himself as a successful athlete and perhaps even a movie star but did nothing to realize his fantasies. In fact, suppose that he stayed in bed most of every day, merely daydreaming. That, too, would have been living in bad faith, a life of resignation coupled with a fantasy life that never actually engaged with his freedom (that is, apart from the freedom of mere imagination, which may be the first step to intentional change). Bad faith, in other words, *is the denial of either one's facticity or one's transcendence.* It is conceiving of oneself as *nothing but* one's facticity—such as the fact that one is a helpless and hopeless cripple, or as *nothing but* one's transcendence, ignoring the realities of one's situation.

Sartre sometimes suggests that bad faith is the *confusion* of one's facticity and transcendence:

> The basic concept which is thus engendered utilizes the double property of the human being, who is at once a facticity and a transcendence. These two aspects of human reality are and ought to be capable of a valid coordination. But bad faith does not wish either to coordinate them or to surmount them in a synthesis. Bad faith seeks to affirm their identity while preserving their differences. It must affirm facticity as being transcendence and transcendence as being facticity, in such a way that at the instant when a person apprehends the one, he can find himself abruptly faced with the other. (B&N, 98)

I will discuss this variation in what is to follow, but I think that Sartre's claim here that facticity and transcendence are and ought to be capable of a "valid coordination" is overly optimistic and against much that he suggests later on. This idea also seems to sit uneasily with both the idea that bad faith is an unstable (or "meta-stable") project and the idea that bad faith may be ultimately unavoidable. I would be happy to give up the latter, but I see good Sartrean reasons for continuing to insist on the former.

The facticity and transcendence formula provides a nice simple model, and it is the one Sartre uses (for the most part) throughout the chapter "Bad Faith." It is also used to explain most of the examples in the section "Patterns of Bad Faith." The waiter in the café, for instance, is described as in bad faith because he imagines that he *is* just a waiter, that is, he is thoroughly defined by the fact of his job and its duties. (That heavily ontological "*is*" is characteristic of Sartre's discussion.) One can imagine similar but more serious cases in which Nazi soldiers or Vichy policemen conceive of themselves as thoroughly defined by their jobs and their duties, who thereby refuse to disobey or even to scrutinize orders, no matter how immoral, cruel, or criminal. So, too, the homosexual discussed toward the end of the chapter has to decide, on the basis of the facts (that he has performed many homoerotic acts with many partners, that he continues to have strong desires for further liaisons), whether or not he *is* a homosexual. But his identity is not wholly determined by the facts, and as he resolves not to engage in such behavior any more (like Sartre's character Daniel, in the novel *Age of Reason*), he would be in bad faith if he were to accept his facticity as defining who he is.

The second form of bad faith, according to this formula—ignoring one's facticity in favor of some fantasy—plays a much smaller role in Sartre's philosophy, and for an obvious reason. What concerns Sartre most, not just as a philosophical thesis but also as a vital, living concern in the midst of the Nazi occupation of France, is the denial rather than the mere neglect of personal freedom and responsibility. Sartre looked around him in the early 1940s and saw his fellow citizens collaborating with the Nazis and making all sorts of excuses for their behavior. ("I couldn't help it. I just found myself in this situation, and I had no choice.") Bad faith, in its typical and most disturbing form, is pretending that one has no choice. One *always* has choices. Of course, the choices may well be repellent. The consequences may be ghastly. It may take real courage or firm psychological resolve to be able to do what one comes to see should be done. But what one cannot and should not do is to wave one's hands helplessly and declare, "I have no choice." Even looking down the barrel of a gun, one has choices. They just turn out to be rather terrifying and quite possibly fatal.

It is thus easy to understand both why Sartre thinks that bad faith is so central to his overall defense of freedom and why he tends to be so moralistic about it. I take his insistence that he is not doing ethics but rather only ontology (which I read as parroting Heidegger) to be both absurd and self-undermining. But the facticity and transcendence formula, as neat as it is, also has some rather disturbing implications, and it fails to capture the complexity of the phenomenon that Sartre seeks to understand. For one thing, Sartre makes it very clear throughout *Being and Nothingness* that facticity and transcendence are not so easily distinguished, and that confusing them is a matter not simply of bad faith but of the human predicament as such. Here is both the wisdom and the pathos of that well-known Reinhold Niebuhr (1892–1971) "Serenity Prayer": "God, grant me the serenity to accept the things I cannot change; the courage to change the things I can; and the wisdom to know the difference." Unfortunately, there is no decision procedure to discern the difference. Johnny Weissmuller would not have been wrong to take his doctors' prognosis as definitive. Who was in a position to definitively say what was possible and what was not? People who try to do the impossible sometimes succeed.

But what is the status of the "facts"? Was Weissmuller's incapacity simply a fact? Consider an unequivocal fact in our personal histories: we were born at such-and-such a time. But people lie about their age all the time. They even acquire false pieces of identification to "prove" that they were born a year or two earlier (more rarely, later) than they actually were. Having lied about it long enough, they may forget (and everyone else may, too) just when they were actually born. One can fantasize some metaphysical book, of the sort that only philosophers and theologians imagine, in which *that fact* is engraved forever. But if everyone in the world comes to believe that one's birthday is one particular day (and suppose that there is no scientific method or evidence that could disprove this), does it really matter what the metaphysical book says? In what sense, then, is there any such *fact*?

But from the other side, the side of transcendence, even the most fanciful fantasies are grounded in our experience and in the facts of our situation. There are limits to imagination. One cannot simply make up a birth date. One can imagine but not really believe that one was born in the fourteenth century (unless one is stark raving mad), or that one was born in the distant future (a science fiction possibility but a logical tangle). Just as Plato's merely imagined ideal Republic looked quite like his contemporary Athens, our fantasies hug pretty close to the facts of our reality. One can play with one's birthday within a small span of years, but one cannot just reinvent it from scratch. Our transcendence, as Sartre often reminds us, is an extrapolation from our facticity and is grounded in the facts. We are always, he says, "in situation."

These complications are particularly pronounced when we consider what we might call "psychological" facts, such as the "fact" that one is depressed, or resentful, or happy and satisfied with one's life. These facts ("of consciousness") are constituted in part *by* our consciousness of them. In this realm, there is a genuine insight in the familiar slogan "Thinking makes it so." Whether one is grieving or merely sad or depressed is determined, in part, by one's consciousness, one's outlook, one's thoughts, including what one thinks and perhaps says about how he or she is feeling. (I say "in part" because, clearly, the facts of one's situation are not irrelevant. In order to be grieving, for instance, one must have recently suffered a serious loss.) Whether one is embarrassed or ashamed depends, in part, on what one thinks one is feeling. Part of this is the authority of first-person reports (about one's own mental states), but it is also because many psychological states, emotions in particular, are (partly) constituted in our consciousness of them. (This is less true of those emotions that are commonly called "basic," which have substantial nonpsychological, neurological, and behavioral components.)

What one feels in such cases also depends on one's culture and language, on the social context, but also on whether there are even conceptions of shame and embarrassment operative in that culture. So, too, whether one is motivated by greed or selfishness or genuine compassion is partly (but surely not wholly) determined by the consciousness one has of his or her motives and intentions and attitudes toward other people. It is also determined—and this is a much larger issue—by what the concept and boundaries of the self are in the culture.[4] None of this is to deny, of course, that one can be in bad faith and self-deception about such matters. Indeed, there is no realm riper for bad faith and self-deception. But the issue cannot be clarified using the simple formula "denying either one's facticity or one's transcendence." In the realm of psychology, the difference is rarely clear (indeed, even regarding those more or less attitude-independent feelings such as physical pain[5]). To a significant extent, our psychology is self-created.

A particularly powerful example has to do with the very important distinction that Sartre makes in the chapter "Nothingness" between fear and anxiety (*peur* and *angoisse* or angst). In chapter 3, we said that the difference is that fear is apprehension about something happening to oneself, whereas anxiety concerns what one might *do*. It is a difference that turns on the difference between victimization and responsible activity, obviously a central concern of Sartre's. I am afraid of being fired, but I am anxious about what I might say to my boss in a moment of fury: for example, "Well, I quit!" But the distinction may be problematic in practice even if it seems clear in theory. Impulses, urges, and other "spontaneous" bursts of motivation may well be prompted or triggered by external events, and the speed with which one reacts may make the difference quite uncertain. To what extent are such outbursts voluntary?

Already apprehensive, I am frightened by a sudden sound. Like Meursault in *The Stranger*, my hand naturally tightens around the grip of the pistol I just happen to have in my pocket. I am in a state of high tension. Am I afraid of what might happen, or of what I might do? Like Meursault, I fire. (This is a prudential argument against carrying firearms as well as an abstract philosophical argument.) Or do I? As in *the Stranger*, one can easily imagine a description that makes little use of agency-talk and speaks only of my physical reaction. How do I conclude that I have in fact "done" anything (although, to be sure, I will probably take the blame)? Where does "suffering" a passion become a "doing," and when vice versa? Even with a good deal of warning and preparation, for instance, if I am to meet my ex-wife's new boyfriend, do I know what I will do, or indeed whether what I "do" is my doing at all? (To be sure, my agreeing to the meeting is my doing, and I am responsible at least for that.) Clearly these questions take us deep into the heart of bad faith, but the issue is not whether I understand or refuse to correctly apply the distinction. Spontaneous action, as Sartre is all too ready to tell us, confuses the issue of responsibility. And facticity and transcendence, more generally, cannot be so easily distinguished

But if facticity and transcendence cannot be readily distinguished, then we can see how Sartre might have concluded that we cannot escape from bad faith. If bad faith is the confusion of facticity and transcendence, the denial of one or the other, and if facticity and transcendence cannot be adequately distinguished, then we might well find ourselves doomed to bad faith. Couple this with Sartre's rather infuriating but typical philosophical bad habit of thinking in stark "either/or" dichotomies, and it becomes clear why he seems so hesitant to evaluate bad faith in terms of degrees of blameworthiness. In ontology, some "this" is or is not (the classic formulation of Parmenides, unfortunately with us still). There is no room for "sort of," "more or less," "in a way," or "in a sense." But we are not talking ontology here but ethics, and we are talking about a very common yet problematic range of human experiences in which we are not straight with ourselves about who we are and what we can and should do. Sometimes our self-deception is merely a matter of willful distraction, choosing not to attend to my irritation at the student crinkling a potato chip bag during my lecture. Sometimes denial is pathological; I refuse to acknowledge my own proven ignorance in a domain of expertise. Often the facts are uncertain, or even indeterminate: our options are limited in ways that are not yet clear. The huge range and the multitude of experiences that fall under the rubric of "bad faith" cannot be captured by so crude a set of dimensions as "the facts that are true of us" and "our possibilities." At the same time, however, this dichotomy allows us to understand and appreciate some of Sartre's most provocative and broadly philosophical declarations about human nature.

There is, first of all, the tantalizing thesis that *there is no human nature*, if by that we mean set behavioral tendencies that are inborn and beyond the bounds of human effort and control. "Man makes himself," Sartre famously tells us. We are, to be sure, embodied creatures, and we always operate within biological, situational, and personal limitations. But those limitations never fully define us. We do that through our actions. Second, and consequently, there is the profound but discomforting idea that human nature is *always in tension*. We live this tension. It is a continuous struggle between two impossible ideals: the solidity of being "thing-like," complete within oneself, being set and settled in a role and a way of life, on the one hand, and the imaginary fantasy of being totally free and not bound by any limitations, including not only the facts about our age and our health and our social situation but even the brute facts about being a living, vulnerable, mortal human being, on the other hand. Thus, we would like to wholly accept our lot in life and the way the world is, what Nietzsche calls (in bad faith) *amor fati*. But we would also like to be free to be whatever we are not. In other words, *we would like to be God*, as Sartre rather blasphemously suggests when he playfully describes the ultimate human project. But the sad truth is, to be human is to be neither what one is nor to be otherwise. It is "to be what one is not and not to be what one is." This is the essential tension of the human condition. We are unable simply to resign ourselves to our lives as they are, and we cannot be and do all that we might desire and imagine.

The importance of this claim notwithstanding, the facticity and transcendence formula oversimplifies the complexity of bad faith in yet another way. We can start suggesting this by means of a number of very Sartrean questions: Does one willfully get into bad faith or does one just "fall" into it? Must one be conscious of being in bad faith (and what does this mean)? How does one keep from becoming conscious of the fact that he or she is in bad faith? *What* is the self that is engaged in bad faith, and how much of the self is in question? (Surely it is not one's facticity as a whole that is in question. Nor is the entire scope of one's transcendence, that is, *all* one's possibilities.) Furthermore, what is the role of other people in bad faith? Sartre's discussion in the chapter looks, at least superficially, as if bad faith is just a matter of the facts about oneself versus one's opinion of oneself that others might enter only as observers, faceless partners, or provocateurs. (Examples would be the young woman's date at the café, the "frigid" woman's husband, her sex partner, and the "Champion of Sincerity" who teases the homosexual resolving not to be a homosexual.) But bad faith, we will see, is not nearly so simple nor so solipsistic.

Bad Faith as Self-Consciousness

Bad faith is a product of self-consciousness or, more accurately, of consciousness of one's self. Sartre thinks that self-consciousness is the case in *all* consciousness, insofar as consciousness is necessarily and immediately aware of its being aware. But consciousness of one's *self* as the subject—or as the object—of conscious activity is a special case of "mediated" self-consciousness, and that is what I will be referring to here. To put the matter simply, if we were not self-conscious beings, there would be no question of bad faith, or of good faith ("authenticity") either. Animals can be neither self-deceived nor inauthentic, although, of course, they can be deceived. But bad faith as self-deception is a peculiar phenomenon of self-consciousness, and whether or not animals have any sense of self (a hotly debated topic, with various species each having their champions), they cannot achieve self-consciousness. And self-consciousness is, indeed, a remarkable achievement.

Many philosophers, linguists, and social scientists would say that self-consciousness is the product of language, and not just any language, but a special self-referring language. There must be first-person pronouns in some sense (whether singular or plural is a further concern). There must be not only some sense of self but also some *conception* of self, and this does indeed require language. Sartre does not exactly commit himself to this, but he does insist on the importance of "reflection," which he more obscurely refers to as "thetic" consciousness. I take it that "thetic" involves a "thesis," and a thesis must be couched in language. But Sartre also tries to retain a purely phenomenological, as opposed to a linguistic, interpretation by further identifying the "thetic" with the "positional," presumably because once the "I" appears, one "takes a position" in the experience. I would suggest that the "thetic" and the "positional" mark out very different positions in phenomenology, however, the one having to do with language and "spelling out" one's experiences and engagements, the other having to do with taking a personal role in them or "avowing" them. (The language of "spelling out and avowing" comes from Herbert Fingarette, who will appear several times in this discussion.)[6] Presumably, the link between the phenomenological and the linguistic interpretations is that by articulating the "I" via language, one thereby takes a positional role in experience.

In any case, to have a conception of oneself requires language, and the conception one has of one's self in bad faith presupposes reflective consciousness and the ability to articulate or "spell out" that conception and avow one's engagements in the world. Again, the realm of the psychological should be our focus here. If our psychological states are in part constituted by consciousness, and in particular by our conceptions of those states, then it will make all the difference what our language and vocabulary are regarding them. One can argue convincingly that to be ashamed as opposed to embarrassed, for instance, depends in part on having the *concepts* of shame and embarrassment.[7] But this is not to say that bad faith must itself be a reflective or a linguistic phenomenon or the product of reflective consciousness any more than our emotions are generally reflective as opposed to prereflective (which, in his *The Emotions*, Sartre insists they must be). Sartre is very clear, in fact adamant, that bad faith is often "spontaneous" and prereflective. (He compares it, rather dubiously, to falling asleep.) But it is the *possibility* of articulating or spelling out and avowing one's engagements and one's consequent conception of self that is the key to bad faith. It is always possible to "see through" one's own bad faith, and bad faith is precisely the *refusal* to do just this. And yet, while I am in bad faith, I may not be reflectively aware that I am.

But there are several different conceptions of one's self in play here. There is the conception of one's self as the *subject* of consciousness, the "I" reflected upon so ceremoniously by Descartes and Kant, and presumably the "I" as agent that is responsible not only for one's actions but also for the refusal that constitutes bad faith. But this is by no means a univocal or unproblematic concept (as David Sherman has pointed out to me in considerable detail). It is not at all clear, by Sartre's own account, that there is any personal "I" at all. But then there are the various conceptions of one's self as the *object* of consciousness, as the "me" that has various physical, personal, and psychological features, including the virtues and vices. It is the "me" self that is, presumably, the object of the distortion imposed by bad faith, the self as a hero or a coward (in Garcin's pathetic case in *No Exit*), the self as homosexual or straight (as in Daniel's case in *Age of Reason* and as in the example in the *Being and Nothingness* "Bad Faith" chapter), and of the self as free or as "bourgeois" (as for Mathieu, in *Age of Reason*). The "me" self is also the self of one's autobiography, or any significant segment of that story. Indeed, it is also the stuff of one's biography as told by other people (as the plot of *No Exit* makes painfully clear). But it is the self as the agent in bad faith and of bad faith that raises the biggest problems for Sartre.

Regarding the self as personal subject and agent, David Sherman and I have discussed for years the problems surrounding the commonsense presumption, merely implied by Sartre, that the "I" is in some sense the author of its (our) actions. David holds that there is *no* "I" as such, but only the "I" as a thin "me," and thus not so clearly an agent at all. When one refers to oneself as the agent of an ongoing activity (for example, when David complains, "I am having trouble with my jump shot"), he notes, "This thin 'I' might then be expanded to a thicker 'me,' . . . I have trouble with so much in life, . . . why do I bother, etc.?"). But *both* the "I" and the "me" are *reflective* here: one thin, one thick, and both are "empirical" in the sense distinguished by Kant (as opposed to the "transcendental" ego). But the first "I" is merely lexical, a placeholder. (In this sense it has traditionally been argued not to be empirical, in that it has no empirical content. Nevertheless, it can be responded, it clearly has an empirical *context*, namely, the particular person doing the referring.)

Sartre attempts to finesse the problem of the (thin) "I" by identifying it with the prereflective "cogito" or consciousness, both of which are said to be *impersonal*. In prereflective consciousness, Sartre says, neither the "I" nor the "me" has yet appeared, but both, according to this analysis, are objects of consciousness. (Thus David claims that I am wrong to say that the "I" is the subject of consciousness even for Descartes and Kant because the "I" that thinks is not the "I" that exists. But what this means is that the "I" that exists is *the person*.) But Sartre retreats problematically to the prereflective cogito and then relies on his claim that it is consciousness and not the self that is the agent of and in bad faith. But then we hit the other, even more serious problem, and that is in what sense Sartre's consciousness can be an agent at all. In what sense can his "spontaneity" be compatible with responsibility?

My self-consciousness of myself as an agent is clearly central to Sartre's entire philosophy, as well as to his conception of bad faith. If I am responsible for everything that I do, and if what I do encompasses far more than what I will usually admit to, and if it is in bad faith that I refuse to ac-knowledge my responsibility, then my agency is very much at the core of Sartre's existentialism. No agency, no responsible self, no responsibility. But insofar as bad faith is "spontaneous" ("the instantaneity of the pre-reflective cogito" [85]), this suggests (and Sartre even says) that it is not something voluntary and willful. Indeed, insofar as my project of bad faith can be spelled out, it almost looks as if it can be spelled out only as an aspect of the "me," not the "I." It must be admitted that in Sartre's ontology, as in grammar, this distinction between the "I" and the "me" is not always clear or rigorous. But, to wrap up this point, whether self-awareness involves the "I" or the "me," Sartre says, bad faith requires reflection, for (in Fingarette's terms) it is only against the possibility of spelling out and then avowing one's engagements, one's self-conceptions as well as one's bad faith, that bad faith is possible at all. Nevertheless, Sartre insists that bad faith is spontaneous and prereflective, and this, I suggest, threatens to undermine his entire philosophy. What would it mean to say that freedom and responsibility do not involve or require agency?

Furthermore, there are least two different and quite opposed conceptions of self-consciousness that are evident in Sartre's discussions. The first is a matter of more or less "immediate" reflection (that is, consciousness of myself which I achieve just by being aware of myself). This is not just the awareness of awareness that Sartre insists is essential to all consciousness, but also that reflection which brings the self as an "I" into the picture. (Sartre's examples: "I am counting cards," "I am running for the streetcar." This is what Sherman calls the "thin" reflection of the "me.") But second is that sense of self that Sartre inherits from Hegel, of reflection *mediated* by the awareness or the possible awareness of others. One might argue that neither sort of reflection is strictly immediate, in that all reflection involves the mediation of the "me," but in the first third of *Being and Nothingness*, which includes the chapter "Bad Faith," it is the first conception of self-consciousness that gets most of the attention, in the guise of the "For-Itself." But beginning with part III, in which "Being-for-Others" is formally intro-duced, it is the Hegelian conception that is most in play (though we might point out that in Sartre's discussion of "The Reef of Solipsism," Hegel is shown to be *aufheben*'d [overcome and improved upon] by Husserl, Hei-degger, and, finally, Sartre).

Sartre's discussion of "Concrete Relations with Others" is notoriously dependent on Hegel and on his "Master–Slave" parable in the *Phenome-nology* in particular. In that parable, selfhood emerges only out of a life-and-death conflict as each tries to gain the "recognition" of the other. The outcome of the battle is mutual personal identity; one becomes the "master" or "Lord," the other, the "slave" or servant (*Knecht*). Indeed, one might well insist that, in Sartrean terms, if the slave yields to the greater strength of the master and *chooses* life as a slave over death, but then represents his choice as part of his facticity, he is in bad faith. (It may or may not be true that the slave is bound by his facticity to be the loser of the fight, but it is his transcendence that he decides to live as a slave.) But getting back to the Sartrean picture, I think that this is yet another juncture where Sartre is torn between his inherent Cartesianism and his admiration for German philosophy. Both of these conceptions of self-consciousness cannot be primordial, but Sartre does not choose between them. Thus I see a major rupture in his great book, or at the very least the peculiarity of presenting what I take to be the derivative sense of immediate self-reflection long before the true origins of self-consciousness in interpersonal mediation are even mentioned.

The above suggests a distinction also suggested by Hegel in his parable, between self-consciousness *as such*, the self-consciousness of the self as agent, "the self in itself," what Kant called "the Will," and having a *particular* self-consciousness, that is, self-consciousness of oneself *as* such-and-such, as the bearer of certain features, of being ugly, of being out of place in an elegant restaurant, of being the smartest kid in the class, of being the loser in Hegel's mythic battle for recognition. Such features are clearly constitutive of the "me." There is some question whether the first and more general sense is presupposed by the latter more or less particularized senses or is, rather, derived from them. A pack animal (a wolf or a dog) might be self-conscious of itself as the loser of a battle without becoming self-conscious as such. But a person has both identities, and this, one might suggest, would be the source of Hegel's slave's bad faith, shifting his claim from the supposed involuntariness of the self as loser to the alleged helplessness of the self as such. Where a particular conception of self is concerned, we might add, the tense of the verb makes all the difference. *Having done* something wrong or inappropriate is straightforwardly a characteristic of the "me," of my awareness of my self in my recent past as an object, not as a subject. But when I think back to the moment of action, or when I plan to act in the immediate future, it seems impossible to think of myself as anything other than an "I," even if it is now remembered or is anticipated as a "me." This tangle, I think, also permeates much of Sartre's early philosophy. It is, again, a dimension of the agency problem.

The origins of self-consciousness by way of mediation by other people, finally, suggest one more problem with the facticity and transcendence formula of bad faith. I suggested that Sartre's discussion of bad faith makes it look as if bad faith might be just a matter of one's opinion of oneself qualified, in some troublesome way, by the facts about oneself. Other people seem to enter in only as dates, sexual partners, or provocateurs. But if self-consciousness is itself the product of one's relations with other people, as in Hegel's parable, it is easy to see how other people might not be at all tangential or incidental to bad faith and to one's opinion of oneself. In fact, even the chapter "Bad Faith" is shot through with considerations of bad faith via the looks and opinions of others, including virtually all of Sartre's examples. So bad faith turns out not to be a two-way tension but a three-way tension among one's facticity, one's transcendence, and what Sartre calls "Being-for-Others." But as we saw with facticity and transcendence, the distinction among these supposed dimensions of human reality is none too clear. So what the facts are and what people widely believe (about one's age, for example) are often problematic, and what one thinks of oneself and what one "internalizes" as other people's opinions of oneself (as in Freud's "Superego") turns out to be an enormous issue and a new source of tension.

Bad Faith as a Real Problem, Not a Paradox

I am trying, despite the technicalities, to capture the heart of Sartre's concern about bad faith. It is not essentially a technical question, but a heartfelt and indignant response to the very upsetting situation in Paris during the Second World War, people not taking responsibility and making excuses for what are clearly their own personal choices. When Sartre introduces the issue in *Being and Nothingness*, however, he does so in strikingly technical terms, not only in terms of facticity and transcendence but also, first, as a kind of transcendental argument (with Kant clearly in mind) and then, worse, as a kind of a logical paradox. The transcendental argument (which actually appears just before the chapter begins) is stated in familiar (Kantian) terms: "How is bad faith possible?" That is, bad faith is a fact about human beings, so what else must be true of them to account for this? But Sartre seems to forget about this peculiarly Kantian question as the chapter gets under way (though it briefly reappears at the beginning of the second section, "Patterns of Bad Faith," 96). The real question isn't how bad faith is possible, but the practical concern of how we use it to deny our freedom. However, Sartre presents this urgent practical problem as a philosophical paradox, and the nature of the paradox is quite false to the phenomenon as well as to the analysis that Sartre goes on to give us.

As the chapter opens, Sartre presents bad faith as a problem about knowledge and belief rather than about self-consciousness and freedom. He sacrifices his hard moral stance to play with a simple logical dilemma. He tries to turn "self-deception" into a paradoxical notion, "a lie to oneself," in which one must both know and not know one and the same proposition. The emptiness of this formulation and the problems it seems to generate would not become clear for a good many years, through the work of Herbert Fingarette, Alfred Mele, and others, but it is evident that Sartre saw through it himself. (Indeed, this alone would explain and justify his calling the phenomenon "bad faith" instead of "self-deception.") As self-deception, bad faith *can* be presented as a paradox, and we all know how enamored philosophers, including Sartre, are of paradoxes. (This started well before Plato—Heraclitus, Parmenides, and Zeno, for instance—and continues via both Continental and "analytic" philosophers of the present day. "Poststructuralist" philosophers, in particular, may pretend to reject much of mainstream and traditional philosophy, but they certainly share this love of paradoxes.) The paradox in question here derives from a long and illustrious list of "liar" paradoxes of various kinds, and it turns on the problematic formulation that self-deception is *a lie to oneself*: to lie, one must know the truth, but to be lied to, one must not know the truth. So self-deception requires one both to know and not to know the truth, a seeming contradiction.

Now, on the one hand, people often hold contradictory beliefs. They just don't see the implications of one or both of them, so in the absence of juxtaposition the contradiction doesn't get noticed. The fact that people hold contradictory beliefs is not itself a contradiction or a paradox. It's just a curious but familiar fact about the limited thinking of most human beings. But, on the other hand, bad faith would seem to require just such a juxtaposition, insofar as the one belief is the active denial of the other. It is not as if one might not notice that he or she is denying what he or she knows to be important, urgent, and true. One might invoke here what Sartre calls the "translucency of consciousness," but one need not. As I noted, people frequently entertain unrecognized mutually incompatible thoughts. But here, it is enough that a person seems to be focusing on precisely what he or she is denying, and if this is not just plain cynicism—namely, *pretending* to believe what one does not (or not to believe what one does in fact believe)—it would seem that one is thus both believing and not believing one and the same proposition *at the same time*, holding the truth in mind just in order to not believe it. So if bad faith is, as Sartre sets it up, "a lie to oneself," in which one is both the deceiver and the deceived, it looks as if bad faith does involve simultaneously both believing and not believing contradictory beliefs.

But self-deception, a real phenomenon, cannot involve, much less require, self-contradictory beliefs. Indeed, Sartre quickly shows how such a conception is nonsensical. So when Sartre begins his chapter on this false note, suggesting a phony paradox instead of a very real life problem, he aims us in the wrong direction. To be sure, "I am a homosexual" and "I am not a homosexual" are contradictory statements, but it is not the *belief* in both of them that characterizes the dilemma of bad faith. Rather, they indicate different ways of acting, different ways of conceiving of oneself, different ways of being and becoming. Furthermore, if there is one thing that philosophers have come to agree on—excepting only those who are so mesmerized by the appeal of a paradox that they no longer care about the phenomenon being so misdescribed—it is that *neither* self-deception nor bad faith is to be understood on the model of one person deceiving or lying to another.[8] Thus, insofar as it tends to lead us down this path to paradox, "self-deception" is a very problematic and not at all innocuous translation of "bad faith." Sartre goes into considerable detail about what is involved in lying, as if to drum in not only the problem but also the appropriateness of the model. Nevertheless, he recognizes that this is not his concern at all. So what is really going on here?

Bad faith cannot be self-deception because it is not primarily about belief. It is about our modes of engagement in the world. Of course, beliefs often follow, but to say that our engagements can become reflective is not the same as saying that we necessarily formulate beliefs about them. Insofar as we do formulate beliefs about our engagements, we may well choose to formulate a set of beliefs that describe the admirable course of behavior we would like to see ourselves as following rather than another set of beliefs about a more disreputable or shameful course that other people may see us as following. But "I am a homosexual" and "I am not a homosexual" are not two beliefs but two projects, two different ways of presenting and being myself.

Here is a less controversial example. Immediately following an award ceremony, I spell out (to myself and to others sitting near me) my indignation about how unfair it is that the prize was given to some undeserving fool, but I do not spell out (either to myself or to others) my envy, my resentment, and my belief that I deserved that prize just as much (and just as little) as he did. I avow (admit and stand behind) my indignation, but I neither admit nor stand behind my resentment. Needless to say, I like to see and present myself as a fair-minded fellow, and I do not like to see or present myself as an envious, resentful person. So I choose the one way of spelling out and avowing my engagement rather than the other. Serious cases of bad faith, of course, involve much more serious situations and much more disturbing conceptions of oneself. But the model in this relatively harmless example is instructive. Bad faith is not primarily about beliefs. It is (in this case) about feelings and emotions and competitiveness, how one is engaged in this particular world of honors and other people competing for them. But so, too, the Vichy and Nazi collaborators spelled out their engagements in terms of a carefully delimited number of seemingly reasonable choices and commitments that they could then avow and stand behind. What they refused to spell out, especially to themselves, was the wider range of choices and commitments regarding their wartime duties to their country and their countrymen.

To finish this up, much ink has been spilled on the so-called paradox of self-deception, but by the turn of the twenty-first century, it has become evident that, like most philosophical paradoxes, this one may seem logically tantalizing but is quite off the mark and false to the problem. Sartre, at the end of the chapter preceding "Bad Faith," asks the quasi-Kantian question, "What must we be that we are capable of bad faith?" But what he is really asking is how we can so subvert our freedom and be false to ourselves, a practical moral problem and not a logical dilemma. Self-deception is very real, and any suggestion that it is logically impossible is laughable. But, of course, laughter never stopped any philosopher. The bottom line, however, is that self-deception is not primarily a matter of beliefs, much less contradictory beliefs. It is not (literally) a matter of self-deception. It is, rather, a question of *taking responsibility*. Luckily, after a few pages of discussing the "lie to oneself" paradox, Sartre recovers, and having fiddled a bit with the problem of "knowing and not knowing," he happily moves beyond it. He has much bigger game in mind.

Another Roadside Distraction:
Sartre versus Freud

Despite the false start of Sartre's conception of bad faith as a lie to oneself, his consideration of the paradox of self-deception allows him to engage in one of the most titanic intellectual contests in the twentieth century—his monumental opposition to Sigmund Freud. The excuse is that Freud can be interpreted as trying to resolve the paradox of self-deception, although it is obvious that Freud, like Sartre, is not concerned with a mere paradox at all but with the deepest issues of human motivation and responsibility. Furthermore, in the face of Sartre's notoriously harsh critique of Freud, we should note that Sartre was a very sympathetic reader of Freud. Sartre, in fact, was entangled with Freud through his entire career. Later in *Being and Nothingness* he presents an outline of his own conception of "existential" psychoanalysis, one focused on "not only dreams, failures, obsessions, and neuroses but also and especially the thoughts of waking life, successfully adjusted acts, style, etc." (734). He notes, with atypical false modesty, "This psychoanalysis has not yet found its Freud." But the truth is and was that Sartre learned a great from Freud, and he was worried about many of the same issues and proposed some similar solutions, although in existentialist rather than quasi-physiological and dubious anatomical terms. Indeed, although he does not even bother to employ the phrase, the section on "existential" psychoanalysis is all about bad faith, the conflict of facticity and transcendence by way of desire.[9]

Bad faith—in the form of self-deception—plays an obvious role in Freud's theory. Nevertheless, Sartre (in a late interview) claimed to be appalled by Freud. As a good Cartesian, he claimed to have had no patience or comprehension of what Freud might mean by the fragmentation or opacity of consciousness, one part of the mind hidden from another. And as a good humanist, he was similarly appalled by Freud's attempt to "naturalize" and even "mechanize" the mind. Thus he opposed what he called "psychic determinism" in Freud. He also criticized this in William James (in his essay on the emotions). It is worth noting, however, that in that earlier essay Sartre praised Freud for having improved upon James insofar as Freud recognized the *meaning* of emotions and to that extent rejected the mechanical model. But one of the main themes of Sartre's philosophy is to combat "mechanism" wherever he finds it if it might be used to compromise our sense of responsibility.

In this discussion, however, it is not Freud's determinism but his appeal to the "Unconscious" that Sartre attacks. The driving force of Freud's psychoanalysis is his observation that people seem not to know what is obviously most troubling to them, not because it is unimportant or because they are not paying attention, but, to the contrary, just because it is so important and upsetting that they *cannot* forget it or get over it. By distinguishing between the conscious and the unconscious mind (where the former does not have easy access to the latter) and, later in his career, among Ego, Id, and Superego, three separate "agencies," Freud seems to explain how one can hide an awkward or awful truth from oneself. But the disagreement between Freud and Sartre does not turn on the translucency–opacity issue, even if that is how Sartre sets up the debate. Sartre has his "pre-reflective consciousness," and this plays at least some of the role played by Freud's conception of the "subconscious." (Although this is Freud's "preconscious" and not the "Unconscious," which is the product of "repression." I capitalize "Unconscious" to mark this special, technical meaning.) Sartre's prereflective consciousness, like Freud's subconscious, explains how something can be "in the mind" but not reflected upon, attended to, or acknowledged, not "spelled out" or "avowed."

Sartre never pretends that all of consciousness is immediately accessible. If one refuses to accept some description of his engagement in the world, it more or less follows that he will not readily acknowledge the plausibility of that description. Thus the difference between Freud's Unconscious and repression and Sartre's characterization of bad faith is said to be the difference between "cannot" and "will not," an inability versus a refusal. But the idea of a "mechanism" in the Freudian case is not so obviously Freud's own view.[10] Freud, too, takes as his guiding principle the idea that the Unconscious can be made conscious, repression can be undone, and the Id can be converted to the Ego. And Sartre expresses the view that we *cannot* (ontologically) get beyond bad faith. Indeed, the more one looks at the details, the smaller the differences between Freud and Sartre start to seem.

Nevertheless, Sartre's harsh treatment of Freud reveals some real insights that are important for understanding both great authors. For example, Sartre accuses Freud of treating the instincts or drives in the Unconscious not as appearances but as "real psychic facts." What Sartre is anticipating here, I suggest, is the idea that the "facts" of consciousness are at least partially constituted by consciousness, which would include the activities of reflection and interpretation. But there are no such facts "in themselves" (90). Sartre also criticizes Freud for "cutting the psychic whole into two. I *am* the Ego but I *am not* the *id*" (91). For Sartre, as I said, the question of how I *am* the self is a knotty question, but I think that he is right to challenge Freud's conception of the "it" as a part of myself that is at the same time not myself.

One of Nietzsche's most brilliant aphorisms (much admired by Freud) is "A thought comes when it will, not when I will," expressing (according to one of many interpretations) his doubts about mental agency in general. We normally think of thoughts as direct expressions of the self, but the fact is that thoughts often "pop into" our minds. Sartre certainly agrees with this insofar as he emphasizes the "spontaneity" of consciousness. But the question to scrutinize is whether Nietzsche is right to suggest that this casts doubt on agency. If it does, Sartre's central theme is in trouble. But so, too, are Nietzsche's idea of a society of selves, disconnected from one another, and Freud's efforts to so neatly divide consciousness (or "the mind," the "psychic whole") into arenas of agency and non-agency. One should notice that all three philosophers thus tend to render the self or consciousness *impersonal.* Sartre does this quite explicitly by turning consciousness into "spontaneity."

For instance, Sartre discusses the impulse to theft (91, which he elaborates in his later book *Saint Genet*) as not clearly the expression of an agent. As prereflective, according to Sartre, it *cannot* be the expression of an agent. So Sartre's example of an impulse raises not only a challenge to Freud but to Sartre's own theory as well. How and where does agency enter into the picture? And *whose* agency, we might ask? If Freud's id is an agent, who is it, given that it is not the "I," the Ego? As Sartre correctly points out, "It is not accurate to hold that the 'id' is presented as a thing in relation to the psychoanalyst, for a thing is indifferent to the conjectures which we make concerning it, while the 'id' on the contrary is sensitive to them when we approach the truth" (93). In other words, the id must be in some intimate relation with consciousness, which seems to be precluded in the Freudian picture.

Sartre's criticism of Freud hones in on one idea in particular: the hypothesis of a censor, "conceived of as a line of demarcation with customs, passport division, currency control, etc., to re-establish the duality of the deceiver and the deceived" (90). One might suspect that this is an unfairly detailed metaphor, but it is Freud, not Sartre, who offers us this analogy. Sartre asks, regarding the "resistance" of the patient (defiance, refusal to speak, lying about his dreams, even quitting the analysis), "What part of himself can thus resist? It cannot be the 'Ego,' ... [but] it is equally impossible to explain the resistance as emanating from the complex the psychoanalyst wishes to bring to light" (92). Sartre concludes, "The only level on which we can locate the refusal of the subject is that of the censor—it alone because it alone *knows* what it is repressing" (93). In short, "If we reject the language and the materialistic mythology of psychoanalysis, [and] if we abandon all the metaphors representing the repression as the impact of blind forces, we are compelled to admit that the censor must choose and in order to choose must be aware of so doing" (93). Thus the resistance of the patient gets located in the censor, and we are right back where we started. It is the censor that is in bad faith, who both knows and refuses to know the same forbidden bit of information, which must, therefore be repressed. The paradox has not been solved.

Furthermore, no number of mechanistic metaphors can disguise the need to understand the repression in terms of its "finality," that is, the purposiveness that Sartre defended in his earlier essay regarding the emotions. The censor must have some comprehension of the end to be attained, which is simultaneously both desired and forbidden (94). Thus there is both the pleasure and the anxiety of the forbidden. (There is some danger here in taking the pleasure and anxiety as ends themselves, but we need not assume that Sartre does this.) One might object that both Sartre and Freud are employing misleading metaphors here, beginning with the spatial ("topological") representation of "areas" of the mind and extending so far as to turn these parts into "agencies" that are, in effect, their own little personalities, "homunculi" of the sort often dismissed in discussions of the mind–body relation. (Even Descartes insisted that "I am not only lodged in my body as a pilot in a vessel, but I am besides so intimately conjoined and as it were intermixed with it, that my mind and my body compose a certain unity"; *Meditations*, Meditation VI.) But insofar as the aim of the Freudian move is the solution of the self-deception paradox, it must be evident that it does not succeed. So given the way that Sartre sets up the problem, the Freudian move to an opaque consciousness, part of which is hidden from itself, is of no avail. This, of course, is not all that there is to Freud, nor, I would argue, does his supposed solution to the self-deception paradox necessarily address the problem that Sartre seeks to solve. The question of responsibility hovers above psychoanalysis just as it does over existentialism.

A more straightforward argument is the one that Sartre makes using the example from Freud's maverick Polish colleague Wilhelm Stekel, of a woman "whom marital infidelity has made frigid." Such patients, Sartre says, do not hide their complexes from themselves. Rather, they practice acts of conduct that are "objectively discoverable." Stekel points out that the husband insists the woman has shown signs of pleasure, but the woman denies this. (We should be very suspicious of both the husband's self-serving assurances and Stekel's acceptance of them, not to mention of Sartre's own notoriously sexist bias in such matters.) But what happens in such cases, according to Sartre, is that these "pathologically frigid" women distract themselves from the pleasure they dread, for example, by thinking of their household accounts while having sex. (Young men, I seem to remember, similarly distracted themselves by thinking of baseball statistics, but for a very different purpose, certainly not to avoid pleasure.) Sartre exclaims, in response to Stekel's case, "Will anyone speak of an unconscious here?" But this is not cynical, Sartre concludes, "*It is in order to prove to herself that she is frigid.*"

Although this quick analysis immediately follows the argument about the censor, it is in fact of a very different nature. Here, Sartre's emphasis on "finality" finally comes to the fore of the analysis, and the argument that it is "*in order to*" prove something to herself takes the place of any effort to hide some forbidden knowledge from herself or deny a painful belief. For bad faith is not, after all, a phenomenon of knowledge and belief, much less a lie to oneself. It is a phenomenon of intention and engagement, of constituting a self in accordance with one's needs and ideals. Freud, I think, can also be so interpreted, and without the dehumanizing emphasis on mechanism, with an appropriately "dynamic" model of the Unconscious.[11] But for Sartre the existentialist, there is little question: bad faith must be understood as a betrayal of freedom, not an epistemic paradox.

II: Freedom Beyond Belief

The first act of bad faith, Sartre writes, is to flee what it cannot flee, *to flee what it is*. Fleeing is very different from lying, and fleeing from oneself is a very different kind of act than lying to oneself, though equally problematic. Bad faith, according to Sartre, depends on the peculiarity of consciousness "to be what it is not, and to not be what it is," but the question here is *being* or, more correctly *becoming*, becoming a self. And this is an ongoing project and process, never completed (while one lives). Bad faith, in its most typical manifestation, is the denial of this unwanted "freedom" in favor of coming to terms with a settled self that one simply *is*. I think that Sartre at first errs, along with a great many other writers on "self-deception," by focusing on the beliefs that may or may not be involved in one's articulation and avowal of one's conception of the self rather than the engagements in which one *constitutes* that conception of self. What is at stake, in other words, is the matter of responsibility. After all, it is *my* consciousness and it is *my* self that are being described. And so with every conception of self or, more specifically, with every unwanted or distasteful realization of who and how one seems to be, there is the pressing question, "*So what do I do now?!*" Typically, that is a responsibility we would rather ignore or not take on (at least, not right now).

Just suppose I leave a 13 percent tip at one of my favorite restaurants. I was distracted, but I also tend to be "tight," and I fear that this is a serious flaw in my character. My undertipping tonight may well be evidence, if not proof, of my miserly tendencies. I am also well aware that my waitress is quick with numbers and recognizes the shortfall as soon as she picks up the check, even if she does not say or show anything. I get very embarrassed— or am I ashamed?—but she walks away, and I turn toward the door. Now what do I do? In one sense, the damage is done. But in another, of course, I can call her back and make amends. I fluctuate between prosecuting myself for my momentary inattention (a mere source of embarrassment) and for my miserly tendencies (a clear source of shame), but after a few moments (that seem like many minutes) I rationalize, "There is not much to be done about it now." Or so I tell myself.

I would say that there is no question that I am in bad faith. Nevertheless, it has nothing to do with a lie to myself or, for that matter, hiding anything from myself. It has much more to do with the fact that I am unwilling, for whatever reason, to get up and undo what I have done, even though I feel guilty about it and I am now very worried about my "reputation." I think now that I shall never again be able to come back to this restaurant, although then I think (inconsistently) that next time I will have to leave a very large tip, and I briefly debate with myself whether 25 or 30 percent will do, assuming that I get the same waitress, and so on. But underlying this beside-the-point inner debate is the fact that I feel quite insecure in my conception of myself and very wary of repeating this behavior in the future.

Then, I quickly distract myself from dwelling on my behavior and its meaning, perhaps by finding something to get enraged about. (In the lot, someone has parked only inches away from my new car.) But the point of my distraction is not *not knowing* what I have done and what it signifies. Rather, it concerns my ongoing behavior: what I *could* do, and what I *will* do, and who I *am*. That is my concern, and that is the subject of my bad faith. One need not talk about anything "unconscious" here, nor need one say very much about belief. It is enough that I am torn in my motivation and between embarrassment and shame and about what to do now. It is not a matter of contradiction but of deciding how I feel and what I am to do. Needless to say, I much prefer embarrassment to shame, to pretend it was a negligible slip-up rather than a definitive demonstration of a flaw in my character that will manifest itself again and again. Note that there is nothing impossible or paradoxical about this scenario. The critical "facts" of the case, whether I am blameworthy or not, whether I feel shame or embarrassment, are at this point not yet determined. They will be settled, if at all, by what I do now. Thus my anxiety is about what I will *do*, not what is true of me. But since my momentary "project" is to not take responsibility or even to think about what it is I've done or might do, I take refuge in distraction, a bit of "escape behavior."

My bad faith project, Sartre insists, is bound to be "meta-stable," that is, subject to sudden disruption. Hazel Barnes notes that it is a term that Sartre invents, but it comes from chemistry and refers to momentarily stable but ultimately unstable compounds. Some chemical compounds are famously unstable (nitroglycerin, for instance), but they may, like bad faith, maintain stability for a substantial period of time. Then, with a mere jiggle or a spark, they explode. Freud, too, often notes the tension and the "leakage" that can be detected in all repression—odd rituals and compulsions that have no rational explanation, slips of the tongue, dreams, and occasional explosions of violent behavior. Such "Freudian slips" are a familiar experience for most of us, when our artfully constructed wall of defenses and distractions springs a leak or "explodes" in frustration or anger. The slips are not only the result of repression; they threaten to undermine it, letting us know that something is very wrong. Of course, Sartre does not buy into the "mechanisms" of Freudian defensiveness, but in the terms I have been suggesting, I think that there is much to say about the tentativeness of one's refusal to spell out and avow one's engagements and conceptions.[12]

For the most part, such behavior is more or less "translucent" or "transparent" in the sense that, to oneself, at least, one is always in some sense aware of what one is doing, and one can become so much more so with just a moment's reflection (for instance, in response to the somewhat rude question, "What in the world are you doing?"). But in bad faith, everything depends on a subterfuge, pursuing or pretending to pursue one project while in fact pursuing another and, if asked, I misdescribe what it is I am doing. Thus I fume about the inconsiderate parker even as I worry whether anyone else in my party noticed the poor tip that I just left. Thus the resentful loser of the prize acts as if he is standing up for justice and fairness instead of expressing his bitterness. And the collaborator insists that he is only doing what is necessary and that he does not fear for his life or favor his personal advancement over his friendships, his citizenship, or his solidarity with his neighbors. But such pretenses are not secure, and though one might explain this by appeal to the translucency of consciousness, a more plausible explanation is that it is juggling too many balls in the air. It is not that one is not conscious of all of them, but rather that it is more than one can handle—one cannot even keep track of them.

This has much to do with the complexity of the bad faith project. As we noted, Sartre insists that bad faith would reduce to mere cynicism if one recognized and acknowledged that he or she was in bad faith. So in order to keep up the project, it is necessary to avoid spelling out the fact that we are avoiding spelling out our engagement. Early in his book, Fingarette gives us the stunning example from Eugene O'Neill's *The Iceman Cometh*, in which the protagonist, Hickey, is relating to his pals at the bar the sympathetic reasons why he murdered his wife (to give her peace and free her from the misery of loving him), when he suddenly blurts out the awful truth: that he resented the "damned bitch." He starts, as if shocked out of a nightmare, "No! I never—!" Even the most carefully developed pretenses momentarily fall apart, and when they do, the whole story about one's motivation has a way of pouring out. "Meta-stable" is a good description of this tendency. We all know, if only from a very brief experiment, that juggling balls is an awkward business. All might be going smoothly, until one misses or drops the first ball. And then the whole performance falls apart dramatically. So, too, with our pretenses. Whether it is distraction or repression may be not so important. It is the tangled web we weave when we set out to deceive ourselves about who we are and what we are doing, consciously or unconsciously.

A further consideration is this: it is not as if spelling out what one is doing is by any means automatic, nor is avowing what we do, but neither does it usually take any special effort. We are language-using creatures, and our language pervades most of our activities, even the most habitual. We spell things out mindlessly, often without paying much attention to the fact that we are doing so. (Am I confessing too much when I tell you that I often catch myself giving a running commentary even when I am doing something incredibly routine, such as washing dishes or taking a bath?) So the articulation, the "spelling out," is often already going on, just "below the surface" (that is, just outside of the focus of my fully conscious attention). I "catch" myself doing it. So, too, our avowal of what we do is typically built into the doing itself, with no further "stand" required. But, for many of us, it takes at least as much effort *not* to spell out what one is doing as it does to spell it out. So we can understand Freudian slips without any reference to repression and defense mechanisms in purely Sartrean terms by interpreting them as the natural consequence of distraction or momentary inattention, dropping the ball, in effect. The meta-stability of bad faith is due simply to the fact that our efforts *not* to spell out and avow engagements that are in fact very important and significant to us are always quite vulnerable. We tend to express them in spite of ourselves. Or, if we are quite self-conscious or steeped in psychoanalytic thinking, we will tend to spell out—or at least ask tough questions about—our meta-project of not spelling out our project of not spelling out what we are doing. And once one begins to realize the extent of one's willful "cover-up," there stands naked before us the awful truth about our responsibilities that is the focus of our refusal.[13]

Thus Sartre as I read him holds, much in line with Fingarette's theory, that self-deception has to do not with perception and belief but with volition and action, with the learned skill of articulating or "spelling out" one's beliefs and actions and their implications. Alfred Mele, by contrast, insists that such language is inappropriate. One could argue that he therefore deals exclusively with the phenomenon of "self-deception" rather than with bad faith as such, but I think he clearly appreciates the linkage between the two. Richard Moran, it seems to me, is closest to the mark. He takes the *responsibility* inherent in first-person authority to be the key to bad faith, and he writes convincingly about Sartre in this regard. Consciousness is a matter not of seeing and believing but of looking and attending, intentional *acts*. We are engaged in tasks and projects. We do not just perceive the world and form beliefs about it, and the first-person standpoint, he writes, is not just about observing ourselves from a peculiar perspective. It is always and irreducibly about our sense of responsibility.[14]

Perhaps, one might argue (as Sartre suggests), we do not normally "spell out" or "make explicit" activities in which we are engaged. In Sartre's terms, we only sometimes engage in activities reflectively, but we are often engaged prereflectively. I run for a streetcar, and my consciousness is "streetcar to be overtaken." Only occasionally do I shift my focus to the fact that "*I* am running for a streetcar," and then, Sartre suggests, there is usually some special reason for becoming reflective (for example, when we notice that some stranger is watching us or, worse, laughing at us). But I think reflective engagement is far more common than Sartre suggests, and we sometimes quite reflectively *avoid* becoming reflective and spelling out our activities. (This is where Sartre offers us the misleading analogy of falling asleep. But in trying to go to sleep, we are waiting for something to happen. In bad faith, we do not wait for something to happen but, rather, engage ourselves trying to do something [or refusing to do something].) But then we have to ask, What is the motivation for avoiding reflection and spelling out what we are doing?

There are various reasons for refusing to spell out our engagements to ourselves, from the innocent need to concentrate on something else we are doing (for instance, Merleau-Ponty's example of needing to concentrate on the activity of typing a letter or playing the piano, and thus trying not to reflect on or spell out one's activity while one is doing it) to the not-so-innocent need not to avow or acknowledge what we are doing where that activity weighs negatively on our conception of ourselves. Of course, it is not necessary that such refusal pertain only to presently ongoing activities. Sartre's homosexual is trying to process a whole history of homoerotic activities in his conception of himself as, or as not, a homosexual. Walking out of the restaurant, I am trying to understand my whole history as an undertipping tightwad. But the processing itself is an ongoing activity, and according to many hypercerebral authors, an ongoing activity that most of us are engaged in much of the time. (I think of Sartre as a hypercerebral author who goes out of his way to deny this.) Bad faith is about our self-identifying engagements and activities, whether we engage in them reflectively and articulate or spell them out for ourselves, or not. Bad faith, in its most usual manifestation, is the refusal to take responsibility for our engagements in the world by way of the dubious strategy of refusing to spell them out as such.

"Patterns" of Bad Faith: Sartre's Infamous Examples

I have argued that Sartre starts us off on the wrong foot by presenting bad faith on the model of self-deception and a lie to oneself. But to make matters worse, Sartre's examples of bad faith are for the most part not really worth the fame and attention they have received as illustrations of bad faith. The rather casual Stekel example, which ends the first section of the chapter, is quite convincing, although, to be sure, there is much more to say about it than Sartre has indicated. The point, often made (and I have made it often in this book), is that Sartre's otherwise Teutonic-styled philosophy comes alive in his examples, and the more personal they are, usually the better. Thus I think the most telling (and revealing) examples in the book have to do with his own sense of frailty, for instance, while out on a hike with his friends, or his perennial sense of being unattractive and how he deals with that. It is this that makes the phenomenology in *Nausea* so convincing. But that already suggests what I think is so weak about the examples of bad faith in the "Bad Faith" chapter. Namely, they are not personal. Nor are they, properly speaking, *phenomenological*. Phenomenology is the careful and insightful description of *one's own* experience (leaving aside the difficult questions about how far such personal experience can be generalized). But most of Sartre's examples here are descriptions of *other people's* experiences.

Thus I disagree with Allen W. Wood, who in a critical article attacks Sartre's examples for a very different reason, namely, that he manufactures his examples for his own purposes. "Sartre describes these examples so skillfully and vividly that it is easy to overlook the fact that they do not tell us much about self-deception. . . . In fact, they are little more than a series of illustrations of Sartre's own radical and idiosyncratic views about human freedom."[15] But, of course, all philosophers produce (whether or not they "manufacture") examples for their own purposes and to prove their points. And Sartre does indeed produce these examples as "illustrations of [his] own radical and idiosyncratic views about human freedom," for, as I have argued, the discussion of bad faith is utterly central to Sartre's views about freedom and responsibility (however radical and idiosyncratic they may be).

Perhaps Wood is misled because he buys into Sartre's own misleading presentation of the problem: "Sartre's problem about self-deception arises because it seems that in order to deceive myself I must simultaneously believe and disbelieve the same proposition at the same time, and this looks like a contradiction."[16] That would indeed make the issue of freedom seem tangential and secondary. But if Sartre's analysis is all about the denial of freedom, I would say that his examples do tell us quite a bit about bad faith (and, secondarily, about self-deception), but much more about what Sartre really has in mind (namely, freedom and its denial) rather than what he says he has in mind (that is, lying to oneself). Two of Sartre's examples, in fact, are quite convincing, although the first and most famous, the waiter in the café, is admittedly a bit oversimplified and merely suggestive. The second, however, Sartre's homosexual acquaintance, is both insightful and profound. I also think the short example on sadness is insightful. Regarding the others, however, I think there is much room for serious criticism, but not for the reason that Wood suggests.

Thus I want to look again at Sartre's description and analysis of Stekel's "pathologically frigid woman." I said that I thought that the example is effective and nicely illustrates Sartre's central point about the purposiveness (as opposed to the epistemology) of bad faith. Nevertheless, Sartre's presentation is suspicious. It is obvious that this is not phenomenology but a borrowed and second-hand assumption about another person's experience. In fact, it is a second-hand version of a psychiatrist's report of the woman's husband's dubious claim about what *she* may or may not have experienced. In other words, it is a description four times removed, with built-in biases all along the way. Now Sartre is rightly celebrated for his phenomenological insights (again, *Nausea* is exemplary), but he is not similarly praised for his empathy, his ability to "get inside other people's heads." Especially when they are women. (To protect myself against the charge that I am doing just what Sartre was doing, *presuming* to understand a woman's point of view, let me say that the following analysis was first suggested and then vetted by my wife, Kathleen Higgins.)[17]

Let us review (so far as we have them) the facts of the case. First of all, we are told that this woman may have been made frigid by her husband's marital infidelity. But Sartre goes on to describe her as "pathologically frigid," thus indicating his insensitivity. Moreover, was she "made frigid" in a merely causal way or is her frigidity a strategy for getting back at her husband? Sartre presumes the latter. He may be right in attributing the obvious purpose in her distracting herself from sex by thinking of household accounts (namely, to avoid enjoying sex with her husband). It is no doubt true that sex is amplified by attention (though not necessarily by way of "spelling out"), and dampened by inattention (especially if the topic of distraction is tedious and takes some concentration on its own). But the question, What is the purpose of the woman's distracting herself? and the further question, Does she realize that this is what she is doing? are not so obviously answered by Sartre. It is not clear that he has eliminated the unconscious (that is, purposes and strategies that the woman might well be able as well as might not want to acknowledge). Moreover, why does she not want to enjoy herself? Might there be some further (ulterior) purpose, one that she *cannot* understand?

I think it best to quote Kathleen Higgins here. First, she points with suspicion to Sartre's use of sexual examples:

> The preponderance of sexual examples in Sartre's list is noteworthy. Such examples are convenient for displaying his analytical moves of preference, for sexual interactions often do render problematic the notions of subjective independence and objectification. However, Sartre exploits the reader's ability to identify with fictional sexual desire—the sole feature through which the man in his example is characterized—to present the woman's response and behavior as unwarranted.[18]

Thus my snide inclusion of a predictable Sartrean sexist sidebar, in which Sartre notes that Stekel points out that the husband insists that his wife has shown signs of pleasure, even though she denies this. But Kathleen Higgins rightly points out:

> Sartre apparently considers pleasure to be a mere facticity of someone engaged in sexual intercourse. Thus, the frigid woman is dreading pleasure, and indeed, Sartre goes on to say, experiencing pleasure. It does not strike him that what the woman dreads may indeed be dealing with her husband. Given the allusion to marital infidelity, however, she may well associate her husband with feelings of betrayal, emotional abuse, rejection—strong emotions that bear little relation to pleasure.[19]

Furthermore:

> Even if one were to agree with Sartre that the woman is avoiding pleasure as such, it does not follow that she is in bad faith. Her strategy, whether consciously or unconsciously adopted, may be the best emotional recourse she has available to her, and indeed one that she might rationally adopt.

Very likely, she no longer trusts her husband. In general, it is a reasonable strategy to avoid depending on an untrustworthy person for anything, pleasure included. Sexual pleasure also renders many women emotionally vulnerable to their partners. Such vulnerability would put the woman in this example at risk of future hurt should her husband be unfaithful again. She might very reasonably be inclined to forgo physical pleasure in order to avoid such emotional risk. Moreover, deliberate distraction from potentially pleasurable activity may be much more easily achieved than the distraction she would require for enjoyment—distraction from awareness of her husband, her emotions in response to him, her disturbance over the condition of her marriage, etc.[20]

And finally:

None of this is intended to suggest that Steckel's patients do not have problems. Indeed, their strategies may be misguided with respect to certain of their goals. A woman's evident sexual disinterest might, for example, motivate her husband to seek sexual applause elsewhere— very likely not the result desired by a woman who responds with such distress to infidelity. Nevertheless, in a situation that might strike a woman as far from ideal, it is not obvious that self-deception is involved in her sexual resistance. Sartre's account is deficient in that he does not seek to understand the concerns of these patients.[21]

I have little to add to this. The upshot, even in this example, is that Sartre has shown himself to be insensitive, too quick to judge, and unwilling to ask deeper questions even where they fit his analysis. His use of sexual pleasure is suspect, and his presumption of understanding a troubled woman's strategy is contrary to his phenomenological method. If he had instead talked about his own sense of sexual inadequacy (modestly but sympathetically described on occasion by Simone de Beauvoir), he would have made a much more convincing case.

A similar analysis is appropriate for Sartre's example of the young woman sitting at a café with a date. Bad faith is a function of self-conception, but Sartre feels quite confident saying, from his third-person (voyeuristic) perspective, "We shall say that this woman is in bad faith." Again, the unwarranted empathetic presumption, and again, we shall see, the projection of sexual intentions. Sartre simply assumes that he knows more about this woman's state of mind than she does. But the real problem is the nature of the example. It is terribly confused. Sartre invokes two very different analyses, first by way of the facticity–transcendence formula discussed earlier, and second by the "lie to oneself" analysis that has been the curse of the entire chapter. ("It is a certain art of forming contradictory concepts which unite in themselves both an idea and the negation of that idea.") But the first, even without the second, is multiply ambiguous.

The woman "has consented to go out" with a man she is seeing for the first time, although he is barely described at all. Indeed, Sartre presumes his frame of mind is a singular desire, which if spelled out (whether by him or by her) would be "cruel and naked," and would "humiliate and horrify" her. But we are given a detailed description of her supposed state of mind. (Again, one must imagine Sartre the voyeur, writing all of this down.) She "knows very well" his intentions, Sartre assures us. (Because all men "want just one thing from a woman," one wonders? Or is Sartre betraying his own desire? Does a leer creep across his face?) Sartre says she knows that she will have to make a decision sooner or later. But does she? Perhaps she is naïve. Perhaps she is more confident with men than she looks. Perhaps she has already made a decision. (As the comedian Paul Rodriquez plaintively observes, quoted by Higgins, "Women are psychic. They always know if you're going to get laid.") But Sartre assures us that "she does not want to realize the urgency; she concerns herself only with what is respectful and discreet in her companion." (What was she supposed to do, ask him matter-of-factly about his intentions?) She does not think about what might happen (Sartre again assures us). Indeed, Sartre even imagines the date saying to her, "I find you so attractive!" but assures us that she would "disarm this phrase of its sexual background." The man appears to her as pure facticity, as "sincere and respectful as the table is round or square" (99). This indicates "a permanence like that of things." But all of this, Sartre again assures us, is because "she does not quite know what she wants."

All of this is brazenly presumptuous, even if Sartre made it all up. Then the facticity–transcendence formula kicks in, but not in any obvious way. Sartre tells us that in order for him to satisfy her, she would have to be addressed in her "full freedom." But at the same time, this feeling would have to be "wholly desire; that is, it must address her body as an object." This impossible "either/or" choice already condemns the woman, assuming that she is as ontologically flat-footed as Sartre is. But in any case, the situation changes. He takes her hand. Now she has to make a decision. "To leave the hand there is to consent to flirt. . . . To withdraw it is to break the troubled and unstable harmony which gives the hour its charm" (97). Her aim (Sartre supposes) is "to postpone the moment of decision as long as possible." So she leaves her hand there, but "she does not notice that she is leaving it." She is at that moment all intellect, "drawing her companion up to the most lofty regions of sentimental speculation." (Why "sentimental speculation"?) "The divorce of body from soul is accomplished, the hand rests inert . . .—a thing."

It is at this point that Sartre confidently asserts, "We shall say that this woman is in bad faith." But this is also where the account gets even more confused. She has reduced her companion's gestures to being only what they are, the "in-itself," but she will enjoy the desire as not being what it is, as its transcendence (98). Finally, she is aware of her own body ("as being aroused, perhaps"), but as if from above, "as a passive object." What then follows is several pages of distraction of literary references, ontological speculation, a too quick introduction of the problem of Being-for-Others, and an even quicker mention of sincerity as the antithesis of bad faith, the impossibility of being what we are, and the consequent necessity ("obligation") to "make ourselves what we are" (99). All of which has the intended effect of making us lose track entirely of the young woman in the café, her bad faith, and the probable sexual outcome of the afternoon.

But let us not forget her. What is the nature of her bad faith? Is it that she considers herself pure transcendence as she rattles on enthusiastically about matters of high intellectual significance? Or is it that she treats herself (that is, her body, her hand) as mere facticity, as a thing, to which events can only happen but which do not in any way provoke or invite them? Is it the way she treats her date, as a thing, and his desire as yet another thing? Or is it the way she thinks of his desire as transcendence (although it is by no means clear whether it is his transcendence or hers that is in question)? Is she in bad faith insofar as she recognizes (what Sartre supposes as) her arousal, or insofar as she does not? Is Sartre so much a sexist that he presumes a young woman could not possibly be so entranced by intellectual matters when the possibility of sex presents itself? Or, for that matter, that a man cannot remain intellectually involved when the possibility of sex is on the horizon? And what is she to do with her hand, once it has been grasped by her date? Pull it away (a sure way to break the "charm" of the afternoon)? Grasp his hand in turn (marking the end of the conversation and distracting both of them, indicating a decision that she possibly has not made yet)? Higgins notes that there is no indication of any negotiation, verbal or nonverbal, between the couple. His desire is just an unproblematic fact, and her treating her hand as a thing, possibly her arousal, too, is just a launch pad for a transcendence that leaves them both behind.

But if Sartre's treatment of the example is deeply troubling, Fingarette's attempt to straighten it out is even more problematic. He asserts what Sartre at most implies: that it is *her* "flirtation project" that drives the plot of the encounter, and that she does indeed know what she is doing with her hand, which makes her cynical rather than in bad faith, on Sartre's analysis. He also adds that she is "playing the role of the intellectual" though she disavows this role, and she "carries on her amorous invitations without reflecting." Fingarette presumes that, unless she is very skillful, there will be "a certain artificiality, a certain glib irrelevance about her conversation," "even momentary eruptions of patently flirtatious phrasing, expression, or gesture." This makes the young woman's project transparent, all right, but only by turning her into the sexual predator, the very opposite, I presume, of Sartre's intention.

Of course, men know women like that, and men have all acted on occasion like the callous cad that Sartre casts in the male role of this little drama. But the net result of the example is to wholly confuse the issue of bad faith, in large part because Sartre is in no position to tell us what this young woman is thinking and feeling. It is all made up, and not very well, if the purpose is to illustrate the dynamics of bad faith. In this case, Wood is absolutely right, but the example fails to shed any more light on Sartre's radical view of freedom than it does on the perplexing and pervasive phenomenon of bad faith in sexual encounters.

But finally, the more convincing examples: the waiter in the café (Sartre spent a remarkable amount of time in cafés), Sartre's own experience of sadness, and the homosexual who questions his own homosexuality. In the first and last cases, one can put forward a version of the above complaints: What did Sartre understand about the menial and solicitous job of being a waiter? (Sartre, the self-appointed working-class spokesman though he may be, pretty much admits as much.) And what did he know about being homosexual, even if he had homosexual friends and acquaintances? But at least they both are males. The most powerful and appropriate example, however, is the personal one, Sartre's analysis of his own emotion. Oddly enough, this is the one that rarely gets talked about in the commentaries on Sartre's bad faith, and Sartre gives it relatively scant attention.

The waiter example is a plausible example of bad faith according to the facticity and transcendence formula, and it is a good illustration of what Sartre means when he says that "we have the constant obligation to make ourselves what we are" (101). But since we "are what we are not and are not what we are," this, too, will always be meta-stable, will always betray "leaks," will always be tinged with artificiality. Thus, he notes, the waiter's movements are "a little too precise, a little too rapid," his step is a bit too quick. He bends a bit too eagerly, his voice is a little too solicitous. Sartre comments, "All of his behavior seems to us a game." The waiter pretends that he is a mechanism. "He is playing at being a waiter in a café" (102). So, too, grocers play at being grocers, soldiers play at being soldiers, and philosophers, to be sure, play at being philosophers. But of the waiter, unlike his female patron from the preceding example, Sartre does not simply exclaim, "We shall say that this man is in bad faith." Surely Sartre knows (from his own grocer example) that the waiter is just doing what is expected of him by his customers. It is enough to say, now appropriately in the first person, "I am a waiter in the mode of *being what I am not*" (103). Sartre throws out some plausible, because more personal, analogies: the student who tries so hard to be an attentive student that he exhausts himself playing the attentive role, the lecturer who is a good speaker just because he plays at speaking (an example I find dubious, but I can imagine giving it a plausible interpretation). The upshot is that there are no facts that are simply true of one. "On all sides I escape being and yet—I am" (103).

Now, Sartre's sadness. It is "a mode of being that concerns only myself." This casual admission throws into relief a problem that has persisted through all of Sartre's examples, not just his implausible presumptions of empathy but the fact that all of the examples in fact involve *other people*, and this changes the dynamic of the examples. Sartre does bring in

"Being-for-Others," very briefly, almost silently, on page 100, in his long distraction from the young woman's case, but he doesn't make much of it. I will have more to say about this toward the end of the section, but first, let's appreciate Sartre's personal sadness.

Sartre's description does not begin very poignantly, as he says, "One might think that surely I am the sadness in the mode of being what I am" (103–104). He becomes more insightful when he becomes more phenomenological and less ontological, and tells us that the sadness is the intentional unity that "reassembles and animates the totality of my conduct. It is the meaning of this dull look with which I view the world of my bowed shoulders, my lowered head, of the listlessness of my whole body" (104). But then, Sartre tells us, he realizes that he cannot hold onto his sadness. If a stranger appears, he would show a lively cheerfulness. He would "obligingly" promise his sadness an appointment later. Now this, I think, is deep and insightful. So often, sadness is treated as a *state*. But Sartre suggests that it is something quite different, which he dubiously calls a *"conduct,"* referring us back to his earlier essay noting that it is consciousness affecting itself, a "magical recourse against a situation too urgent." I think that this oversimplifies sadness. Sometimes, we feel sad just because of the weather. Other times it is due to a momentary feeling of loss. But Sartre's insight is that we *make* ourselves sad. We may "receive it" from elsewhere—in other words, we may be caused to be sad by any number of external factors (the weather, a loss), but consciousness affects itself just for this reason. It may not be entirely voluntary, but it is not wholly involuntary either.

Moreover, I must continue to *make* myself sad. My sadness is never a finished product. Here our brief discussion about consciousness constituting the "facts" of consciousness comes once again into focus. Sadness is routinely treated as a "basic" emotion, one largely defined by a neurological syndrome (or "affect program") and all but indifferent to both outside causes and its own intentional objects. It is, in an important sense, inert, continuing without effort once it begins. But Sartre is insisting that there is no such inertia, only renewed investment, and that pretending this is just another form of bad faith ("I can't help it, I'm just sad today").

But isn't my sadness just the way my consciousness is? Or perhaps it is rather the case that my sadness is my chosen *object* of consciousness? But this would involve us in an all-too-familiar tangle, in what sense can consciousness be its own object, etc.? But Sartre at this turn insists that my sadness is neither something that I am nor that I have for myself so much as it is a response to other people—in other words, a phenomenon of Being-for-Others. This takes us far beyond the solipsistic "escape behavior" of the earlier essay and even the seemingly personal nature of sadness he began with here. Sartre's description is rather labyrinthine, but I take it that the essence of it is that my sadness is largely a *presentation*, which is why I "turn it on" for people with whom I am intimate but can readily turn it off, at least temporarily, for strangers. This may hardly be fair to our friends, but Sartre here appreciates and explains how our emotions have an intricate involvement in the intimacy of the roles the Other (friend or stranger) plays in my constitution of myself. My sadness is not just a state but a kind of performance.

Sincerity in the case of emotions might be understood as just *being* what one feels, and then perhaps reflectively accepting or approving of what one feels. (This two-tier model of emotion should remind us of the Stoic theory, in which an emotion is an "affirmation of an appearance.") But Sartre is saying that there can be no such being, and so one's sadness, if I continue the Sartrean jargon, is largely a meta-stable product of our intentionality, something constituted by consciousness that then "discovers" it. I try to figure, via introspection, just what I am feeling. But the attempt, which should be all too familiar to us, is unsuccessful. There doesn't seem to *be* anything there. I look for my sadness, as I have just presented it to my best friend (putting her in a somber mood as well), and what I see is just my own behavior in progress, no sadness at all. So, too, when I am trying to decide whether or not I am in love, especially in the presence of my beloved, I cannot find what I would like to find—and what she is surely hoping for as well—*love*. The bold truth that Sartre is proclaiming here is that we *make* love, as we do sadness, as we do all of the many emotions and feelings we live through. The conditions may present themselves, but it is up to us to decide or, in the Stoics' language, affirm through judgment the legitimacy (or the lack of it) of what we feel. To pretend otherwise is to be in bad faith.

Bad Faith and Being-for-Others

In most of the chapter "Bad Faith," Sartre maintains the misleadingly simple, and therefore seductive, thesis that bad faith is a denial or a confusion of two very different and opposed aspects of ourselves: facticity, the facts that are true of oneself, and transcendence, that which goes beyond the facts. To be sure, there are examples of self-deception that are somewhat like this, and Sartre plays with them, notably with the waiter in the café who pretends *to be* a waiter; in his novel *Age of Reason*, where his character Mathieu insists (à la Sartre) that he is not what he obviously is; and in the play *No Exit*, where the male protagonist wrestles with the question of whether he is (or was) nothing but the sum of his actions (and of *which* actions?). But most of Sartre's examples of this supposed phenomenon are demonstrably something quite different, in which it is the view of *other people* that creates the problem of bad faith, and not just the self-reflection of the subject. In other words, bad faith is the product not only of facticity and transcendence ("being-in-itself" and "being-for-itself") but of what Sartre calls "Being-for-Others" as well. We shall see that this complicates matters enormously.

In Stekel's frigid woman story, the husband is not just a sex partner whose instrumentality the wife fails or refuses to enjoy. The example is all about their *relationship*: how she thinks of him and his infidelity, what she thinks he thinks of her, and how he thinks of her or at least how he treats her (given that negotiation between them, apart from sex, seems to have broken down). We cannot talk about bad faith in such a case without talking about the manipulation and deceit that go on between them and how sex is particularly fertile soil for such manipulation and deceit, especially as, among human intimate activities, sex invites less candor and "spelling out" (and, ironically, less intimacy) than almost any other. Thus the young unmarried woman in the café can hardly express whatever sexual feelings, fears, or expectations she may have, particularly to the man sitting across from her, but her feelings for him, his feelings for her, her feelings about his feelings—not to mention either of their feelings regarding the philosophical pervert sitting at the next table—are all relevant to the question of whether either of them is in bad faith. It is certainly not just a question of whether the young woman identifies with her body and its arousal or, rather, identifies with her intellectual transcendence of her body. (Suppose that the man across the table is her philosophy tutor. What difference would that make to Sartre's simpleminded account?)

The waiter case is much less complicated than the others, but it is pretty evident that he, too, is putting on a *performance*. He may just be "playing," but he is playing as in a theater, and not as in a sandbox. It is extremely doubtful that he would continue the performance after all of the customers have gone off for the evening or when he gets back to his apartment at night. The sadness example is even more to the point. Sartre begins by asking us whether we think that this is an instance that concerns only oneself, but answers with a resounding "no." It, too, is a presentation. My sadness depends for its meaning not on my introspective psychology but on my interplay with others in the world. In other words, Being-for-Others is not a casual third term in the understanding of bad faith, and so the discussion of it in the chapter "Bad Faith" is both misleading and woefully incomplete.

That leaves us with the last and most extended example of the chapter, which we have touched on throughout our discussion. It follows the discussion of sadness, but the emotion here in question is *guilt*, even though Sartre rarely refers to it as such. The point is the same: guilt is not just a psychological fact that we discover in ourselves but is, to a certain extent, something that we make so. But this is complicated by an ambiguity that we keep running into in this book, with both Camus and Sartre. There is legal guilt, which is in an institutional sense "objective"; and there is causal guilt, which in a factual sense is also objective; and then there is moral guilt, which (certain theological and moral doctrines aside) is what we have mainly been talking about. *Feeling* guilty, one might say, so long as we don't take this to be just a feeling (a sensation). What gets us into the homosexual case is his guilt, and his question is Should I feel guilty? Sartre tells us that he has "intolerable guilt," and he is therefore in bad faith. Moreover, all of this is complicated by subsequent discussions of shame and guilt in *Being and Nothingness*, where Sartre insists, "My original fall is the existence of the

Other" and "It is before the Other that I am guilty" (352, 531). But we need to slow down and ask whether it is his feeling that he is guilty that puts him in bad faith, or other people and their "looks" that put him in bad faith, or his "conduct" that makes him such. (Obviously, the question of legal guilt cannot be wholly excluded from consideration, and given that he is described not as a homosexual but as a "pederast," we cannot retreat to contemporary liberal sexual platitudes.)

On the one hand, the conflicted person in question—and I again find myself picturing Daniel in the Roads to Freedom trilogy—has a clear and undeniable history of homosexual encounters. Furthermore, he suffers from repeated homoerotic urges and desires. All of this, his past and his psychology, falls into the "facticity" side of the ledger. On the other hand, this man is repulsed by his past behavior and disgusted by his urges. He resolves to act differently. He resolves to be a different person. But temptation and opportunity present powerful obstacles. And so he struggles. Sartre rather unsympathetically describes his evasion and uncertainty as "comic" insofar as he refuses to draw the conclusion that seems so obvious from the facts. But his friend, whom Sartre dubs "the Champion of Sincerity," insists that he declare frankly, "I am a pederast." And Sartre rather evenhandedly but implausibly questions, "Who is in bad faith, the homosexual or the champion of sincerity?" (As if turning another person into an object is also a serious act of bad faith.)

The poor fellow fights against what he fears is his destiny. I often compare him with the inveterate smoker who is trying desperately to quit but is so "hooked" that he always finds another excuse to keep smoking. But however powerful the addiction and its physiological and psychological compulsions, there is always that sense that one can, with sufficient "will power," successfully resolve to quit. After all, millions of others have done it. Sartre describes all of this in some pretty fancy talk about "rebirth" and "being" and the "peculiar, irreducible character of human reality." But without getting spookily ontological, we are all familiar with the pattern. At some point, the smoker denies that he is addicted, denies that anything stands between him and quitting (despite many failures before), and in so denying reality, he is, according to an unsympathetic Sartre, in bad faith. He is condemned whether he identifies himself and his determined destiny according to his facticity or he rejects his facticity and insists on his transcendence. So, too, the homosexual, whatever the pressures of his habits and his urges, and despite the temptations he so readily (but guiltily) gives in to, continues to insist on his transcendence. He, too, can be condemned in either direction.

But there is a further turn in the argument, prompted, in Sartre's version, by the Champion of Sincerity. And that is the reflective turn, or rather, the confessional turn; Sartre even reminds us of the slogan "a sin confessed is half pardoned," as if reflective confession is already an assertion of freedom. But Sartre's cynical take on this has a powerful measure of plausibility: that it is for the benefit of the other (the Champion of Sincerity), and not for the sake of his own freedom, that the homosexual is urged to confess. How much better it would make us feel to say, "He's a hopeless homosexual" (or "He's hopelessly addicted"), thus both celebrating our own freedom and wisdom ("I, at least, have the wisdom not to be a homosexual/not to smoke"). At the same time, we deny the same freedom of choice to the Other. (This, perhaps, is the source of the Champion of Sincerity's bad faith.) Sartre also predictably cross-references his insight to Hegel's master/slave parable in the *Phenomenology*: one is forced to give up his freedom to the other in return for the mere possibility of freedom yet to come.

But apart from this insightful (and cynical) aside, the role of reflection in the homosexual's bad faith is quite significant. For one thing, it is only on the level of reflection that "will power" appears ("*I* have got to stop doing this!"). And despite Sartre's insistence that bad faith must be a prereflective phenomenon, it is only on reflection that certain critical features of bad faith—and human engagement in general—come into full play. Second, it is in reflection, most notably, that one opens up that critical "gap" between oneself and one's engagements, commitments, emotions, motives, and desires. One "pulls back" to reflect upon the fact that one is investing enormous amounts of effort and energy in the pursuit of some trivial activity. One pauses to reflect on one's anger or sense of growing resentment, suddenly aware of how unwarranted and unseemly it is. One may even stop mid-sentence—in either thought or speech—as one "listens to oneself" say something about oneself that suddenly, as if in a flash of insight, seems utterly absurd. Other people, "champions of sincerity" or not, may prompt or even demand such reflection, but as essentially reflective creatures we often initiate it, sometimes spontaneously, ourselves. (Surely it is not always spontaneous. If one decides to go to a therapist or talk to a friend or even spend a quiet hour alone, "thinking things over," one *invites* such reflection.) Surely our homosexual is sufficiently wracked by intolerable guilt so as to be not only prompted but obsessed with reflecting on his nature and his fate. He hardly needs the self-serving Champion of Sincerity to urge him on.

So why does Sartre introduce the champion of sincerity into the discussion at all? I think that Sartre introduces this dubious character in order to make the highly controversial point that even sincerity is in bad faith. It is yet another effort to dissociate oneself from oneself, and therefore even in "good faith," bad faith is unavoidable. But I think that this is a troublesome conclusion, a bad argument, and it undermines the value of an extremely important ethical concept.

Can One Be or Become "Authentic"?

I have been using the word "authenticity" somewhat loosely (usually parenthetically) as more or less a synonym, or at any rate a rough equivalent, of the notions of "good faith" and "sincerity," as the opposite of bad faith (as well as of self-deception). First of all, I bother mentioning "authenticity" at all just because it has become such a cornerstone of popular "existentialist" thinking, although even the two authors with whom it is most correctly associated (Kierkegaard and Heidegger) in fact said remarkably little about it. Heidegger, in particular, spends most of his time cataloging the various forms of *in*authenticity. His suggestions about authenticity [literally "own-ness"] are famously confusing if not obscure. Sartre rarely uses the word, except occasionally to link his own thinking to Heidegger, and in any case he never subjects it to even the most minimal analysis. He does give us an extensive analysis of bad faith, but we should by no means assume that "good faith" or authenticity is the "opposite" of bad faith, despite his contrasting them at the end of the chapter. And to make matters even more complicated, Sartre clearly suggests that there is no possibility of authenticity or of "good faith" or of "sincerity" (which in his writing seems like a variation of cynicism). So at best we might be able to say what good faith would be *if it were* possible. But here again the comparison with virtue and vice might be valuable. Just as no one can be *completely* in bad faith, so no one could be *completely* in good faith. But just as one can be quite honest, or generous, or courageous, so one might be better or worse in avoiding bad faith. To be sure, "no one's perfect." But that is surely not the end of the story.

Bad faith is a bad thing, but like all bad things it admits of degrees and is rarely found in "pure" form. It can be "more or less": more or less destructive, more or less egregious, more or less justified. Refusing to face up to one's cheapness is much less egregious than collaborating with the Nazis. In this, it might profitably be compared with the traditional conception of the vices. (As "sins," the vices may have some claim to absolute status, but even sins are routinely distinguished both by lay folk and church doctrine as "major" and "minor" as well as "mortal," "venial," and "cardinal.")

Like the traditional vices, bad faith has an awkward logical relation with its "opposite," "good faith," just as the vices have an awkward logical relation with the virtues. The "opposite" of gluttony, for example, is what? Moderation at the dinner table? Abstemiousness? Self-denial? Starvation? Is chastity the "opposite" of lust? And what is the "opposite" of anger? For Aristotle, it would be getting angry judiciously— in the right way, at the right time, and so on. For the Stoics, it would be abstaining from anger altogether. For Saint Augustine, it's leaving it all up to God. Again we should not leap too quickly to the idea that "good faith" (or "authenticity") is the "opposite" of bad faith.

Aristotle says that a virtue is "the mean between the extremes [of vices]." What if we were to take the comparison with the vices a step farther and suggest that the "extremes" of bad faith would be (1) total emphasis on one's facticity and (2) total emphasis on one's transcendence? To be sure, Aristotle's doctrine is a matter of considerable controversy, and it is widely held that his list of virtues is ad hoc (or ad hominem, simply a description of the ideals approved of among his peers). Thus his list of virtues and vices has nothing of the elegance of the medieval lists, and so, too, I think that "bad faith" encompasses a wide swath of human failings and weaknesses that cannot be easily unified by any simple criterion. Thus, again, we should be careful about assuming any straightforward relationship between bad faith and good faith, including the idea that good faith is the correct "balance" of facticity and transcendence. Nor should we assume that the absence of bad faith is equivalent to good faith (or "authenticity") and vice versa.

All that having been said, however, I would like to say something about the cluster of concepts "authenticity," "good faith," and "sincerity" in Sartre. "Authenticity" has become the word that attracts the most attention (whereas "good faith" is pretty much restricted to the margins of commentators writing about Sartre on "bad faith"). With "authenticity," the English association with "genuineness" can be misleading. In Kierkegaard and Heidegger, the word might better be understood as something more like "integrity," or even as "autonomy," insofar as both authors explicitly contrast the notion with something like Kant's "heteronomy": in Kierkegaard "the herd" and "the public," in Heidegger *Das Man* and the anonymity of the "they"-self. The word "integrity," we know, has its roots in "wholeness" or "completeness," as does the Heideggerian notion of "own-ness" (*Eigentlichkeit*). But it is important (particularly if we keep an eye on Heidegger) not to render this "own-ness" too subjectively. That is, we should be wary of an overly "internalist" understanding of integrity or "own-ness" in which it might be said of someone that he or she has integrity or "own-ness" if only he or she is perfectly consistent and coherent in thought and feeling.

To any such "internalist" understanding there is a ready sophomoric rejoinder: What if a person is completely *evil*? Is "integrity" enough? Is it necessarily a good thing? Heidegger is famously obscure on this, especially considering his own political history. But I think that there is a good answer. It involves a version of what Aristotle called "objectivity" in ethics, in other words, not just consistency of personal values but consistency involving the *right* values as well, including the values of one's community and, ultimately, basic human values.[22] Describing authenticity this way would seem to violate Sartre's views, since in his more theoretical writings he seems to reject "human values" along with "human nature." But in his political writings, and in *Being and Nothingness* as well, it is evident that he takes freedom to be just such a value and not just as an abstract matter of ontology. Whether or not this value can serve in turn as a fulcrum for a more general conception of universal human values is a difficult question, and Sartre's toleration and even defense of violence certainly raises even more difficult questions.[23] But on the basis of that one value, freedom, I think there is a good argument to be made that Sartre is no "relativist" or "subjectivist." Thus the concept of "authenticity" may have some genuine purchase in his philosophy.

I distinguish "authenticity," however, from "sincerity." The two terms have been played off against one another a great deal since Sartre's work.[24]

"Sincerity," like "authenticity," also involves something like consistency and coherence in one's thoughts and feelings. But "sincerity" does allow for ethical failures of just the sort that "authenticity" excludes. A person might indeed be evil and sincere, and he or she might be thoroughly self-deceived and quite sincere. I noted earlier that Sartre, at least in the "Bad Faith" chapter of *Being and Nothingness*, suggests that sincerity is cynical, or at least his "Champion of Sincerity" is self-servingly so. But I would argue that the one thing that a sincere person *cannot* be is cynical, on Sartre's own analysis. The coherence of one's thoughts and feelings make that "double con- sciousness" (as in Camus' Clamence) impossible. Thus I think that there is a good case to be made that sincerity is not so much opposed to bad faith, nor is it identical to authenticity, but a noteworthy alternative and neither bad faith nor cynicism. As for "good faith," finally, this is a term that is pretty well restricted to Sartre's own occasional use as a contrast to bad faith, but apart from meaning "not in bad faith," it seems to have little positive content.

So what are we to say about the possibilities of *not* being in bad faith or, more modestly, about the possibilities of being more rather than less in touch with one's engagements in the world? I have already suggested that we should ignore Sartre's "either/or" ontological bias and think in terms of degrees of self-awareness and, as in our talk of virtue and vice, use "being in touch with one's engagements" and "bad faith" as straightforwardly moral terms of evaluation, approbation, and disapprobation. Sartre only pretends to be an amoralist. He is, as I've said, the harshest of moralists. Moreover, I think that Sartre is a "particularist" in these matters. That is, if he does not talk about virtues and vices, it is because he insists on what in more modest ethical quarters might be called "situation ethics." He rejects the very idea of "character traits" because, he would say, these point only to the expected outcome of a history of certain behaviors. They are hypotheses about future behavior, not personality structures. They may summarize the "facts" of our behavior so far and give *other* people an empirical basis for predicting fu- ture behavior, but they say nothing about who or what we *are*. So gluttony points to a history of behaving gluttonously and eating like a pig. It also provides grounds (for everyone except the glutton) to predict future gross behavior at the dinner table. (The glutton is surely in bad faith if he/she resigns him/herself to *being* a glutton on the basis of such evidence.) But gluttony does not capture any kind of "essence" of a person. So, too, being in bad faith is something a person *does* in a particular situation (or sequence of situations). It says nothing about who or what a person *is*. (If one resigns oneself to bad faith, one is thereby and furthermore in bad faith.)

Perhaps it is the case, as Sartre suggests, that we are always to some degree in bad faith. Indeed, the central Sartrean image of human existence as always an unresolved tension between facticity and transcendence, be- tween our conceptions of ourselves and how we are conceived of by others, between different possibilities that keep presenting themselves as choices, or obligations, or desires, would seem to require that this be so. Furthermore, we should question what Sartre calls the "translucency" of consciousness. One cannot pay close attention to both a philosophy lecture and a video game at the same time (however many students may try to do so in class). One cannot focus on one's embarrassing history and the open-ended possibilities of one's transcendence at the same time (however bravely we might try to do so in the name of "authenticity"). But as an inescapable aspect of human consciousness, bad faith is not necessarily blameworthy. Specific episodes and processes of bad faith become blameworthy. How bad they are depends on the context. (The particularist is often a contextualist, too.) Just as one can be a little bit gluttonous, one can be a little bit in bad faith.

There are times, as in some of Sartre's literary examples, when bad faith may devour the whole of one's life. But even so, it is not as if one just *is* in bad faith. Again, people might say this ("Well, I guess I'm just in bad faith"), but this, quite palpably, is just another case of bad faith, another way of refusing to face up to one's responsibilities. No one, however, is "just in bad faith." Some people are more conflicted, less consistent and less coherent in their values and their ideals, and more willfully distracted. But it is the nature of consciousness that, short of extreme trauma or psychopathology, few of us are all that conflicted, inconsistent, or incoherent. (This is what I take Sartre to suggest by "translucency.") Our lives (more or less) "hang together," and the right hand usually has a good idea what the left hand is doing. We may all occasionally fool ourselves about what we are doing with our lives and conceptualize ourselves in self-serving (or in some cases self-denigrating) terms, but there are almost always limits to how extensively we can do so.

But if bad faith is always a matter of more or less, we might think, too, of good faith or authenticity as a kind of ideal that no one can actually be expected to achieve. It would require a kind of full transparency and lucidity about oneself that is so rare that it is truly amazing when we discover it even "to a large extent" in someone. (We would rarely claim this for ourselves, for the very thought regarding oneself is very likely to be in bad faith.) But if no one can really be in good faith or be fully authentic, we surely recognize more or less in virtually all virtuous human behavior. Saints are people who tend to rate very high on the authenticity meter. Liars and hypocrites tend to do very badly. Most of us have our good days and our bad days. But "in bad faith" and "in good faith" are two dangerous Sartrean locutions insofar as they lead us to assume that a person *is* or is *in* one or the other. If, however, we were to think in terms of a person's being "more conflicted" or "less conflicted" (with regard to some particular course of action and the conception of self with which it is correlated), more or less consistent and coherent in his or her desires and impulses and emotions and ideals, I think that we would have a much more workable model (or set of models) of what it means to "be in" bad (or good) faith.

So, is good faith or authenticity possible? Is bad faith unavoidable? The answer to both questions is "yes, to a degree." This reply is not nearly so dramatic (nor so ontological) as Sartre, following Heidegger, would lead us to wish for, but it renders these moral categories imminently useful in the everyday real world. This is not the place to discuss some of the even more dramatic suggestions regarding authenticity, Heidegger's linking it to "Being-unto-Death" and Sartre's vague hints at the value of "purifying reflection." But with regard to the mundane, and occasionally even the heroic and the scandalous, we can say without mystification both that authenticity is possible and that bad faith defines and pervades the human condition. The matter comes down to particulars and particular contexts. Who is conflicted about what issues in what circumstances, and what rides on it? As many authors have pointed out, notably the two early existentialists Kierkegaard and Nietzsche, a little bit of bad faith may be not only unavoidable but also necessary for human flourishing.

Are We Responsible for Bad Faith?

I have evaded the question, Is bad faith something we do, something for which we can be held responsible? Or is it simply something that happens to us, for which (therefore) we can make excuses? That question is critical, at least for Sartre, for whom *doing* is the prerequisite for responsibility. If we *suffered* from bad faith, we would not be responsible, any more than we are responsible for getting sick (though, to be sure, we might well be responsible for not taking care of ourselves, exposing ourselves to pathogens, etc.). But Sartre remains caught between his uncompromising insistence on "absolute freedom" and his problematic conception of (prereflective) consciousness as "spontaneity." Whether or not we are willing to go all the way with Sartre in his admittedly harsh and radical notion of freedom, it is clear that he would make no sense at all if we were to conclude that, given his conception of consciousness, we are *never* responsible for what we do. Nor would the moral condemnation attaching to being in bad faith make much sense if it was merely a "character flaw" or a misfortune, and not our own responsibility.

Accordingly, I think we are forced to give up at least some of Sartre's conception of spontaneity. And the best way to do this, I think, is to weaken his insistence that consciousness is by its very nature spontaneous. I think Sartre is right about the fact that most of our acts and engagements are not deliberative, not reflective, not fully self-conscious. Much of our behavior is habitual, practiced, "thoughtless," but it does not follow that human consciousness is spontaneous. I think that Sartre is trying to embrace Nietzsche's aphorism "A thought comes when it will, not when I will," extended to intentions and actions, but in doing so, Sartre downplays reflection too much, as if it were just an occasional accompaniment or embellishment of consciousness. We are, as Merleau-Ponty so clearly pointed out, obsessively reflective beings (some people more than others, needless to say). I suspect that Sartre's motive in downplaying reflection is to dramatize the important point that he makes in his *Transcendence:* that we are not *always* reflective.

The fact that we are obsessively reflective beings does not mean, as Sartre rightly insists, that we are reflective all the time. But I think we need to bring reflection back to center stage.[25] Our consciousness would be incomprehensible to us without reflection (and not just in the trivial sense that we could not *comprehend* anything without it). Without reflection, I have argued, there could be no bad (or good) faith. Without reflection, we would not be human.

Bad faith, I have insisted, has to do with our engagements in the world and not merely with our beliefs, but it has a great deal to do with our selectively "spelling out" and "avowing" one's engagements. These are *actions*, which sometimes seem to be automatic or "spontaneous." When we are talking to someone or even teaching a class, it may well seem as if the words just pour out of our mouths. Indeed, paying too much attention to one's speaking interferes with, and may even stymie, one's talking. But there is no question whether or not one is *doing* something. So, too, when we spell out or avow our engagements, no matter how spontaneous or even seemingly involuntary this may be, there is no question that one is *doing* something. But refusing to spell out or avow our engagements is also doing something, and we are therefore responsible for it.

When Sartre argues that bad faith need not be reflective or articulate, I think that he is trying to solve a number of problems. First, a basic practical problem: if someone is responsible only for "possibilities" that he or she has considered and articulated, that would eliminate from consideration many of the most egregious cases of bad faith: the rich person who never even thinks of his or her effects on the poor or of the inequities of which he or she is the beneficiary; the SUV driver who just never thinks about, nor has ever articulated, the damage his purchase is wreaking upon the earth; the soldier or policeman or prison guard who has never even thought of the possibility that he could refuse to obey an unethical command. So opening up the arena of responsibility to include matters not reflected upon or articulated serves an essential purpose for Sartre, one at the very heart of his theory of freedom.

It may take considerable effort *not* to spell out one or another of one's engagements, and at some stage along the way this needs to involve a fully conscious decision. To be sure, it will probably not be of the form "I had better distract myself in order to not pay attention to . . . ." But it does not follow that no step in the project of bad faith can be fully conscious, nor does it follow that the number of steps might be unending. The amount of prereflective activity involved in most cases of bad faith may be rather modest, and most of the process tends to be reflective if not necessarily attended to. I think that the distinction between a conscious process being reflective and being attended to is extremely important, although it slips between Sartre's clumsy categories of reflective and prereflective consciousness.

Alfred Mele writes at length about self-deception and the question of whether it is willful or voluntary, and he, too, is tempted by the "anti-agency view" that "no motivationally biased beliefs are intentionally produced or protected" in self-deception.[26] The advantage of such a view is that it avoids the unpalatable conclusion that I must be aware of my motive and my strategy in maintaining some unwarranted conception of myself. Sartre is right, in his essay on *The Emotions*, that awareness of one's motives may well undermine an emotional strategy. The disadvantage of such a view, of course, is that it seems to leave the obvious "why?" question unanswered: "Why would one bother to do this?" It seems to be one of the data of both bad faith and self-deception that it is motivated behavior, not something that simply happens to us. Sartre writes, "One does not undergo his bad faith; one is not infected with it; it is not a state. But consciousness *affects itself* with bad faith."

The problem, again, lies in Sartre's dichotomous ontological thinking: bad faith versus good faith, motivated versus nonmotivated, reflective versus prereflective. I noted a moment ago that I consider the distinction between a conscious process being reflective and being attended to as extremely important, even though it slips between Sartre's categories of reflective and prereflective consciousness. One might note that there is also *noticing* what is going on, and "barely noticing" as well. There is no simple dichotomy here, but several complex dimensions of self-awareness. From our more or less habitual behaviors to fully conscious, deliberate actions there is an enormous range of senses in which one can be "conscious" of one's engagements. Insofar as an engagement is articulated or "spelled out," there are also many ways in which one can describe it, some of them evasive, some of them insightful, some of them cynical, some of them unwittingly revealing. Insofar as an engagement is avowed, there are always alternative avowals, ranging from straightforward "taking ownership" to devious acknowledgments and admissions that evade the issue at hand. (Think of the now standard political phrase "Mistakes were made....")

Sartre is probably right that we do not usually attend to, spell out, and avow our actions and our engagements. It is only on rare occasions—such as when we are trying to break or alter a habit—that we actually attend to the habit and its accompanying sensations. But even where it is a deliberate action (which already involves "spelling out" as well as avowal), we do not always or even usually pay close attention or continue to spell out our action once the action or engagement has been "launched." But these various levels of attention and reflection form the complex fabric of consciousness. Most of the time, we may barely notice what we are doing and what we feel, but this would still seem to count, in Sartre's phenomenology, as reflective consciousness. You see, I hope, what I am suggesting, that there are many "levels" of (self-)consciousness and it is the interaction and shifting between them that explain most cases of bad faith. Full consciousness (wholly articulate and avowed consciousness) is perhaps rare, but prereflective consciousness in the strong sense that Sartre defines it plays a negligible role in any instance worth talking about.

The Reiteration of Bad Faith

The discernment of dimensions and levels of reflection is important for another aspect of bad faith, one I have alluded to several times, and that is the "reiteration" of bad faith. Bad faith is not simply a prereflective phenomenon. It is not a one-stage, one-dimensional psychological, much less an epistemic, act or state. Bad faith is a process, a project, an engagement that takes time and preparation, whatever its seeming "spontaneity." But as part of this process, Sartre tells us, bad faith must "reiterate itself." That is, one must further be in bad faith about one's being in bad faith. (Freud also faced this complexity. That is, the mechanism of repression must in turn be repressed.) But it is difficult to see how bad faith might reiterate itself without at the same time betraying itself, since this would involve self-consciousness in further convolutions. Indeed, there is the obvious question of whether one must furthermore be in bad faith about one's being in bad faith about one's being in bad faith. Then there is the immediate question: Doesn't becoming reflectively aware of one's being in bad faith undermine the bad faith and make it unsustainable, the way that (in *Emotions*) Sartre insists that one's emotional strategies must remain prereflective or else be "seen through" and thus lose their "magic." (There is nothing magical about just pretending that the grapes are sour.) This is why Sartre insists that bad faith is "*meta-stable*" and liable to "disintegrate" at any time. But Sartre presents this as the result of the impossible project of holding in consciousness two contradictory beliefs. The real problem lies elsewhere.

The project of bad faith would certainly fail insofar as one fully recognized that one was acting in bad faith. Such recognition is possible, of course, but it is no longer bad faith. It is rather what Sartre refers to as a *cynical* consciousness, one that sees through its own pretenses but maintains them just the same. The cynic, unlike the person in bad faith, is a fully *self-conscious* hypocrite. Thus my opening quotation from Gide's *Counterfeiters*: "The true hypocrite is the one who ceases to perceive his deception, and lies with sincerity." This is a depiction of cynical consciousness. But to be in bad faith is not to be cynical or to be hypocritical or to be conscious (of one's bad faith). It is to be *sincere* (whereas the cynic is thoroughly insincere). And the only way not to be cynical is to "cover up" what one is doing and hide it from oneself. To be in bad faith is also to be in bad faith about one's being in bad faith.

Fingarette rightly invokes the figure of Clamence in Camus' *The Fall* to illustrate such cynicism. Clamence knows full well what he is doing, and for that reason he is cynical rather than simply self-deceived. He confesses,

> I have been practicing my profession at Mexico City for some time. It consists, to begin with, as you know from experience, in indulging in public confession as often as possible. I accuse myself up and down....I navigate skillfully, multiplying distinctions and digression too—in short I adapt my words to my listener and lead him to go me one better....When

the portrait is finished, . . . I show it with great sorrow; this, alas, is what I am. But at the same time the portrait I hold out to my contemporaries becomes a mirror. (*The Fall*, 139–140)

From politics, we know all too well the hazards of cover-ups. They are rarely successful, and the consequences of a failed cover-up are often more devastating than the original fault covered up. There are almost inevitably "leaks," whether by way of Freudian verbal slips or uncontrolled gestures or facial expressions. There are also anxiety and nervousness, which signal the cover-up, not to mention tell-tale eye movements and other "tells" that poker players are so quick to recognize. But the most serious leaks and betrayals are not so much leaked to or picked up by other people so much as they are evident to the person in bad faith, from uninvited thoughts to noticing inconsistent or incoherent bits of behavior to the explosive realization that one does not in fact accept what one is doing or how one is behaving. This may creep into one's self-consciousness in fits and starts of self-recognition and reflection, or it may seem to burst in all at once, "spontaneously." In such a fashion does cynicism give way to regretful sincerity.

But the reiteration of bad faith presents Sartre with a problem (as it does Freud). So long as there is some compartmentalization of consciousness, whether in the difference between prereflective and reflective consciousness or in the "topography" of consciousness and the Unconscious, it makes some sense to suggest that what (self-) consciousness doesn't know is that which is outside of its domain. But once we begin talking about reiteration, it is no longer clear where or how the secondary bad faith is to be identified or located. If bad faith is the refusal to reflectively spell out and avow one's engagements, is this refusal itself reflective? (Thus Sartre seems caught in the same dilemma that he finds in Freud.)

Sartre is surely right that *some* aspects of bad faith are prereflective (i.e., not spelled out) but others are fully reflective. As I have interpreted him, one must be *capable* of self-reflection—of having some conception of who or what one is—in order to be in bad faith. It is in the complexity of the reflection that bad faith is maintained. But we all know what a philosopher will ask at this point: Where will this reiteration end? If one now has to be in bad faith regarding one's meta-project of denying that one is in bad faith about one's bad faith, isn't there an infinite regress argument, the bane of philosophers since Aristotle? But the regress *does* come to an end, sometimes quite quickly and simply when one just loses focus or interest. Sometimes it is only by way of using elaborate and ingenious subterfuges such as massive distraction and putting oneself in emotionally or even physically harrowing situations. But we can agree with Sartre that bad faith does indeed require reiteration and a "cover-up," and this in turn makes bad faith an extremely complicated phenomenon, its recursive complexity denied or at least hidden behind the simple formula of "facticity versus transcendence."

Sartre sometimes seems to assume that in order for the further project of reiteration to succeed, it is necessary that bad faith *never* become reflective at all. This, I think, is a serious mistake. On some level, at some point, bad faith has to become reflective—it is not enough that it is *capable* of becoming reflective—if it is to be bad faith at all. But how can this be if bad faith is not to betray itself? If bad faith were just a matter of belief, it might be represented as denying that one believes what one believes. But insofar as it is more akin to *not knowing what one is doing*, it is much less obviously a problem and involves nothing so obviously unstable as a straightforward or even a twisted contradiction of beliefs.[27]

Conclusion: Bad Faith as the Human Condition

Sartre is right that human life is a struggle and always in tension and that we can never get it permanently in balance. Fingarette dubiously argues a resolution for Sartre: by way of "pure reflection," choice coincides with and "endorses the system of the self." The problem is that for Sartre there is no such systematic self. The self is an "impure reflection" that is always in question. I think that this is the strongest single point of Sartre's theory, and it is a shame that he polemically (but mistakenly) seems to insist that to have *any* conception of self is therefore to be in bad faith. Sartre as ontologist has once again belied his own phenomenological insights by insisting on the clumsy categories of ontology instead of the keen analytic lens of phenomenology.

Authenticity ("good faith") should be conceived of not in terms of the absence of bad faith but rather as an optimized sense of self, consonant with one's reflective ideals and values as well as prereflective emotions and desires. This may not be very easy, "flawed" creatures that we are. But it is by no means impossible; rather, it is a more or less essential part of being human—trying to "get it together" or cultivate one's integrity or express one's human dignity or *ren* or whatever one may call it in whatever culture. But authenticity is not an illusion, and inauthenticity (bad faith) is not in any reasonable sense unavoidable. Can we be perfectly authentic, that is, "wholly one's own person?" No, of course not. According to Sartre, not even God can do that. But can we *strive* to be clear about who we are and what we are doing, about our self-conceptions and our self-deceptions? I think that most of us do that most of the time. It is one of the more obnoxious pretensions of contemporary European philosophy to make authenticity (like "genuine thinking") seem like something rare and unattainable except for the exceptional philosopher (or, for the postmodernists, something laughably naïve). True, there remains an ideal of total transparency and transcendence that is unattainable, as are perfect virtue and final truth. But to be cynical in the face of that ideal is at least as serious a mode of bad faith as not recognizing or trying to pursue the ideal at all.

7

NO WAY OUT

Sartre's No Exit *and "Being-for-Others"*

The distinguished theater critic Eric Bentley, writing of Sartre's *No Exit* (*Huis clos*) many years ago, noted that "having assembled all the elements of a bad and deeply conventional play, Sartre has gone on to make a good play out of them."[1] *No Exit* does indeed have all of the ingredients of a cheap formulaic melodrama, and it is important to appreciate that this is exactly what Sartre intended. The bourgeois setting, plot, dialogue, and theme are what Bentley calls "commodity literature," which Sartre uses as raw material. But Sartre, as we know, was anything but sympathetic to bourgeois culture, and it is the bourgeoisie that is his target rather than (or as well as) his intended audience. The setting (leaving aside its extraordinary location) is a cliché: A Second Empire drawing room with kitsch décor down to the details, especially the massive bronze ornament over the mantelpiece, the three brightly colored and uncoordinated sofas. (The tacky furniture is a target of ridicule as the play opens. One of the characters [Garcin] confesses, "I had quite a habit of living among furniture that I didn't relish" [3]. A few moments later another character [Estelle] expresses horror at the thought of sitting on a vivid green sofa that would clash with her pale blue dress. These are trivial concerns, but Sartre goes out of his way to make this look like a usual bourgeois drama.)

The plot (leaving aside the extraordinary circumstances) is standard drawing room drama, a triangle of mutually antagonistic characters going at one another and trying to maintain their dignity if they cannot achieve victory. The three main characters, Joseph Garcin, Estelle Rigault, and Inez Serrano, are not unfamiliar types. Not one of them is a bourgeois (although Estelle clearly aspired to be accepted as one, having grown up in poverty). Garcin is an intellectual and a self-styled "revolutionary" (note that only he gets the formality of being called by his last name). Inez is lower class and self-righteously vulgar. But their behavior and their ways of treating and dealing with one another would have been perfectly familiar to a Parisian bourgeois audience. They are all three flawed and nasty individuals, each in his or her own way, and consequently they will not, and could not possibly, enjoy either heavenly peace of mind or one another's company. They are, all three of them, self-centered manipulators. They are adulterers, deceivers, marriage wreckers. Estelle is also, we find out, a murderer, a baby-killer, who provoked her lover to kill himself. Inez drove her lover to murder and suicide. (Her guilt-ridden lover killed both Inez and herself by turning on the gas.) Garcin was not only an adulterer but much worse. He tortured his wife by bringing his women home with him and making her serve them break-fast. There is no question of innocence for any of them, despite their initial protestations. The philosophical theme, familiar to us from *Being and Nothingness*, is the impossibility of attaining authenticity, especially given the extraordinary circumstances.

And what are those extraordinary circumstances? Garcin, Estelle, and Inez are recently dead, and the drawing room is in Hell (or Purgatory, Sartre's onto-theology not being very committal one way or the other). Sartre is on record, of course, as a vehement atheist, making the setting and the circumstances deliciously tongue in cheek. His attitude toward eternity is also predictably indifferent and merely ironic. The play starts on a casual note, "Hmm! So here we are?" and ends similarly, "Well, well, let's get on with it. . . ." The peculiar logic of a play set in Hell, of course, is that nothing can ever happen and no one can ever do anything, ever again. Toward the end of the play, Estelle tries to stab Inez, and they all end up laughing at the absurdity of this act. These people are already dead to the world, even if they seem very much alive—to us.

"Hell is other people" (*l'enfer, c'est les autres*) is the well-known punch line of the play, but the piece does not depend on being set in Hell to evoke a profound and disturbing truth about people and their relations with others. It is all about what Sartre calls "Being-for-Others," and the play summarizes and dramatizes one of the most contentious and upsetting aspects of Sartre's philosophy. (Being-for-Others, Sartre emphasizes, is a basic ontological category, on a par with Being-in-Itself and Being-for-Itself, despite its late treatment in *Being and Nothingness*.) "Being-for-Others" is not a dimension of human existence that we have dealt with much in the course of this book, except, notably, in our discussions of Sartre's bad faith and, as an absence, in Camus' *The Stranger*, but it runs through both Sartre and Camus like a powerful underground river, only rarely surfacing but always a major de-terminant of the experiences that are misleadingly described as individual and "for-itself." For the thesis, sporadic and inconsistent in Camus but an explicit and fundamental dimension of Sartre's phenomenological ontology, is that our interpersonal relations with others are always major determinants of our experience, including, especially, our experience of ourselves. "Being-for-Others" also invites bad faith, even as it makes it increasingly confusing exactly what bad faith is. But the centrality of Being-for-Others is often underestimated in the shadow of existentialist "individualism."

Furthermore, Being-for-Others plays an important role in Sartre's view of death. Death is not exactly a topic in No Exit, but it is obviously its underlying theme. Sartre elaborates his view of death (by way of an attack on Heidegger) in Being and Nothingness. The thesis demonstrated in No Exit, however, is more indirectly suggested in Sartre's popular 1947 essay, "Existentialism as a Humanism," where he casually notes that "the genius of Proust is nothing but the totality of the works of Proust." That is, all that remains of the great French author are his works and his reputation, which are now entirely in the hands of other people. This is quite different from the usual understanding of Sartre on death, which is most directly opposed to Heidegger's supposed celebration of Being-unto-Death. In general, and against Heidegger, Sartre adopts a line from Epicurus, that "death is nothing." But unlike his ancient Greek counterpart, Sartre does not draw the overly simple conclusion that "death is therefore nothing to fear." No Exit gives us a very poignant and insightful reason why we should fear death, and that is the total loss of control of our own identities. Heideggerian authenticity aside, our fear of death has nothing to do with "Being-unto-Death" or "nothingness." Death, too, has a good deal to do with the hellishness of "Being-for-Others."

Three Characters in Search of Each Other

One does not expect Sartre to come up with appealing characters. His Roquentin in Nausea, for example, is about as unlikable as a protagonist or a narrator can be, making even Dostoevsky's Underground Man look rather kindly by comparison. The major characters in the Roads to Freedom trilogy are either cardboard, hypocritical, arrogant, or pathetic—or some combination of these. They are not particularly admirable or even memorable (cf. Camus' Meursault or Clamence. Of course, they both have the advantage of having the stage to themselves). But it would be a big mistake to read No Exit just in terms of the characters or the play as a multiple-character study, as, for instance, The Plague is a multiple-character study despite the overriding concern of the epidemic. No Exit is a drama about relationships and Being-for-Others. It is not a posthumous bildungsroman. There are no tales of self-discovery or personal development. These characters are done with, with nowhere to go, nothing to learn, and nothing to do. The story is about how they interact. We learn little of much interest about Garcin, Inez, and Estelle, except that they are creepy people who bring with them dark but hardly submerged secrets. *No Exit* is a play about poisonous relationships, and what we see is how three poisonous and finished characters relate to each other. The play is all about being recognized, characterized, and identified by other people, both the other characters in the play and the characters outside of it—in the wings, so to speak—*the still living* who appear only in the three deceased persons' otherworldly visions. Nevertheless, the opinions of the survivors weigh heavily on the thoughts of the deceased. The deceased are, we come to see, nothing but what is made of them, both by the living and, in this curious situation, by the dead.[2]

Thus I disagree with Daniel Maxwell's suggestion that "*No Exit* is the perfect existentialist 'laboratory' to study three separate individuals who are divorced from the world and people they knew. Left in an empty room/cell, their actions and feelings will thus define exactly who they really are."[3] This misses and at the same time underestimates the severity of the problem and the dilemma that Sartre wants to present to us. The problem is that we *cannot ever* "define exactly who [we] really are," either with or without the help (or intrusion) of others. As conscious beings, "We are what we are not, and we are not what we are." Moreover, we are not immune to what others think of us, we are necessarily "for-itself-for-others." But the dilemma is that we are not what others make of us, either, nor are we ever free from what others make of us. This is the dilemma of freedom in the face of Being-for-Others. Am I what they think of me, or not? To what extent are "they" right about me?

At least two of the three characters, Garcin and Estelle, are particularly and pathetically "interested" in the opinions of others. (Inez is oddly resigned both to her fate and to her lousy personality. Garcin pretends to be indifferent to the views of Inez and Estelle, but he is anything but indifferent to what his still living comrades are saying about him.) Theirs is a shared destiny, however, they have a collective as well as an individual problem, and they are anything but "three separate individuals who are divorced from the world and people they knew." They are transfixed by what is happening "below" (or "above"—Sartre's eschato-topography again being none too clear). Estelle spends her first moments spying on her own funeral (but how long is a moment in Hell?). She is appalled by the fact that no one is crying, and then she watches helplessly as her "best friend" goes off with one of her former lovers. And Garcin listens intently (but also helplessly) as his former comrades gossip about him and abuse his memory. Inez, of course, has no one left, but even she watches helplessly and in horror as her old room is rented to a heterosexual couple who lie down on her old bed. She has "disappeared." She really is dead to the world. (She realizes, "All of me's here, in this room.")

But are they "separated from the world and people they knew"? Well, yes and no. They can no longer act in the world. They have no effectiveness.

They cannot even make their views and opinions known. But nevertheless they remain vulnerable to the views and opinions of others. (In that sense, perhaps, they are very much like some victims of divorce.) Indeed, in sharp contrast to the dialectic of arguments, views, and self-definitions that they engaged in while alive, their lives are now wholly defined by other people. Eventually, it is true, the world fades away, and the three are left on their own. But who they were (and consequently who they are), what their lives amounted to, that remains in the hands of the living, who will soon forget about them. It is that, of course, that we fear most: not death, not nothingness, not dying, not "missing out on the party," but being wholly forgotten. Which raises the curious question, although Garcin seems determined not to consider it, of whether it might be better *not* to be remembered than to be misunderstood. Would it be worth it to be immune to the pricks of criticism, misinterpretation, anger, resentment, envy, and jealousy of the living, which even the most carefully managed reputation cannot prevent, but at the cost of being—nothing? Ecclesiastes might thus be read as an odd bit of optimism.

To say that the play is about relationships and to complain that the characters are cardboard is not to say that *No Exit* should be understood by way of an abstract schema in which the particular characters are of no particular importance. Their particular personalities fuel the tension among them. But what are these personalities, and what do they represent? Many years ago, when I first read the play, I was told that each of the three characters of *No Exit* represented one or another basic element: Estelle was "airy," Garcin was fluid (watery, I guess), and Inez was made of stone. But however attractive such an interpretation might be in some forms of literary criticism, I do not find it very convincing. Since then, I have more philosophically seen the three characters interpreted as each representing one of Sartre's three ontological categories, and thus as abstractions. In one version, Garcin is said to represent Being-for-Itself; Inez, Being-in-Itself; and Estelle, Being-for-Others. Thus it is argued that Garcin is wholly absorbed in his identity crisis ("A man is what he wills himself to be"), Inez is the most solid and straightforward of the trio, and Estelle is wholly dependent on male admiration and support.

But despite his pretensions and objections, Garcin is anything but independent and "for-himself," and Inez is hardly just a "thing." It could even be argued that she is the only one who is not in bad faith (or is least in bad faith). She matter-of-factly echoes Sartre: "You are nothing else but your life" (*Tu n'es rien d'autre que ta vie*), but Inez has no one left to make anything of her. This leaves entirely unanswered, however, the question of what *we* are to make of her (and what she is to make of herself) in the very peculiar postmortem situation in which she finds herself. If she is in "good faith" regarding her life, does that put her in bad faith about her current state? This much is true: the dialectic among the characters is at the same time a dialectic among the ontological categories. It is just a naïve oversimplification to identify each character with one and only one logical category. The dialectic is not just among the characters but also, like Hegel's "master–slave" dialectic (to which Sartre frequently alludes), *within* the consciousness of each of the characters. Indeed, the tensions would be unintelligible otherwise.

The three "inmates" (or whatever) are diabolically thrown together, as Inez points out. They do indeed act as torturers of one another, and this is virtually guaranteed by the arrangement. Just to say the obvious, Garcin is a womanizer, Estelle is a coquette, and Inez is a man-hating lesbian. Any sniggering sexual fantasies the reader or the audience member might fancy about some eternal ménage à trois is ruled out from the beginning, whether or not such an arrangement might be possible with three more compatible sexual partners. (I see no reason to rule this out a priori. We are routinely if unconvincingly assured that our standard heterosexual two-party romances can last "forever" and the blessed couple will live "happily ever after.") Estelle makes a play for Garcin and he responds, to be sure, but Inez's murderous looks and verbal barbs are more than sufficient to deflate any arousal. Inez attempts to seduce Estelle, but Garcin's presence is enough to keep that from happening.

Not that sexual entanglement would have improved matters, even for a few moments. Even if we do not accept Sartre's cynical view of sexual desire, and even if we could ignore the vicious triangle, the personalities of the characters would ensure the quick and disastrous failure of any attempted liaison. Garcin is not only habitually unfaithful but abusive, Estelle is both flighty and unfaithful, and Inez openly admits that she enjoys making others suffer. Sexuality, we all know, just increases the pressure and the problems that two (not to mention three) already troubled and troublesome people face together. And it is hard to imagine even a civil conversation among these three misfits. One need not accept Inez's fatalistic and slightly paranoid speculation that "they thought it all out to the last detail" (14), or Garcin's belated and unacknowledged echo, "everything's been thought out" (45), to appreciate that this particular "concrete" arrangement will have a dialectic that is fated to have a disastrous outcome.

Nor can they simply ignore each other, as Garcin so strongly urges. ("No, I shall never be your torturer. . . . So the solution's easy enough; each of us stays put in his or her corner and takes no notice of the others.") He would like to reduce the complexity of the situation to his wrestling only with himself, removing the tension among the characters, and just trying to resolve the tension between his facticity and transcendence, his Being-in-Itself and Being-for-Itself. But Estelle needs his approval, or at least his recognition, and she keeps intruding on his solitude. And Inez is not one to leave well enough alone. "When I say I'm cruel, I mean I can't get on without making people suffer. Like a live coal. A live coal in others' hearts. When I'm alone I flicker out." So when Inez and Estelle soon find things to talk about, Garcin's futile attempt at isolation is destroyed. He feels the eyes of the others "burrowing into his back." But even he needs an audience, and he comes to realize that they are caught in a kind of web. If any one of them moves, the others feel a little tug. "Alone, none of us can save himself or herself; we're linked together, inextricably." This, for Sartre, is a general and genuine ontological insight. The one-dimensional tension between facticity and transcendence is always interrupted by Being-for-Others. Relationships always determine—even if they do not always trump—personal identity.

It has often been commented that the setting of the play is not unlike the forced entrapment of the citizens of Paris during the Nazi occupation, when *No Exit* was written, suggesting the unrelenting surveillance by the Gestapo in Paris. It is because we are trapped and dependent on one another, not just for spooky effects or on some peculiar eschatological whim of Sartre's, that no one can leave the room. It is a situation that would have felt all too familiar to Sartre's early audiences. At one point, fairly well along in the play, the door of the room suddenly opens (just after Garcin has complained, "Anything, anything would be better"). Inez teasingly urges him to go, but he won't ("No, I couldn't leave you here, gloating over my defeat"). Inez finds the situation a "scream." Estelle sets to push her out the door, but Inez begs to stay, and Garcin surprisingly defends her ("It is because of her I'm staying"). One is reminded of that delicious Luis Buñuel fantasy, *Exterminating Angel* (1962), in which the bourgeois dinner guests find themselves unable (for no obvious reason) to leave the dining room. In the Buñuel film, the guests slowly starve to death, whereas in Sartre's play the inmates of Hell seem to be beyond any need for food. But it is of considerable significance that they more or less retain their need for sex. Sex is, unlike hunger, not just an appetite, a physical need. It involves a need for other people, a kind of recognition, an ontological need which does not end with the end of mortal life. Interminable confinement does not lessen this need but, rather, inflames it.

The Tangled Web: Deceit and Self-Deception

No Exit is a morality play in which the peculiar moral (as in most morality plays) is a very general one, "Being with other people is Hell." But, more specifically, *No Exit* is a play about truth and deception, confession and disclosure, self-deception and self-revelation, alliances and enmities; and its rather perverse but perceptive moral is "Everybody lies," both to themselves and to others. Philosophers usually talk as if lying and deception were the ultimate moral transgressions and, as a precondition for living together, not all that pervasive. Australian philosopher Tony Coady probably speaks for most philosophers when he writes, "Dishonesty has always been perceived in our culture, and in all cultures but the most bizarre, as a central human vice. Moreover the specific form of dishonesty known as lying has generally been scorned, and the habitual liar treated with contempt. There are perfectly good reasons for this."[4] But, he adds, "We should note that this perception is consistent with a certain hesitancy about what constitutes a lie and with the more than sneaking suspicion that there might be a number of contexts in which lying is actually justified." He reminds us that Plato defended "the noble lie," and the ultrarespectable English ethicist Henry Sidgwick suggested that a "high-minded lie" in the direction of humility might do us all a good deal of good.

It was Nietzsche who asked, "Why must we have truth at any cost anyway?"[5] It was an odd question from the philosopher who prided himself, above all, on his brutal honesty. Nietzsche is famously skeptical about truth, and consequently cynical about truth-telling, even if he more often than not celebrates his own (unusual) virtue of truthfulness.[6] In fact, philosophers have often enjoyed fantasizing whole cultures composed of liars, if only as a source of deliciously self-referential paradoxes. The neo-Marxist notion of "false consciousness" has further reinforced the idea that a whole society could be in self-deception (a view with which Sartre is quite sympathetic). And insofar as self-identity must be characterized in terms of some personal narrative, Sartre would insist that we are all prone to self-deception, fooling ourselves, in particular, about who we are. And because the narratives we tell about ourselves and about others are so closely and often confusingly linked to the narratives others tell about us and themselves, deception and self-deception cannot be easily separated. Bad faith, which makes use of both self-deception and the deception of others, pervades our lives and our relationships.

Garcin, Estelle, and Inez talk to each other, fraudulently declare their innocence to each other, then hesitantly and inauthentically confess their crimes to each other. With the possible exception of Inez, they are profoundly self-deceiving. With the possible exception of Garcin, they blatantly lie to each other. (I allow for a possible exception here only because his Garbo-like withdrawal allows him to say nothing for much of the play.) Garcin, Estelle, and Inez form shifting coalitions to exclude the third party (for the dubious reason that it is easier to fool one person than two). To be sure, they are an unusually deceitful lot, but whatever their individual vices, the play is also about the logic of disclosure and deception, including bad faith. The presumed ideal of human communication (doggedly defended, for instance, by such diverse philosophers as Jean-Jacques Rousseau and Jürgen Habermas) is *transparency*. But Sartre, following Nietzsche, does not buy this for a moment. Not only is bad faith inescapable but, because bad faith is inescapable, the deception of others would seem to be inescapable, too. Or, put the other way, because the deception of others is necessarily a critical feature of our living with each other (*What would it be to tell everyone everything?*), bad faith is always a logical temptation, if only to make what we think consistent with what we say.

And yet, Sartre seems to share the Rousseauesque ideal. (So does Nietzsche, which is how he can praise his own truthfulness as a virtue.) For

Sartre, that is why bad faith is "bad" and blameworthy. And certainly in the realm of public discourse, Sartre insists on truthfulness. Indeed, it would otherwise be impossible to understand his fifty years as a journalist and his participation in the Vietnam War Tribunal with that other skeptical champion of the truth, Bertrand Russell. But one can be philosophically skeptical about the existence of the external world and nevertheless be careful not to step in front of a truck. One can also be philosophically skeptical about the possibility of avoiding bad faith but nevertheless be outraged at being deceived and be ashamed of lying. One can get indignant when a friend is in denial, and become filled with anxiety and anger when one is accused of doing the same. Even if the complexity of the self (including Being-for-Others) is such that there is no ultimate "truth" about the self to be told, there may yet be good reason for aspiring to clarity about oneself and transparency with others. For the characters in *No Exit*, clarity and transparency are not just the price of getting along but the only possibility of salvation, whatever that may mean in Hell.

Garcin, Estelle, and Inez may all recognize the truth of this, but it is not what they do. It is in the shadow of the Rousseauesque ideal that we watch Garcin, Estelle, and Inez unfold their deceptive and self-deceptive strategies. Garcin, of course, both endorses and promotes the strategy of non-disclosure, thus avoiding deception but embracing and protecting his own self-deception. When he is forced to disclose, he lies to the others by way of lying to himself. But his lies are more in the form of half-truths and selective focus rather than outright lies. Estelle is so deeply in denial that there is no logical space between her self-deception and what she says to the others. Nevertheless, she is quite willing to lie to get the sympathy and attention of the others. Inez does not seem at all self-deceptive, but she obviously thinks of truth-telling in merely instrumental terms, as when, acting as Estelle's mirror, she viciously lies just to be upsetting. At the end of the play, she threatens to do the same thing to Garcin, with far more harmful consequences.

Among the strategies of deception and self-deception are the characters' strategic alliances, shutting out the third person, however tentatively and temporarily (especially given "the auspices of eternity"). To eliminate someone as a recipient of disclosure can be an effective means of protecting oneself not only from his or her lies but also from his or her *mattering*. If a person does not matter, what he or she thinks does not matter. And if one dismisses the person to whom one lies as not mattering, one can more easily deny being a liar. While it may sound cynical, this strategy has a distinguished pedigree. Saint Thomas of Aquinas made the point that a falsehood does not count as a lie if the question is unwarranted or if the questioner does not deserve to know the answer. (So Kant's Good Samaritan would not be lying if he refused to answer illegitimate questions about the whereabouts of the man hiding in his cellar, and Bill Clinton did not lie when he refused to answer personal questions about his sex life.) By dismissing another as "not mattering"—and all of the characters in *No Exit* do this at one time or another—one can maintain one's version of one's own identity without being subject to the opinions of at least one other. However, one cannot do this with everyone (despite adolescent bravado to the effect that "I don't care what anyone says"), so forming strategic alliances is a way of selecting and controlling one's audience, like a politician who insists on speaking only to loyal members of his own party.

Thus Garcin initially attempts to isolate himself from the others and isolate Estelle and Inez from one another as well, but this strategy fails. He cannot insulate himself from both of them, nor do they have any interest in isolating themselves. In fact, as soon as Garcin withdraws, Inez sees her opportunity to come on to Estelle. But Estelle senses the trap and starts to withdraw from Inez, who responds by going on the attack. Estelle tries to shut her out by turning to Garcin, who, defeated in his initial strategy, responds to her seductive pleadings and joins her effort to isolate Inez. But Inez refuses to be ignored, and in the end, it is Garcin and Inez who seem doomed to spend eternity together, as Estelle becomes irrelevant—at least for the moment (but a moment in eternity, remember). At which point Estelle tries to eliminate Inez altogether, by killing her (stabbing her repeatedly with a conveniently placed paper knife). But—the "joke" of the play—is that she is already dead. (Both women break into laughter, and eventually Garcin joins them.) It is not news that we will do almost anything not to be reminded of our own self-deceptions, but ultimately, there is no escape. There is no isolation, no insulation; and no strategic alliance will hold.

Garcin and Estelle have plenty of reason to lie. It's not just that they have secrets that they are ashamed of; they obviously do not know how to come to terms with those secrets themselves. Inez, by contrast, has no secrets but plenty of shame. She has suffered a lifetime of disrespect, abuse, and humiliation. Better in such circumstances to come right out and define oneself as mean and vicious, beating the others to it. It is also easy enough to imagine pretty Estelle as the serial object of desire of many men, but being desired is addictive, and while one might consider it a position of great control, it more often than not turns out to be oppressive, putting oneself at the absolute mercy of others. "They all want me, but what do they want of me and why? And what about that one?" Thus one turns out needing to be wanted not just by those who do want one—who are always plentiful—but also by those who do not. But the very idea of appealing to no one, after a lifetime of lovers! So Estelle is needy and confused. She will do anything to be appealing. She turns to Garcin, and is even briefly drawn to Inez. She is, indeed, as close as one can imagine to pure Being-for-Others. The awful thing is that she is not at all exceptional, except perhaps in her very limited Hell-bound range of choices.

And then, of course, there is Garcin, needy and existentially confused Garcin. It is not a woman he needs (although he will gladly take one if available), but confirmation, salvation, validation of his lionlike boldness (as Inez so teasingly points out). He is even willing to accept validation from

Estelle, who will gladly trade it for a little affection, but he realizes all too well what such bought and traded affirmation is worth. "Yes-men" (or women) are worthless as outside evaluators. Their opinions, as mere reflections of what one wants to hear, no longer count as Being-for-Others. And Inez, of course, is quite happy to stand by and shout the contrary opinion.

It is one of the most familiar sources of bad faith, the desperate need for other people's good opinion of us, our willingness—often unwittingly—to take other people's opinions about us at face value and as simply true, the pressure to conform. But we are not so simply defined or molded by others, and if freedom means anything, it means being able to resist the views and opinions of other people. "Standing up for one's own convictions" (for example, political or social opinions) is but one of many forms of such resistance. Closer to home is our ability to resist the views of other people about our own characteristics: whether we really are as dumb, or as slovenly, or as ignorant (or as smart or charming) as they say we are. One aspect of this, in turn, is not only our ability to counter their observations and evidence with evidence of our own (and redefine the selective process for picking out such evidence) but also our ability to make resolutions and resolve to be different and act differently in the future. To be sure, there are considerable individual differences between us: how much "willpower" we have, how desperate we are for approval from others, how independent or autonomous, but the problem of Being-for-Others is not dependent on any particular character traits, strengths, or flaws. We should note that all of this interplay of deception and self-deception takes place in a context in which, one would think, the truth no longer matters. After all, Garcin, Estelle, and Inez are dead. But it is the nature of Being-for-Others that what people believe to be the truth will always matter, even long after it could possibly matter *to* the person in question.

One might well object, as Garcin does, that their reputations do not reside just in the hands of the living. There are also *the facts*. So it was a fact that Garcin ran an underground newspaper for many years. It was a fact that he wept and pleaded before the soldiers shot him, that is, it was a fact, at least, that he acted like a coward. And it was a fact that he treated his wife cruelly. It was a fact that Inez seduced her cousin's wife. It was a fact that Estelle had an affair, it was a fact that she had given birth to and killed her baby, and it was a fact that her lover committed suicide. But the problem of the play is that the facts are not self-defining, and they do not simply present themselves. Nor are we (in the audience or on the stage) entirely clear what they are. It certainly doesn't help that all three characters begin by lying to each other, and they continue to do so. But neither is it evident whether they are also lying to themselves about the facts. Even in the world of the living, the facts are subject to selection, weighting, and interpretation. What do the facts signify? What does running an underground newspaper for years amount to? Is it necessarily courageous, or could it, too, be a matter of camaraderie, a left-wing version of conformity, as it is for so many young "radicals"? What counts as "seduction," if the result is by mutual consent? Compare the troublesome problem of "date rape." What counts as "consent" in such circumstances? And at what point—before, during, or after— is consent to be ascertained? Consequently, at what moment does the "fact" of seduction take place?

Even the most deceitful people feel compelled to appeal to facts (whether or not they have to make them up). The facts seem to be the anchor points for whatever narrative fabric we want to weave. But the facts do not "speak for themselves." The facts don't speak. And when we are talking about human behavior, of course, it is rarely a question just of facts. It is also about intentions, and intentions are not themselves facts. What was the intention behind Garcin's extended commitments? Need there have been any such intention? Certainly we would not expect that among his intentions was "to be courageous" or even "so people will think I'm courageous." Indeed, any such explicit intention would detract from his subsequent claim to have been courageous, and often our intentions are not explicit at all, even to ourselves. (One need never formulate much less articulate the thought of what one intends to do.) Intentions require interpretation, extrapolation, speculation, even on the part of the agent. They are not given as "facts."

This is even more the case when the intentions in question are not one's own but those of another party. It is a fact that both Estelle's and Inez's lovers committed suicide, but who was to blame? Even if the suicide follows the offending act immediately (Estelle's killing the baby) or the cause is otherwise obvious (Inez's relentless pestering of Florence), it does not follow that the one act causes the other. The intervening variable is the suicide's own intentions and his or her interpretation and signification of the acts or events in question, and these, too, will be a matter of interpretation, extrapolation, and speculation. Inez tells us that her cousin, too, died because of her affair. After she seduced Florence, the cousin's wife, he was killed by a tram. This wasn't suicide, but it could be argued that nevertheless his death was caused by their actions, perhaps due to his extreme distraction and despair—a point that she evidently never tires of pushing on poor Florence. But here, it seems, there is not even an intention to focus on, just one unfortunate fact following another unfortunate fact. Even in the case in which the suicide leaves a note, we should remember that this may be his or her last opportunity to affect and manipulate his or her immediate world. Sobering, too, is Camus' Clamence's observation in *The Fall*: "What's the good of dying intentionally, of sacrificing yourself to the idea you want people to have of you? Once you are dead, they will take advantage of it to attribute idiotic or vulgar motives to your action" (75–76). The awful truth is, killing oneself is handing oneself over to Being-for-Others, abandoning any continuing effectiveness in one's world on one's own behalf. And Estelle and Inez both illustrate this by simply dismissing the significance of their lovers' suicides (and their lives as well).

The underlying, inescapable point of *No Exit* is that we are stuck with each other. Like the characters in the play, we, too, cannot leave each other alone. We need each other, not just for comfort but for our very existence, that is, our human existence, our existence as one human being among others. We care about (though not necessarily *for*) each other, and we are therefore vulnerable to each other. Indeed, it is even misleading to suggest, as Sartre does, that "existence precedes essence," as if each of us is born into this world alone. We are born of and into a world populated by other people, and, in the words of St. Exupéry (quoted by Sartre's existentialist colleague Maurice Merleau-Ponty), "Man is a network of relationships, and these alone matter to him."

Moreover, we want (or think we want) transparency in our relationships. But we have all wondered, at least on occasion, "Who really knows another human being?" Even with those with whom we are most intimate (or, perhaps, especially with those with whom we are most intimate), we sometimes find ourselves facing a cipher. And the more we care, the more likely this is to happen. The more we care, the more intensely we interpret, we interrogate, we speculate, until the distinctions between what we need, what we want, and what we see have utterly disappeared. When we really need each other, deception and self-deception are virtually inevitable. When the network becomes a web of entrapment, what Sartre often summarizes as *viscosity*, it is not as if this mutual dependency eases up. The ferocity of relationships makes them all the more intense. As Sartre points out in *Being and Nothingness*, hatred makes for more intimate bedfellows than does indifference, and in *No Exit* he demonstrates this in painfully "concrete" form. It is not just that "Hell is other people." It is that Hell is always *these* other people, whoever they may be.

Being-for-Others and the Metaphor of the Mirror

We want to get other people to define us as we would like to define ourselves. This is the dynamic of Being-for-Others, the idea that the self is in tension between what we would make of ourselves and what others would make of us. The other, one might imagine, is a mirror in which we not only see but also define ourselves. Consequently, we put on fronts, we "make faces," we present ourselves and "pose" selectively, and we often use deceit and duplicity as strategies, sometimes combined with self-deception. But one could reasonably charge that as soon as one starts to think in terms of presenting ourselves and "posing," we are already in the realm of deceit and duplicity, if not of self-deception.

The characters in *No Exit*, who are not very virtuous to start with, continuously present themselves and pose to each other, often lying whether or not they also lie to themselves. After refusing to acknowledge that she did anything wrong, Estelle eventually confesses to having cheated on her husband, getting pregnant, running off to Switzerland to have the baby and drowning it in front of her lover, who then shot himself in the face. It is hard to imagine a more gruesome scenario, but Estelle seems genuinely perplexed about why she should have ended up in Hell. When she tries to look at herself, by way of presenting herself to the others, she holds the pose of the confused innocent. So, too, Garcin feigns innocence and presents the others with a very well-edited selection of facts about himself, omitting the critical facts about how he died. He wants to see his courage and boldness reflected in the eyes of the others who are now his mirrors, or if not that, his ruth-lessness, his cruelty. (Remembering his wife, by contrast, he bitterly recalls, "She never uttered a word of reproach. Only her eyes spoke. Big, tragic eyes.")

Inez, the most forthright of the three, unhesitatingly admits that she seduced her cousin's wife and drove her to murder-suicide, but precisely in order to challenge the confabulations of the others. She uses the others as mirrors, but she expects to see no more than what she has put there, her mean and nasty working-class soul ("I prefer to look you in the eyes and fight it out face to face"). She, unlike Estelle, needs no mirror to confirm that she still looks "all right." Her role in the play is to call the others on their lies, to act as their mirrors, reflecting the truth. But she also ends up lying. Not about herself (she is so filled with self-loathing that no truth is too awful to see) but to the others, and especially to Estelle, who "interests" her. In what is possibly the most impressive scene in the play, Inez offers to be Estelle's "mirror" (in the absence of any physical mirror) and describe in detail her appearance (18–20). This is a profound bit of writing, and it illustrates better than anything else in the play the complexities of Being-for-Others. Estelle looks into Inez's eyes, but she hardly sees herself at all. (This is an old vampire movie scene: the dead don't see themselves in mirrors.) Since Estelle can't see herself "properly," Inez acts as her "eyes," reporting what she sees, guiding her hand with the lipstick, approving ("far better, crueler, your mouth looks quite diabolical that way"). Already, the "mirror" is not just reporting but interpreting. But then the "mirror" lies outright. Inez asks, with mock horror, "Is that a pimple?" This cuts to the heart of Estelle's conception of herself and establishes Inez in a position of absolute power ("Suppose the mirror started telling lies? Or suppose I covered my eyes and refused to look at you, all that loveliness of yours would be wasted on the desert air"). To someone who exists only by being reflected by others, the mirror is the reality. There is nothing else.

The metaphor of the mirror, however, applies not only to Being-for-Others but also to the nature of self-consciousness and Being-for-Itself as well. The metaphor has much to do with the metaphor of reflection/*reflexion* that can often be found at the base of philosophical theories and ordinary talk of self-consciousness. The phrase "mirror of nature" as a metaphor for consciousness (adapted by Richard Rorty in the title of his most impressive book[7]) reflects the idea that (as Rorty puts it) "pictures rather than propositions, metaphors rather than statements, determine most of our philosophical convictions" (12). Rorty traces the metaphor back to the *speculum obscurum* of St. Paul and finds it in Shakespeare as well as throughout modern philosophy. But the crux of the idea as Sartre employs it is the mirror as reflective not of nature but *of the self*. It is the self that exists only through consciousness, self-consciousness. Sartre's notion of intentionality, furthermore, includes a denial of any such "representational" view of our knowledge of the world. But the metaphor of the mirror suggests something profound about the peculiar "double" nature of self-consciousness.

On the one hand, it is one of the special peculiarities of first-person experience that we are "immediately" aware of ourselves. On the other hand, we are aware of ourselves through the perspective of other people. In short, self-consciousness is not mere awareness of oneself (one's "consciousness of consciousness") but a reflection of the self (or ego), "a being outside, in the world, like the self of another" (*Transcendence of the Ego*, 31). We have already suggested the complexities and difficulties of this separation of consciousness and the self, but for our purposes here we need not concern ourselves with the nature of consciousness. Our concern is about the self and (in that sense) *self*-consciousness and its relation to "reflection." But there are two very different senses of "reflection" here, the sense in which one "reflects" on him/herself and the sense in which one is "reflected" in the eyes of other people. The mirror imagery plays on the visual dimensions of this metaphor, starting with the idea that one is literally reflected, mirrorlike, in the pupils of another person's eyes. (Estelle comments that she can see herself in this literal sense in Inez's eyes, but, she notes, "I'm so tiny.") But this, of course, is just the beginning of how one person is "reflected" in the eyes of another.

Sartre's basic thesis, which has formed one of the underlying philosophical structures of this book, is that there are two different perspectives for viewing the self: the first-person viewpoint and a third-person point of view. The first-person point of view is the only one that accounts for *experience*, as one can be directly aware of only his or her own. (There is no way of saying this that doesn't sound trivial, but it is anything but a trivial thesis, and it has profound implications.)[8] But reflection, by contrast, seems to have no such "privileged access." To the contrary, its theses and perspectives are open to others as well. For example, the reflection "I am a selfish person" is not "privileged" in any evident sense. Others may recognize this (of me) more readily than I do myself. As a practical matter, of course, no one else may be in a position to know all that there is to know about a person, *in part* due to the fact that one has only his or her own experience. (I try to be the only one around most of the time that I am acting selfishly.) But this is, one could argue, merely a contingent matter. A mind reader or psychic might well have as much relevant information as the person him- or herself (avoiding the question whether such knowledge might count as one's own experience). In cases of bad faith or self-deception, furthermore, a person may well know or acknowledge considerably less about one's self than others do. So reflection or "thetic consciousness" might just as well be the product of good information as of personal experience. ("Positional consciousness," by contrast, would seem to be limited to the first person.)

This distinction between first- and third-person perspectives, however, leaves out what is most significant in our concern with Being-for-Others, the *second*-person point of view. Thus Sartre has to radically amend his phenomenology. That is what is at stake in the mirror scene in *No Exit*. Estelle might have experienced a sore spot on her cheek and known right away that it was a pimple. Or she might have noticed one of those brief looks of disgust or disapproval by Garcin or Inez as they glanced at her cheek. In real life she could have adopted or accepted the thesis that she had a pimple on the basis of all sorts of evidence or third-person testimony. (For instance, she could see a photograph of herself or read a gossip column in which this was commented upon.) But in the play it is in the *interaction* between Inez and Estelle that the scene gets its power via the peculiarities of the second person. Without understanding the willful *manipulation* that is involved, one would not understand the scene at all. It is not what Inez sees or what is the case, but *what she tells* Estelle, that makes all of the difference. Being-for-Others, as the very phrase makes clear, is not a mere factual matter, nor could it be a merely first-person phenomenon. Philosophers have long argued over whether one could even have a *concept* of other people if there were in fact no other people. The consensus is that, at the very least, this requires what *seem* to be other people, even if (as only philosophers and bad science fiction writers would imagine) they are only robots or holograms. Being-for-Others is about relationships, but not about relationships as such, relationships as matters of fact. (It is a fact that *X and Y are married.*) It is, rather, a question of what relationships are like "from the inside." It is still a matter of phenomenology, but it is not just a question of *first*-person experience. It is *second*-person experience—experience of others experiencing oneself—as well.

In *Being and Nothingness*, this is the focus of Sartre's well-known discussion of "the look" (*le regard*). Sartre begins with an analysis of shame, and in chapter 3, shame provided us with a third example of an experience that overwhelms all arguments. The arguments in question have to do with the skeptical challenge of *solipsism* in which the philosopher is unable to prove the existence of anyone other than himself. In shame, there is no doubt about the existence of the other. In *No Exit*, the characters may be narcissistic, but their proximity and confrontation with each other make any semblance of solipsism, which presents itself to Garcin, at least, as a welcome escape from other people, utterly impossible. Not that Garcin, in particular, doesn't try when he suggests that they all retreat to their separate sofas, look away from each other, and keep silent. In *Being and Nothingness*, Sartre refers to the philosophical problem as "the reef of solipsism," and he focuses on

Husserl, Hegel, and Heidegger and argues that the problem can be solved only by giving up "the affirmation that my fundamental connection with the Other is realized through *knowledge*."[9] That is, we do not know other people by observing their behavior and then inferring that this is caused by consciousness (as is our own). From the point of view of "knowledge" (evidence and inductive logic), it is possible, at least "logically," that I am in fact the only conscious being in the world. But we are aware of other people in a very different way. This is exemplified in shame.

In shame we do not observe or "know" other people so much as we are observed, we are judged (negatively, in this case). We are *looked at*. In shame, Sartre says, we are *immediately* aware of the other person's consciousness. No philosophical argument to the contrary could convince us otherwise. And so it is on the basis of shame and other such experiences that the reef of solipsism is phenomenologically dissolved. In the scene with Inez and Estelle, one might object, the emotion in question is not shame but embarrassment. After all, Estelle is not *to blame* for her pimple. But the principle is exactly the same: it is an emotion (a form of consciousness) that is constituted by (and only by) one's direct awareness of oneself by another. This need not involve blame. Embarrassment does not involve blame, only self-consciousness induced by another. There is also that form of shame, distinguished in French (*pudeur*), which consists of feeling naked or inadequate or ugly but nevertheless without blame. For the sake of Being-for-Others it does not matter that Estelle is being manipulated, that she has no pimple, or that her awareness of herself is so pathetically focused on what is most "superficial" about her. It is enough that she is forced to "see herself" through the eyes of another. What she sees, horrifies her, but even if it pleased her immensely, her being nevertheless remains in the hands (eyes) of others.

Estelle's problem is in fact more general, as it is not just her appearance that worries her. It is her very existence. "When I can't see myself I begin to wonder if I really and truly exist. I pat myself just to make sure, but it doesn't help much" (19). We can understand the power of Inez's manipulative lie as putting into question Estelle's very existence, not just her good looks. The implied thesis is that she exists (as we all do) only by being seen by others. It matters less how we are seen than *that* we are seen. Shunning is a well-known way of reducing someone to virtual non-existence. It is not just a matter of *pretending* that the person is not there. It is making the person feel as if he or she is utterly absent, irrelevant, insignificant, and to make people feel thus is an essential step to making them *in fact* thus. Not calling on a student in class, I have to keep reminding myself, is an extremely cruel and destructive matter, no matter how annoying or disruptive he or she may be. And it is not just a question of "hurt feelings." Exile was treated by the ancients, and continues in many tribal societies, to be a fate as terrible as death. And it is not (as independent Americans like to fancy) just a matter of sheer survival, which sufficient skills and "self-reliance" might resolve. It is existence itself.

Sartre on Death: Why We Should
Still Be Afraid

Although Sartre playfully sets *No Exit* in Hell (since he himself does not believe in an afterlife), he is not so playful about death. Epicurus wrote that death is nothing, and therefore nothing to be feared. In *No Exit*, Sartre is perversely suggesting that death might be something, but that something is merely a shadow of existence, an odd perspective on our lives about which we can do nothing. Heidegger, writing only a few years before Sartre (in *Being and Time*), had seemingly celebrated death and highlighted it, that is, celebrated and highlighted our existential awareness of it as the key to authenticity (*Eigentlichkeit*). Sartre takes this very seriously, and an entire section of *Being and Nothingness* is devoted to the consideration and, ultimately, the rejection of Heidegger's view.

Sartre sides with Epicurus. Heidegger, writing two thousand years later, demurred. Death, he can be taken to be saying, is everything, and not to be feared so much as appreciated as an essential existential insight. That is a hyperbolic interpretation of Heidegger, to be sure, who is by no means clear about these matters and in any case retreated from this morbid philosophy within a few years (after writing *Being and Time*). But there are plenty of examples of what I call "death fetishism" in modern philosophy and culture: the French playwright Antoine Artaud, for one; much of the nihilistic "grunge rock" movement, for another.[10] According to some of these advocates, death is the ultimate (and not just "the last") experience, a view that would have made even Heidegger cringe. But Sartre's view, like that of Epicurus, demands more scrutiny as well. Is it possible or reasonable to be as blasé about death as he would have us believe?

In *No Exit*, death is a setup that involves the mutual self-identities of the three characters, despite the fact that they are dead. One might think that the problems of self-identity end with death, but that is only insofar as we think in terms of the limited phenomenological worry that begins with "Who am I?" and continues to work through that question in life decisions. Nevertheless, there is a larger-than-life matter in question here. I noted that in his popular essay "Existentialism as a Humanism," Sartre tells us that "the genius of Proust is nothing but the works of Proust," that is, there is nothing left of one's potential once one is dead. In the curious context of *No Exit*, this has a bizarre implication. If we were to outlive ourselves, as in the play, the question of self-identity becomes all the more urgent in the absence of any future actions and any possibility of undoing or apology or redemption. Limited to what we have already done in our lives, however, the difficulty of the question is by no means lessened: What is to be remembered? What do we make of it all? what emphasis do we put on this as opposed to that? How do we interpret one's habits and routines (as opposed, for example, to one's more dramatic pronouncements, one's most self-glorifying or self-denigrating self-assertions)? And how do we appraise a person's last moments, which are given such emphasis both in epic literature and in Christianity? In Homer, as in so many American westerns, *how* one dies is of the ultimate importance. In Goethe's *Faust*, as in so many lesser Christian dramas, a last-minute confession changes everything and a soul is "saved." Thus, in one sense, the drama of *No Exit* centers on the man, Garcin, who is tortured by the question self-identity, and how he died. But the question isn't the how as much as *whether* this moment carries any special weight. And the answer is, entirely, it depends what others make of it.

What we most fear in death, I submit, is far more the pain, the process, the indignities of dying rather than death itself. But *No Exit* begins only when all three protagonists are already dead, and we might note that their deaths were quick and there was no suffering. (Estelle died of pneumonia and was only half conscious. Inez succumbed in her sleep to the gas from an unlit stove. Garcin was shot by a firing squad.) In short, two of the main causes for fear about death, the twin agonies of anticipation and suffering, would not have applied. Moreover, as a proponent of the Epicurean thesis, Sartre would not have worried much about the "nothingness" of death, for there would be nothing to worry about. Indeed, in *Being and Nothingness* Sartre suggests that death is nothing more than the termination of life, again, nothing to worry about. Nevertheless, *No Exit* provides us with a very powerful reason to fear death, one that, unlike the more solipsistic reasons above, refers us directly to Being-for-Others. We fear death because we fear what others will make of us. Thus neither Garcin nor Inez will leave the room when they (seemingly) can do so, as neither wants to concede the modicum of remaining control over their lives. It is bad enough to be dead, but to willfully walk away from what remains of one's identity is unthinkable.

But perhaps this burning "existential" question of self-identity also betrays, unintended, that all of this is typical male narcissism, and the real identity questions are more subtly settled by women, whose identities are routinely swept to the sidelines, whose obsessions are therefore not so merely *self*-absorbed, who are more gracefully accepting of Being-for-Others as the human lot in life. Thus Sartre, like Camus, though admittedly with considerable resistance, approaches the distinctively nonexistentialist position that we are, without embarrassment, Beings-for-Others, defining ourselves through other people and our relationships with them. When Sartre's friend Simone de Beauvoir complained (in *The Second Sex*) that women were defined in terms of men, she may have started an extremely important movement to redefine women in terms of themselves, but she also stumbled onto the Confucian sore spot of Sartre's macho existentialism. We are not first of all Beings-for-Ourselves, but Beings-for-Others, and men (as well as women) are nothing but networks of relationships. These alone should matter to us.

8

PATHOLOGIES OF PRIDE

Camus' The Fall

What is Hell? Here is one answer: five straight days of conversation with a garrulous, narcissistic, rather depraved lawyer. This is the text, in fact the entire content, of Camus' brilliant quasi-religious novel, *The Fall*.[1] It is, as the title promises, something of a "downer," a tale of horrid descent, a moral parable for our sick and absurd times. And there is another definition of Hell: it is having "fallen" from the heights of happiness to the depths of despair, from success and virtue to failure and depravity, and bitterly, exquisitely remembering it. On this account, there is no Hell without a Heaven, and it is the contrast between them that makes it so.

Jean-Baptiste Clamence (not his real name) is the garrulous lawyer. He calls himself a "judge-penitent," an ironic but poor description, I will argue, of his current profession. Once a noble and immensely successful "defender of widows and orphans," he now more resembles a black widow spider, waiting as predator for the fly-by tourist in the seediest bar in the seediest section of the seedy inner circle of Amsterdam. His predation consists of entangling the victim (in fact, the reader) in a web of eloquently spun words, demonstrating his unabated skill in presenting, at length, a "brief," protesting simultaneously his guilt and his innocence, and quickly establishing his superiority in the relationship. He is obsessed with his own innocence, "even if we have to accuse the whole human race and heaven itself." But although Clamence (and Camus) offer us a soliloquy on guilt and innocence and judgment and repentance, I think that the more straightforward interpretation of the novel is that it is all about the sources and pitfalls of pride, *self-confidence, amour propre*. Clamence displays a curious pride in his descriptions, first, of his superiority through innocence in his earlier Parisian life, and then by way of his protestations of guilt in the seedy setting of the Mexico City bar in the bowels of Amsterdam.

More gloomily, one could readily conceive of *The Fall* as a meditation on the "deadly" sin of pride. Pride as a sin perhaps need not entail self-confidence, much less superiority, but it is certainly entangled with them. And that introduces a host of ethical (not to mention theological) questions. Is pride indeed a sin, or is it only "false" pride and such that are sinful? Is pride necessarily about something in particular (some accomplishment or achievement), or is it, as David Hume argued, ultimately about The Self *simpliciter*? Do self-confidence and a sense of superiority have to be competitive, a "zero-sum game," or can one feel self-confident and superior without thereby demeaning anyone else? Can anyone be really self-confident in a fickle world, or is every display of self-confidence really a cover for self-doubt and insecurity? (To be sure, this is sometimes the case, but as a general diagnosis, is it anything more than an expression of envious projection on the part of the admittedly insecure?) Do self-confidence and superiority entail invulnerability, or are they, rather, a setup for a "fall"?

It is this last question that defines the plotline in *The Fall*. The implication of Clamence's story is that his fall and his move from Paris to Amsterdam demonstrate the falseness of his sense of earlier self-confidence and superiority and his sense of innocence. It is, thereby, a moral lesson for all of us. Insofar as we maintain a sense of our own self-confidence, superiority, and innocence, we, too, are vulnerable and therefore "false." Instead of pride, perhaps, we should adopt the "monkish virtue" (Hume again) of humility, and embrace the Christian view of humanity as fallen but redeemable.

This interpretation of the book as a meditation on the "falseness" of pride has been powerfully presented by the late Phillip Quinn.[2] Quinn is perfectly aware that the Christian symbolism that pervades every page of *The Fall* is but a tease. Camus is an atheist, and the philosophical setting of the novel is pointedly devoid of the Christian promise of redemption. Indeed, in the final pages Clamence goes into a feverish rave in which he holds up (and takes the role of) Christ himself as an example of the falseness he has been "outing" throughout the book. Quinn, we should note, was a devout and prolific defender of the Christian promise. Accordingly, he suggests at the end of his review a stark choice: "Christianity or nihilism." He ends by softening this and suggesting that there may be some nonnihilistic yet non–Christian way of thinking about all of this, but in the scope of the novel he finds no possibility of redemption. Thus, for Quinn pride is, as it was for Saint Augustine and Pope Gregory, the worst of the sins. It is never defensible, even where it is (in some more limited sense) warranted. Thus even the pride of well-earned success should be subdued by the humbling force of humility, that all-embracing sense of ourselves as essentially flawed and vulnerable beings.

I do not share Quinn's Augustinian Christian viewpoint, and I find the self-image of this pervasive humility offensive. I prefer Nietzsche, whose views on this matter are well known, or Aristotle, in whose ethics pride is a virtue, not a vice. Of course, for Nietzsche or Aristotle, pride may be misplaced. It might be based on literally false self-description, and is thus canceled out by Aristotle's virtue of "truthfulness" or it might be inappropriate to the circumstances or based on defensive resentment, incurring Nietzsche's criticism. But pride as such is neither "false" nor defensive. To the contrary, the ideal of pride in Aristotle's ethics is the *megalopsychos*, the "great-souled man." To us, perhaps, a *megalopsychos* would be obnoxious, but perhaps because we are all so steeped in Christian culture (which is what Nietzsche was so vehemently about). But what *megalopsychos* represents is pride as a virtue and as a primary ingredient in happiness. It is not that the *megalopsychos* cannot fail or fall, but he (or she) does not dwell on that, focusing, rather, on the joys of a successful life, including the exercise of the virtues. This, I think, is how we should view Clamence in his Parisian incarnation, not as an example of false pride but as a striking example of a *megalopsychos*, a virtuous, self-confident, and rightfully proud man.

Clamence's Tragic Flaw

I think the main point to make about Clamence is that in Paris, he is indeed a truly virtuous, fully contented, enviably successful man. His self-confidence is fully warranted. The temptation, especially given his embittered perspective on his past, is to understand Clamence as deeply flawed and as a "two-faced" hypocrite, the view that he presents of himself. But insofar as one can "read through" his deceptive self-description (as one must "read through" Meursault's descriptions in *The Stranger*[3]), there is no reason for accepting this view of Clamence as deeply flawed or as "two-faced." Indeed, the power of the novel is the "fall" of a nearly perfect human being into bitter despair. If it can happen to him, we are forced to realize, it can happen to any of us. On the other hand, if we can discern some basic flaw, for example hypocrisy, in Clamence's character, then we can attribute his fall and subsequent unhappiness to that flaw. And we, who are relatively flawless in that respect, are off the hook.

This temptation to find the tragic flaw (*hamartia*) in the tragic hero goes back to Aristotle, who in his *Poetics* insisted that tragedy should be structured around a powerful, lofty hero with some tragic flaw or disproportion of character that brings him down. It is important that nothing external does this, although external forces might enter in as an afterthought to solidify the failure wrought by the flaw of character. Aristotle was thinking of such tragedies as Sophocles' *Oedipus*, but the analysis might just as well be applied to more modern tragedies, such as those of Shakespeare, *Hamlet* and *Othello*, for instance.

Oedipus, we are told, was obstinate, and would not listen to the sage advice of Tiresias and his wife/mother, Jocasta ("Best to live lightly, as one can, unthinkingly"). Hamlet, we are told, was "a man who could not make up his mind" and Othello was irrationally jealous. But should we see either Oedipus or Hamlet or Othello as flawed? To be sure, they are human, perhaps all too human. But Oedipus is a king out to cure the curse that is afflicting his people. His obstinacy might be better described as perseverance. Hamlet wanted proof. It was not indecision that made him not accept at face value the murderous moanings of a ghost who pretended to be his father. It was prosecutorial integrity. He then faced insurmountable difficulties, not least of which was the fact that his beloved mother was now married to the man he felt obliged to murder. His hesitation before murdering Claudius as he prayed (as distinct from his utter impulsiveness when he thought he was killing Claudius behind the arras) had nothing to do with indecision but was an essential part of his plan to send his uncle to Hell without redemption. And with Othello, would any of us not exhibit the same jealous rage that Iago had so successfully set Othello up for? Othello had no one else to answer to, and isn't the name of that tragic flaw love?

So what work is the theory of the tragic flaw and Aristotle's insistence that the tragic hero must be lofty (a king or a prince, for instance) doing here? It blocks the likelihood of seeing Oedipus, Hamlet, and Othello as people like us, not perfect, perhaps, but tragic despite their virtues, not because of their vices. Thus, insofar as we buy into Clamence's description of himself as overly self-confident before the fall, we find ourselves with a ready rationalization. He fell because he was flawed and because he lived more loftily than we do. It is not that his vulnerability is all of our vulnerability. His pride and extraordinary self-confidence make him exceptional. Quinn is certainly right about Camus' novel being a morality tale on the pathology of pride. But what is that pathology, if it is not (as I contend that it is not) the pathology of pride as such? I would suggest that the pathology of pride, even when it is "true," is rather the pathology of fallen pride, in other words, the pathology of that famously bitter emotion of resentment (*ressentiment*). And resentment would like nothing better than to be convinced of the viciousness, even the sinfulness, of those compared to and contrasted with whom it feels humbled. In Clamence's case, the comparison and contrast are with his earlier self.

Two Worlds, Two Truths

Camus' *The Fall*, like its earlier complement, *The Stranger*, is divided into two parts. In *The Stranger*, the parts are quite clearly divided by the incident (for lack of a better name) of Meursault's murder of the Arab. Before that, he was blithely innocent, essentially mindless, whether one takes that to be simply his nature or the result of a duplicitous prior act of "bad faith."[4] After that, he is in prison and on trial, leading to the development of a Self in this hitherto seemingly selfless and wholly unreflective character. The two parts of *The Fall* are not textually separated, yet are starkly distinct. The first part, which we discern only through Clamence's jaded descriptions, is his self-confident life in Paris as an eminent and successful lawyer. The second part is his subsequent life in Amsterdam as a "judge-penitent," in which he displays a very different and rather dubious form of self-confidence, much of which is taken up with redescribing and reinterpreting his prior life in Paris.

Philosophically, the division is essentially the same in both *The Stranger* and *The Fall*. The first part offers us a life that is devoid of reflection, and thus happily devoid of judgment and guilt. Throughout, Meursault seems as incapable of moral judgment as he is unable to muster up the slightest passion. Clamence makes a big deal of the fact that in his role as defense attorney he is neither judge nor judged. Of course, Clamence's life is much more reflective than Meursault's, if by that we mean that he is thoughtful and clearly knows what he is doing. But it is unreflective in a more serious and contentious sense. He may, unlike Meursault, have a keen sense of his life as a whole. Indeed, that is the nature of his pride. But he maintains his innocence and does not take seriously the possibility of failure or his vulnerability. He refuses to see, or at least take seriously, the palpable presence of other people's envy and resentment. And that innocent sense gives way to part II, in which both characters are held up for judgment by others (and by themselves!) and in which their guilt is made transparent. If the first part is the world of unreflective "lived experience," the second part is the world of reflection, a world defined by self-condemnation. Meursault (perhaps) manages to escape self-condemnation, though the last line of the novel, about being greeted at his execution by "howls of execration" (*cries d'haine*, "cries of hate"), seems to undercut this, whereas Clamence gives himself wholly over to it. It is through self-condemnation, in place of his public courtroom victories on the behalf of others, that he comes to define his new and depraved sense of self-confidence and his superiority over all others.

Lived experience and reflection are presented as contraries in Camus' works. They are not just complementary, nor do they simply represent the complexity of consciousness. The one interferes with the other. Thus Clamence, despite occasional lyricism about the Dutch weather and the quality of Dutch gin and his superior references to the vulgarity of the bartender, is pretty much oblivious to his surroundings. His life in Amsterdam is "caught up" in reflection. Far from him is Queen Jocasta's philosophy—"Best to live lightly, as one can, unthinkingly." He lives heavily, like the gloomy Dutch weather, through embittered and resentful thinking. And through that embittered thinking, he remembers and interprets his earlier, seemingly innocent and noble life as so much of a sham. He offers us several metaphors, all of which point to a "double" life. If he had a professional business card, he tells us, it would be Janus-faced, with the slogan "Don't rely on it." Don't rely, in other words, on the apparent face of innocence and nobility, for the face of the Amsterdam devil is on the other side. He tells us that when he looked in the mirror (after a humiliating experience), his smile was "double." The duplicity refers to his presumed hypocrisy, to the alleged fact that he is guilty while pretending to be innocent, to his apparent selflessness which is in fact, he tells us, motivated by the sheerest self-interest and vanity. On the one hand, there is the world of innocence and nobility, the world of Rousseau's "noble savage" and Nietzsche's ancient noblemen. On the other hand, there is the world of reflection and guilt, the world of Rousseau's corrupt courtiers and Nietzsche's resentful slaves.

Each of these worlds has its own "truth," although the latter world has a decisive advantage over the former. The reflective life is, as Nietzsche tells us, exceedingly "clever," and it can incisively comment on (judge) the relatively naïve world of mere experience. From within the innocent world—that is, a world not yet infected by self-doubt and the fear of failure—the truth is simply the goodness of life, the joy of flourishing, and one's own moral and extramoral excellences. It views the resentment and envy of those who do not share that joie de vivre, that sense of flourishing, and those excellences as sad, even pathetic, but it does not take seriously (or perhaps even notice) their condemnation. But this means that it lacks the means to defend itself against accusations of "elitism" and "superiority," for it does not see these as accusations at all. Thus Aristotle presents his aristocratic ethics "for the best" without succumbing to egalitarianism—though he is keenly aware of the importance of equality within certain well-defined contexts—and he presents his list of virtues (excellences) without defending them. Compare this to the "Why be moral?" obsession that defines modern ethics, as justification becomes needed for what Aristotle saw as simply obvious.

Through reflection and resentment, however, "elitism" and "superiority" are damning accusations, and the resentful critic can easily discern ulterior and underlying motives that the noble soul either would not recognize or (if differently described) would not take seriously. Thus an innocent act can be interpreted as a self-serving one, and a generous or heroic act as a selfish one. All philosophy students are familiar with this game. One *feels* no hint of self-interest in a virtuous act, but this may be self-deception. One's subsequent good feelings betray this, for, after all, mightn't the anticipation of those good feelings (or the possibility of bad feelings of guilt or shame) have motivated the act in the first place? There is no defense against such suspicions, for even Kant was willing to acknowledge that we are in no position to know the actual motivation of our actions. Within the innocent world, it might not matter what the motives are. The act (or the nobility of character) speaks sufficiently for itself. But from the point of view of the resentful world, motives really do matter, for even the best acts and characters can be scrutinized for ulterior motives and the basest actions and personalities can be defended in terms of their good intentions.

To move to the text itself, let me pick one simple example of how Clamence plays this game with himself—and with us. He first mentions how happily he helps those in need, for example, helping elderly or blind people across busy boulevards. He enjoys exercising these simple virtues so much, he tells us, that he goes out of his way to find opportunities to practice them. In this, he perfectly exemplifies Aristotle's virtuous person, who exercises his or her virtues not out of duty or obligation but because he or she *enjoys* doing so. But it is easy to see the vulnerability of such a virtuous person to the scrutiny of the resentful critic. Taking the enjoyment itself as the motive rather than as a secondary consequence (as Aristotle argues in his *Ethics*, book X, sec. 5), the resentful critic rejects the protestations of the virtuous person—if he or she bothers to protest at all—to the effect that the action was "for its own sake" and not for any ulterior motive.

Moreover, small details provide further evidence for condemnation. Returning in his narrative to the same situation, Clamence notes that after helping a blind man across the street, he doffs his hat, an extra courtesy that the blind man could not possibly have appreciated. It is easy to imagine this. One practices such virtues as courtesy until they become unthinking, second nature. In this incident, the gesture was amusingly inappropriate, but certainly innocent for all of that. But from this small oddity, accusations of hypocrisy are quickly forthcoming. It had to be vanity, the argument goes, not a merely automatic gesture. It was *showing off*, despite the claim to be mere courtesy. Thus the seeming virtue of the entire behavior, not just in this incident but in all such incidents, is undermined. Clamence's former courtesies, along with his other virtues, are thus displayed for what they "really" were, the acts of a vain and selfish man and, worse, a hypocritical and "two-faced" man, pretending to be one thing while really being another.

The virtuous Parisian cannot defend himself. He has passed through the novel and exists now only in the memories of this bitter, resentful Amsterdam bum. The Parisian and his world are vulnerable. Just as Aristotle and his virtues come off as elitist and far from moral from the perspective of Kant and his cronies, the virtues of the younger Clamence are dismissed as "false" from the perspective of his later incarnation. The world of innocence is always vulnerable when it is viewed from within the world of bitter reflection. Unless, that is, the world of bitter reflection is itself exposed to its own "truths," and its own motives of envy and resentment are displayed for all to see. This is what Nietzsche does. It is also what Camus does, through his ultimately crazed character Clamence. *The Fall* is not a condemnation of pride, self-confidence, or superiority, but a condemnation of *resentful* pride and superiority, false self-confidence and pride that refuse to recognize themselves as such, superiority that proves itself only by stealth and subversion. In the noble world, one is rightly proud of his or her excellences and accomplishments. In the resentful world one takes pride (if that is the word) not in winning but in bringing the other low. The fall is not due to a tragic flaw at all, but to conniving and self-deception, in this exceptional case the conniving of Clamence's later self against the former.

The Pathology of Pride
(Why Is it a "Sin"?)

If the theme of *The Fall* is self-confidence, superiority, and pride, the book is not a condemnation of self-confidence, pride, or superiority, but a condemnation of resentful pride and resentful superiority, self-confidence based not on achievement but on resentment. It is also about judgment and repentance, which are not irrelevant to the sin of pride—or, rather, to false pride, unwarranted pride, phony self-confidence, and an unwarranted sense of superiority. Such pathologies of pride involve judgment (or, rather, meta-judgments, that is, judgments about the warrant of emotions and judgments). Pride is not, as Hume suggests, merely a pleasant feeling or a pleasant feeling about oneself, which "contains not any representative quality." But, he adds, passions may be "accompany'd with some judgment or opinion," and in this sense they may be "contrary to reason" or "unreasonable."[5] I would add that the emotions are not "accompanied" by judgments but *constituted* by them, so the question is ultimately whether the judgments that constitute pride are themselves defensible. I agree with Hume that they are, or at least can be.

Pride, in particular, is subject to judgment, both within (as constitutive of) the emotion and as meta-judgment about the warrant of the emotion. Ultimately, it is difficult to distinguish these, at least in one's own case. To feel pride is already to judge that one's Self and one's accomplishments are worthy of pride. If others do not or would not agree with that assessment, the possibility of "false" pride, pride that is unwarranted by the circumstances, is quite likely. This is how Christian psychology gets its hooks into pride. By starting with a cosmically unflattering comparison and contrast between a God "greater than whom none can be conceived" and mere human beings, even noble, virtuous, and accomplished human beings, it is easy to see how one might conclude that none of our nobility, our virtues, or our accomplishments are worthy of pride. But why should we accept that humiliating comparison? There is a chicken-and-egg problem here: it is only by accepting the Christian (or some comparable) worldview that one is compelled to conclude that nothing about us is worthy of pride, but the feeling of humility and unworthiness may well impel someone to accept the Christian worldview. This concern is something other than the accusation that pride is a sin because it involves the neglect of worship and awe of God (which is a link to another deadly sin, *acedia*, badly translated as "sloth") or that it implies a kind of narcissism and consequent neglect of both God and other people. If one does not accept the Christian worldview, the neglect of God is no vice, and one can accept the fact that narcissism is no virtue without so tightly linking it to pride. Clamence, in particular, takes great pride in his virtues, and these consist in turn of his attentiveness and aid to others.

The pathologies of pride begin, no doubt, with false pride, unwarranted pride, a sense of self-confidence or superiority that is misplaced or inappropriate. Thus Aristotle opposes boastfulness to truthfulness and counts it a vice (not a sin) because it is either not true to the facts or is inappropriate. But the fact that it is a version of pride does not count against it at all. Only that it is—quite literally—false. But Aristotle's vices typically come in pairs, one of excess, one of deficiency, in contrast to the virtues. Excessive pride—that is, more pride than one deserves—is evident enough. But it does not follow that all pride is excessive or false, that there is nothing for mere human beings to be genuinely proud about. If we tighten our worldview to what Nietzsche called a "this-worldly" perspective, an essentially human perspective, then human virtues and accomplishments are to be judged on their own merits, not in comparison and contrast with God Almighty or the supposedly perfect exemplar of Jesus. Surpassing even Nietzsche, Clamence makes his blasphemous attack on Jesus himself, denying him the perfection that he supposedly represents. Within our human framework, we know perfectly well what is worthy of pride and what is not. Genuine accomplishment and virtuous deeds are worthy of pride, and the life that Clamence has led in Paris warrants and justifies pride if anyone's life does.

Severed from the Christian account in which all localized enjoyment of human life is mere vanity, we can even appreciate what is worthy in vanity. Vanity (as opposed to pride) involves advantages and "blessings" that are not due to one's own efforts or virtues but are rather, one might say, matters of luck. One's good looks, for example (without neglecting the pride one might take in good grooming), or one's natural wit, charm, and intelligence (again without neglecting the pride one might take in hard work and the constant exercise of those gifts). Pride and vanity are thus intertwined and, again, so long as one doesn't condemn all human enjoyment as vanity and all sense of human virtue and accomplishment as false pride, both are to be enjoyed, or rather, to coin an ugly word, they are to be meta-enjoyed, for in pride and vanity we both enjoy our virtues and our blessings, and, in innocent reflection, we enjoy the fact that we enjoy both our virtues and our blessings.

To appreciate the range of such meta-enjoyment, compare what Milan Kundera says about kitsch: "Kitsch causes two tears to flow in quick succession. The first tear says: how nice to see children running on the grass! The second tear says: How nice to be moved, together with all mankind, by children running on the grass! It is the second tear that makes kitsch kitsch."[6] Many human emotions are not only amplified but also transformed through reflection. This may be true of enjoyment as well. Reflection on how one is enjoying oneself may not only enhance the enjoyment but also transform it into something quite different: self-satisfaction, for example. But it can also undermine it, compromising pleasure or even turning it into pain. That is what Kundera would like to do. Thus the cynic that Camus sometimes seems to play suggests that there is something essentially kitsch-like about our enjoyment of our lives, and that reflection on the meaning of life and "the Absurd" reduces all such enjoyment to self-deception. But the details of life are not absurd, as Camus well knew, and human virtues, accomplishments, and "blessings" are apt subjects for reflection, producing the "positive" emotions of pride and vanity.... They need not be matters fit for humiliation.

The corresponding vice of deficiency, in Aristotle's terms, is the Christian virtue of humility, for it is a refusal to enjoy what one deserves to enjoy and is thus detrimental to happiness and the good life. It also leads to an even more serious vice, which Aristotle does not much deign to consider, and that is the viciousness of resentment. For the true "opposite" of pride is not the mere monkish virtue of humility, it is that bitterness with life and all of its blessings that Nietzsche so strongly if not "bitterly" criticizes as the weapon of the weak and those who are sick of life. It is this that Clamence represents.

Clamence's Resentment: Why Did He Fall?

Simone de Beauvoir writes, "When Gods fall, they do not become mere men. They become frauds." Clamence is not a god, nor did he think of himself as one, at least until his over-the-top display of megalomania during his fever in Amsterdam. But he is clearly something of an *Übermensch*, and this is how he thinks of himself when he is "on the heights" in Paris. But for an *Übermensch*, Clamence seems unusually vulnerable. That Nietzschean image certainly carries with it the veneer of invincibility, and it quite explicitly excludes the vulnerability to resentment to which all of us are prone. But this is just to say that perhaps that Nietzschean image is itself too overblown and uncritical, that here Nietzsche himself falls prone to that same "otherworldly" posturing that he so criticizes in the Christian worldview. For is not the image of the *Übermensch* just another comparison and contrast with a superhuman ideal in which we are bound to come out poorly? Indeed, this is what Nietzsche praises as "going under" in the prologue to *Zarathustra*. It is a kind of self-humiliation in conscious comparison and contrast with the "superman" that is not unlike the self-humiliation of the weak and mediocre in conscious comparison and contrast with the nobles that Nietzsche criticizes as "slave morality." But I am willing to chalk this up to Nietzsche's never well-hidden misanthropy, and nevertheless endorse a good deal of his neo–Aristotelian (or in any case aristocratic) ethics, an ethics of excellence and of character as opposed to an ethics of universal rules, not to mention of resentment. Accordingly, I think that we can recognize in the Parisian Clamence an extraordinarily enviable and admirable character. He is not invulnerable and (obviously) he is not invulnerable to resentment, but he is, in his earlier incarnation, as close as any of us can imagine coming to the Western urbane ideals he so clearly embodies.

This is not to say that he is perfect, but his imperfections, I think, can be bracketed as those of a macho Parisian man after the Second World War. His treatment of women, for instance, may be objectionable by contemporary American standards, but I have considerable hesitancy applying those standards to Clamence or to Camus or to Parisian society in the 1950s. In any case, Camus' intention was clearly to present us with a portrait of a most admirable man, and one can bracket Clamence's insensitivities in this regard as reflections of Camus' own less than admirable behavior with women.

But why, then, is Clamence (Camus) so vulnerable? It is important to appreciate how virtue is in fact much more vulnerable than vice. There is a kind of guilt to which all "do-gooders" are vulnerable, for instance it is that sense of never being able to do enough. Anyone who receives more than thirty or forty charity solicitations a month knows what is now sometimes called "donor burnout," that sense that one's generosity is and always will be overwhelmed by the needs of others. And such guilt can also occupy a more insidious dimension, even closer to the conscience. Compassion demands that we (in some sense, to some degree) have to share the suffering of others. But it seems that we never feel enough, our suffering is never comparable to the suffering with which we would sympathize. And, of course, there was a kind of guilt to which Camus was particularly prone. It can be summarized in his need to choose between "his country or his mother" in the Algerian war, and his insistence of being "Neither a Victim nor an Executioner" in the political struggles that followed. Sartre could write with aplomb about "dirty hands," but Camus would have no part of it. He felt guilty no matter which way he would turn. And it is in this context that he invented the ultimately good and guilty "judge-penitent," Clamence.

So, too, Clamence seems doomed whether he is innocent or guilty. One can criticize both Clamence's earlier sense of naïvete and his later hyperreflectiveness. First, he seems wholly unself-critical, then he becomes too self-critical. Again, I am tempted to suggest that this reflects Camus' own ambivalence regarding innocence and reflection, but this, I think, is essential not only to both of the novels that we have been considering (*The Stranger* and *The Fall*) but also to Camus' other works (notably *The Myth of Sisyphus*, his notebooks, and his lyrical essays) as well. How philosophical can one be without falling into the gloom to which philosophy is so prone? ("I tried philosophy," noted Doctor Johnson, "but cheerfulness kept breaking out.") To what extent can one live the life of reflection, which, contra Aristotle, both Kierkegaard and Dostoevsky likened to a kind of disease? Does reflection inevitably lead to a sense of one's own inadequacy? On the other hand, is all innocence just waiting for a fall? Such questions readily lead a good sensualist like Camus either to bed or to the beach, and so, too, Clamence (well, not to the beach, perhaps, but certainly to bed and, ultimately, to a period of debauchery that was still inadequate to shut out the pain of guilty reflection). Innocence and reflection are, for Clamence, one more painful dilemma.

I think one apt diagnosis is that Clamence (Camus?) indulged in *the wrong kind* of reflection, reflection that was already tainted with the otherworldly, with comparisons and contrasts to perfection, and consequently with the seeds of failure and resentment. This is the cost of what Nietzsche called the "shadows of God," our continuing insistence on holding up superhuman ideals of perfection and then declaring ourselves failures or frauds in their reflection. Thus the comparison and contrast with a perfect world makes this one seem "absurd," and the comparison and contrast with either God or Christ or the *Übermensch* renders us pathetic, "human-all-too-human." But let us not take this less than perfect aspect of Clamence as his "tragic flaw." It is just another aspect of his being human, his being much like us—only better. His fall does indeed point to a capacity that we all share, and Christianity provides just one version of it. In this, again, I think Phillip Quinn is right on the mark, but Camus rightly raises the question of whether the Christian worldview is the only cure—or, rather, whether it is the cause—of this state of affairs. True, the world of *The Fall* is, despite all of its Christian symbolism, a Godless world in which redemption—or at any rate *that kind* of redemption—is unavailable. But the despair of the novel cuts at least two ways, only one of which can be read as urging us toward the Christian sense of redemption. The other encourages us to reject that or any worldview whose consequence is that morbid sense of guilt and resentment. I, like Quinn, read *The Fall* as a morality tale, but I suspect that Camus intended it as a rejection of Christian redemption and morality.

But why did Clamence fall at all? Many people live their lives as insufferable snobs and never get their "comeuppance." So why Clamence? I think that here Camus does go back to ancient tragedy, not to the "tragic flaw" theory as such but to the more general Aristotelian idea that what brings the hero down are not external circumstances but, in some sense, his own self. This is not to say that he has a fatal flaw (or even a "disproportionate" character) but only that it is *in some sense* the hero's own doing, and it is just as likely that it will be the result of his virtues as of his vices. Or, indeed, that it just focuses on the hero's self-consciousness. This explains the utter triviality of everything Clamence tells us with reference to the "why?" of his fall. Indeed, it is not even clear—nor does it much matter—whether the events he cites are factual or not. He tells us that he heard laughter on the bridge, but he could not find its source. Immediately after, he hears the laughter of youths on his street, but quickly discovers that it is mere camaraderie and has nothing to do with him, as if to suggest that the laughter on the bridge might just as well have had nothing to do with him either. It does not matter, for the echoes of that laughter continue to ring in his head and do their damage. Mere self-consciousness and reflection is quite enough. But this is not the healthy and happy laughter of amusement or joy, but the unhealthy and unhappy laughter of self-humiliation.

So, too, Clamence tells us that before that event or non-event on the Pont des Arts, there was another incident, also on the bridge, this one the seeming suicide of a young woman. I say "seeming" because Clamence's description makes it none too sure that there was such a woman or, if there was, what happened to her. Clamence's failure to do anything, even notify the authorities, becomes one of the threads that ties his narrative together. Although we get the full (though very minimal) description halfway through the novel, he mentions it (abstractly) very early on, and he mentions it again, in bitter reflection, at the very end of his narrative:

> Oh young woman, throw yourself into the water again so that I may a second time have the chance of saving both of us! A second time, eh, what a risky suggestion! Just suppose, *cher maître*, that we should be taken literally? We'd have to go through with it. Brr...! The water's so cold! But let's not worry! It's too late now. It will always be too late. Fortunately! (147; all exclamation points are Camus')

It may be probable that a young woman did take her life by jumping from the bridge and Clamence did not do anything, but, again, I think that there are good grounds for saying that it doesn't really matter. He exclaims, at one point, "But what do I care? Don't lies eventually lead to the truth? And don't all my stories, true or false, tend toward the same conclusion?" (119). Indeed, reflection has already reached its conclusion, and events and evidence are besides the point. His final exclamation makes it quite clear that the damage is being continually done by the poisonous thought that, were such a situation to come about again, he would still be unwilling or unable to do anything about it. Like the laughter, the source of that poisonous thought—in an actual incident or merely in his imagination—is ultimately less important than the self-undermining, humiliating nature of the thought itself. One can imagine the earlier Clamence contemplating, in the absence of any such prior experience, the likelihood of his jumping off the bridge to save a person's life. With his early sense of virtue and his urge to help others, there is little doubt that he would, and saving that young woman would have been genuine altruism. But that is just what the cynical, reflective Clamence cannot understand, and looking back, he can no longer imagine it. And so again it is not as if the incident caused him to lose faith in himself. Somehow he already had, and we are left with just another description of Clamence's vulnerability.

There are several other bits of narrative aimed at explaining this vulnerability—the traffic incident, which Clamence tries to see as insignificant, and his ridicule at the hands of a woman, for which he exacts a brutal revenge—but the vulnerability, we learn, is not to be explained. As in *The Stranger*, where we get little help understanding Meursault's slippage into more or less "pure" prereflective consciousness, in *The Fall* we get little help understanding the actual mechanisms of Clamence's "fall," that is, his elevation into bitter reflection, "clarity" from his perverted (reflective) point of view. Indeed, it is of a piece with his growing sense of failure and fraudulence, of being less than perfect, of being "two-faced" in his masterful way of dealing with the world and his slavish insecurities. It is from the standpoint of this vulnerability that he learns to practice the duplicitous art of the "judge-penitent," which might better be described as his desperate effort to remain proud and feel superior in the face of his ever-increasing humiliation. He learns to "see through" his earlier façade of virtue—as if it were nothing but a façade—and finds beneath it all of the signs of duplicity and hypocrisy. But it is the duplicity and hypocrisy of the critic Clamence, not any duplicity and hypocrisy on the part of the innocent Clamence, that is betrayed.

Innocence Betrayed: The Seduction Motif

Clamence's narrative in *The Fall* is only secondarily intended to tell a story. It is first of all a seduction aimed at his almost silent interlocutor in the bar and ultimately toward the reader. His strategy, as he finally describes it, is to paint a vivid portrait ("of all and of no one") and then hold it up to the viewer so it becomes a mirror. The point is to seduce the listener to reflect on and judge himself. Like all seductions, it proceeds by stealth and indirection. It seems to be doing one thing, but it's actually doing another. Clamence's narrative seems to tell a story and be a personal confession of guilt, but it's actually setting a trap. Here is the real duplicity: not innocent Clamence as two-faced but resentful Clamence as seducer, using his charm and his verbal skills to mislead and trap his victims. "Don't rely on it," indeed!

How Clamence does this (or how well he does it) is of interest to me, but even more tantalizing is *why* he does it is. The *how* gets to the complex dynamic of interpersonal confession, a fascinating question (with which I have little experience, having spent little time with either priests or psychiatrists). But the *why*, I think, gives us the complex key to Clamence's depraved character. The seduction succeeds by way of getting the victim to scrutinize his own less than perfect behavior with the same cruel persistence and from the same perspective that has undermined Clamence. But why should he do this? What does he get out of it? For even if his accusation of duplicity and selfishness against the earlier Clamence is false and unfair, it accurately characterizes him now. Clamence as we get to know him is a cynic and a narcissist. He always has ulterior motives, and he is always looking to his own advantage. We can be sure that his seemingly tireless efforts to seduce have a payoff for him, but we are never entirely clear on what it is, even when he is willing to tell us (on the assumption that we have by this time been caught in his seducer's web).

My first suggestion has to do with the benefits of confession as such. Clamence boasts to us, in his feverish rant: "The confession of my crimes allows me to begin again lighter in heart and to taste a double enjoyment, first of my nature and secondly of a charming repentance" (142). But what is the "charm" of repentance? In this Godless world, without the possibility of redemption, it is hard to figure out what can be so charming, unless repentance is in some sense its own reward (as the earlier Clamence says of his virtues). But confession is not just the lightening of one's burden. It is also communication with another person, and confession yields a strategic advantage. (It is a huge mistake to think of it as primarily a first-person performance.) He tells us, "I was the lowest of the low," and then he imperceptibly passes from the "I" to the "we" and explains, "I have a superiority in that I know it and this gives me the right to speak. You see the advantage, I am sure. The more I accuse myself, the more I have a right to judge you. Even better, I provoke you into judging yourself."

Throughout his narrative, Clamence keeps repeating variations on the biblical "Judge not, that ye not be judged" theme. At this point, his advice seems to be "Judge yourself, and that will compel others to judge themselves." But elsewhere, he seems to be defending a gunslinger's Golden Rule, "Judge others before they judge you," and, at another point, it is the more sage and strategic "Judge yourself before others judge you." But in the end he finds that all such strategies fail in their ultimate aim, which is to evade judgment, period. Perhaps surprisingly, he does not offer the Nietzschean advice not to judge at all: "I do not want to accuse; I do not even want to accuse those who accuse. *Looking away* shall be my only negation. And all in all and on the whole: some day I wish to be only a Yes-sayer" (*Gay Science,* §276). But it is clear that judging is what Clamence does. It is the world of his expertise.

In the absence of his earlier, enviable role in the justice system and his palpable sense of success and superiority, judging others gives Clamence sustenance and a more subterranean sense of superiority, the dubious superiority that comes with resentment. "Once more I found a height . . . from which I can judge everybody" (142). But then again, he says in his later fever-filled rave that "I was wrong, after all, to tell you that the essential thing was to avoid judgment. The essential thing is being able to permit oneself everything, even if, from time to time, one has to profess vociferously one's own infamy." The confession thus becomes not a means but a cost, the cost of utter licentiousness and self-indulgence. "I have learned to accept duplicity instead of being upset about it."

This licentiousness—"shamelessness" would be a good word for it—is Clamence's ultimate "solution to the problem of guilt," for I think that what it really amounts to is his first replacing pride with shame and then shame with shamelessness, wallowing in it. Clamence boasts, "I yield to everything, to pride, to boredom, to resentment, and even to the fever that I feel delightfully rising at this moment." Hardly an attractive list of "everything," but it is through this utter self-indulgence, this utterly adolescent sense of freedom, that Clamence can declare, "I dominate at last. But forever." Even "How intoxicating to feel like God the father." But what a sick and phony sense of superiority this is! What a terrible example of "false pride." Megalomania is not self-confidence and not the pride of a *megalopsychos*. It brutally exemplifies Nietzsche's characterization of the delusions of superiority in "slave morality" and, sadly, sounds like Nietzsche on his really bad days late in his life. Through resentment, one turns noble values on their head, so that strength becomes weakness and weakness becomes strength. It is when one is most infirm, as Clamence is clearly infirm (in fact, mad), that one entertains these illusions of greatness. "I crush everything under the weight of my own infirmity." It is the ultimate Nietzschean "transvaluation," turning noble values upside down. Being totally down trumps (the supposed illusion of) nobility and virtue.

One might well argue that Clamence maintains his earlier sense of self-confidence and superiority throughout the novel, substituting this perverse and illusory sense for his earlier, seemingly more warranted sense of self-confidence, superiority, and pride. But even if one were to make this argument, it comes at a terrible cost. Whereas the earlier Clamence, as a true *megalopsychos* if not an *Übermensch*, simply took pride in his accomplishments and virtues, with considerable benefit to his fellow citizens, the resentful Clamence gains his sense of self-confidence and superiority only at wholesale cost to others. True, much of his sense of self-confidence and superiority is wholly "in his head," without much effect on other people, but we gather from his intent to carry out serial seductions that his ravings and illusions are by no means innocent. In other words, despite the accusations of hypocrisy against the earlier Clamence, he was in Paris a genuinely virtuous man. But the resentful, recollecting Clamence is not only cynical; he is exceedingly cruel, just ineffective.

No doubt Camus is being ironic when he makes Clamence an advocate for what I have elsewhere called *the blaming perspective*," better known, perhaps, through the harsh moralizing of Camus' onetime friend Jean-Paul Sartre. (There are a great many sarcastic barbs aimed at Sartre and his "atheist café" friends in *The Fall*, and we remember that its writing occurred just after their very well-publicized falling out.) Clamence declares his new basic principle, "No excuses ever, for anyone" (131) and "I am for any theory that refuses to grant man innocence and for any practice that treats him as guilty" (131–132). One could not think of a more direct condemnation of Sartre. In his earlier incarnation, of course, Clamence's philosophy and his legal practice had been all about excuses and extenuating circumstances, excuses of poverty and adversity, excuses of perversity. But here is the author of "Neither Victims nor Executioners" putting words in his character's mouth that would make us all both at once. It is easy enough to see why. The *why* of Clamence's campaign of seduction is nothing less. If everyone is guilty, then (by his dubious logic) he who acknowledges that first has the right to condemn and rise above all of the others. It matters not at all that humanity itself is thus degraded.

The novel also ends on a morbid if familiar note. In the midst of his hysterical raving, Clamence turns to his interlocutor with a desperate plea: "I'm happy, I am happy, I tell you, I won't let you think I am not happy." There should be no doubt that Clamence is *not* happy, and the desperation and defensiveness of his plea make that amply clear. But by now we should be deeply suspicious of Camus' declarations of happiness and his kinky linkage of happiness with death. We are not surprised that Clamence finishes off his plea with "I am happy unto death," but that only reminds us that there is no happiness in death, only loss. Camus' "happiness" is the mania of a hysteric, a final burst of desperation and unhappiness that chooses to express itself in the language of flourishing and fulfillment. That is the ultimate pathology of pride, that it prefers even death to humiliation, and if one fails at happiness in life, then happiness unto death would seem to be the last desperate hope, the final gasp of a bitter resentment.

CONCLUSION

Thinking it Through—Experience and Reflection

I have argued that Sartre and Camus together have given us a phenomenology that is an exquisite exploration of personal experience and at the same time a dark vision of human nature. I have also suggested throughout that an important distinction for both of them is that between lived experience and reflection. I have raised many questions about how the two are related, about how or whether reflection clarifies or rather distorts experience, and even whether it is possible or normal for adult human beings to have experience without reflection. As I said in the introduction, in their view experience and reflection are the twin tracks on which their phenomenology travels in order to illuminate what is both ordinary and extra-ordinary in our personal experience, in our "existence," and in our lives.

So what are we finally to say about experience and reflection, reflection and self-consciousness? Are these faculties at war with one another, as Camus suggests in his two most personal novels and Sartre suggests as well? Or are experience, reflection, and self-consciousness interweaving threads in the fabric of consciousness, in which on occasion one weave may absorb us in its pattern and prominence but always with the others in the background? Just as the "I think" hovers over consciousness in Descartes and Kant, according to Sartre, the "I" hovers over all of our experiences, ready to claim them as one's own. So, too, the "me," whether by way of our vanity, our pride, or our sense of responsibility for past deeds, is never far from our attention. Guilt and pride, for example, are rarely just "episodes" in our lives. They pervade our consciousness and our experience, and they also define a good deal of our reflection—its themes and tones. For human beings, a great deal of consciousness is self-consciousness, and whether or not we feel "trapped" in it probably depends to a large extent on the particular nature of our emotions and reflections.

Sartre's good friend and younger colleague Maurice Merleau-Ponty worried at length about what our experience would be like if we could pry reflection and self-consciousness away and were left with just the experience alone. This has much to do with how thoroughly language and linguistic ability transform and pervade consciousness, and a moment's reflection makes it clear that we can't easily think of our world or even experience it without our categories, our distinctions, our metaphors, our choices of verbs—all possible only through language. But "intelligent" animals have experiences that are not so linguistically defined, so it must be "like" something to have an experience without language and, presumably, without reflection. But the question of selfhood is not of a piece with questions about language and reflection. Thus it does not follow that self-consciousness requires language or reflection, and it then becomes important to distinguish these. It might be that if we could pry away reflection and language as Merleau-Ponty suggested we would still be left with self-consciousness.

That said, we need to ask where to situate self-consciousness in the supposed polarity of experience and reflection. Meursault is illustrative. He is minimally self-conscious, compared, say, to Clamence in *The Fall*. But to what extent is self-consciousness constitutive of selfhood? That is one of the problems that Camus (and Sartre) set us. Sartre and Camus write as if reflection on the self is self-consciousness, but then, is self-consciousness a species of reflection, or is it a bridge between experience and reflection? This is by no means clear in either Camus or Sartre, but it does suggest that there is something very wrong with the opposition to start with.

I think the many twists and turns we have explored in this book in the selected writings of Camus and Sartre show pretty clearly that the polarity is overstated, that "pure experience" is virtually an impossibility for human beings, as is pure reflection, however much philosophers since Socrates have pretended otherwise. Nevertheless, the polarity makes a certain dialectical sense insofar as it encourages us to pay more attention to experience and to be critical of reflection and give it the same celebratory status that philosophers have tended to give it (usually under the title of "reason," of course). Moreover, Sartre and Camus push us to explore a much neglected question in the history of philosophy, and that is the nature of *agency*, and with it, freedom and responsibility. But is agency a matter of experience; that is, is it experienced? Many philosophers, for instance Hume and Schopenhauer, have talked about "the Will" as if it were obvious that we are immediately aware of our own agency. But Nietzsche provoked Freud and many of us when he casually declared, "A thought comes when it will, not when I will." Thus he opened up the question of agency in a radical way, one which is taken up in interesting ways by both Camus and Sartre.

Thus the pivotal scene in *The Stranger* is the murder scene. I commented in chapter 1 that Meursault's crime was barely an action. He may have been aware of the heat, the sun, the sea, a black speck that might be a ship, the wind, and the light, but there is little indication of any agency as opposed to his simply being part of the causal chain that led to the death of the Arab. All we are told of the murder is, "The trigger gave, and the smooth underbelly of the butt jogged my palm." There is not the slightest indication of Meursault's *doing* anything at all. So, too, Sartre insists that much of our activity in the world is devoid of an "I," here presumably the "I" of the Will. I experience "the streetcar to be overtaken," but I do not experience *my* doing anything. Nevertheless, this is clearly an action. But whose action is it? It cannot be anyone's other than mine. But then what is the status of agency? Is it necessarily experienced? Is it necessarily experienced as self-consciousness? In Sartre's larger phenomenology of consciousness and action, this problem becomes basic to the whole project. Sartre's aim is to show that we are responsible for everything that we do, and the reason for this is that consciousness *is* freedom. Thus my self-consciousness of myself as an agent is clearly central to Sartre's entire philosophy. But insofar as consciousness is "spontaneous" ("the instantaneity of the pre-reflective cogito") it looks as if what we do is neither voluntary nor willful. So how can we be responsible?

Moreover, we have to ask how much of our self-consciousness is *mediated* self-consciousness—that is, reflected through the eyes and judgments of others? How much of reflection is *our* reflection, as opposed to other people's thoughts and opinions that we have unthinkingly absorbed and adopted as our own? Indeed, it has often been argued by philosophers that reason isn't one's own at all, but rather we share it with everyone else, even with "all rational creatures." It may be a "faculty" of the individual mind, but the principles and insights it taps into are not a matter of the individual mind at all. Thus Hegel argues that human consciousness in general is something we all share. The reflections that constitute his great *Phenomenology of Spirit* are emphatically not Hegel's own (except, of course, for the purposes of authorship and academic tenure) but the reflections of the human spirit writ large and throughout its development. But the first point that Hegel (or Spirit) makes in that book is that there is no separating experience from reflection; there is no "unmediated" experience; that experience is always already reflected experience. Thus we should ask, how much of our experience is *our* experience, as opposed to vicarious or even merely imagined or remembered or surreptitiously shared, borrowed, or just plain stolen?

This might sound absurd—the idea that our experience might not be *our* experience, but think of a typical contemporary experience, watching a movie. What you see and, more important, what you *feel*, is to a very great extent determined by the actors, the director, the cinematographer, the scriptwriter, and so on. There is a trivial sense, of course, in which your experience is *your* experience. But there is also that familiar sense, if the movie is a thriller, or a romance, or a political documentary, that you might well feel "manipulated" (which is why you chose to see that movie in the first place) and that your experience in this critical sense is *not* your own. In a museum, looking at an excellent painting (say, a Caravaggio), what do you see? Odds are that you see what your art or art history teacher or textbook taught you to see, informed by all the knowledge of the artist and the epoch and of Italian art that you can bring to the moment. Again, there is that critical sense that your experience is actually *not* your own. One can raise such doubts even in the most personal perceptions, such as watching a sunset from a rocky crag in Western Oahu. How much of what you see is framed and informed by the postcards you have seen in the Honolulu airport and over the course of your lifetime? Have you ever sat and watched a tropical sunset *as if* it were a postcard? And how often have you entered into a marital squabble only to realize (to your considerable humiliation) you are just repeating the dialogue of any number of unimaginative, even witless, television or theater sitcoms? In other words, the "mineness" of even our most personal experiences is open to question.

On a different note, the early Sartre makes a big deal out of the need to either "live or tell," as if we cannot both be absorbed in an adventure and develop its narrative structure at the same time. But I think that this is more intriguing than Sartre makes it out to be. In one sense, we are almost always our own narrators, even in the thick of action. That is how we make sense of our actions, even as we are absorbed in them. There are levels of narration, however, and indeed we may not see the bigger picture, but nevertheless, we are always living a story. But, as above, it is an open question to what extent it is truly our story, our creation, and to what extent we are living out plot lines that have been inculcated in us for years. The voice we hear may well prove to be the voice of someone else (one's mother or father, one's harshest critic, one's best friend, the anonymous voice of "conscience," or an old cartoon book script). But there is no living without telling, even if only inarticulately and inaccurately. In Sartre's own case, I would say that the telling *is* the living. Thus the tyranny of words that despite his many protests he never left behind.

Experience and reflection are not only not opposed but are inseparable and, to a large extent, indistinguishable. Neither experience nor reflection are clearly our own, so our feelings and thoughts are not so clearly our responsibility after all. But doesn't this leave us all rather like Meursault, who on this analysis emerges not as "strange" but as a genuine representative of the human condition? This is, again, what appeals to all of those undergraduates for whom the novel is their first glimpse into the strange new world of existentialism. But for those of us who want to follow Sartre, at least in his campaign for personal responsibility, this is a huge problem. I want to end the book by saying a few more words about it.

The problem, again, lies in Camus' and Sartre's dichotomous thinking: bad faith versus good faith, reflective versus pre-reflective consciousness. But I noted earlier that there are many further distinctions—between reflection and self-consciousness, between a conscious process being reflective and being attended to—and then there is *noticing* what is going on, and "barely noticing" as well. There is thus no simple dichotomy here but several complex dimensions of self-awareness. From our more or less habitual behaviors to fully conscious deliberate actions, there is an enormous range of senses in which one can be conscious of or reflective in one's engagements. Insofar as an engagement is articulated or "spelled out," there are many ways in which one can describe it, some of them evasive, some of them insightful, some of them extremely misleading, some of them cynical, some of them unwittingly revealing. Insofar as any engagement is avowed, there are always alternative avowals, ranging from straightforward "taking ownership" to devious acknowledgments and admissions that evade the issue at hand. (Think of the now standard political phrase, "mistakes were made...")

Sartre is probably right that we do not usually attend to, fully spell out, and consciously avow our actions and our engagements. In our ordinary behavior, for example, it is only on rare occasions—such as when we are trying to break or alter a habit—that we actually attend to the habit and its accompanying sensations, and it is usually when we are trying to explain or justify ourselves (even to ourselves) that we spell things out in much detail. It is when we are challenged, perhaps when our commitment is questioned, that we actually avow our engagement. But even where it is a deliberate action (which already involves "spelling out" as well as avowal, once the decision is made), we do not always or even usually pay close attention and continue to spell out our action once the action or engagement has been "launched." But the various levels of attention and reflection form the complex fabric of consciousness. Most of the time, we may barely notice what we are doing and what we feel, but this would still seem to count, in Sartre's phenomenology, as reflective consciousness.

The next phase of phenomenology, I would suggest, should include a much more careful and fine-grained analysis of the many "levels" of (self-) consciousness. I want to end by suggesting that it is the interplay between them that accounts for much of the complexity of human consciousness. Fully conscious (articulate and avowed consciousness) may not play the major role that many philosophers seems to presume it does, but pre-reflective consciousness in the sense that Sartre defines it plays a pretty negligible role, too. Nevertheless, the constant possibility of reflection in all its variations is what accounts for the most important single feature of human existence, certainly according to Sartre, and that is *freedom*. When, at the end of his career, he softens his early insistence on "absolute freedom" in his oft-quoted statement, "the idea I have never ceased to develop is in the end that a man can always make something out of what is made of him,"[1] the idea remains that we are free to make something of ourselves and responsible for the result. That is a welcome bit of existential advice for all of us, in this world of victims and martyrs, in which variations of bad faith and cynicism have become something of an art form. There is a lot of empty and hypocritical talk about "freedom" these days, but much too little appreciation of what freedom really means, namely, *responsibility*. For that alone, Sartre (and Camus) remain philosophical beacons, despite their often grim thoughts and dark portraits of human experience.

NOTES

Introduction

1. In a lecture in 2003 ("Sartre at One Hundred"), Thomas Flynn of Emory University mentioned five reasons why Sartrean existentialism would grow in relevance to contemporary philosophical discourse. Coming from a longtime Foucaultian, I took this to be encouragement from an unexpected source. Flynn listed:

The concepts of presence-to-self and being-in-situation
The theme of "committed" knowledge and literature
The theme of existentialist "authenticity" ("the sole existentialist virtue")
The related notion of responsibility
Existentialism as a "way of life," a form of (Greek) "care of the self" (*epimeleia heautou*).

2. In an interview in 1959, Jean-Claude Brisville asked Camus, "What's lacking in your work?" Camus candidly and with a hint of obvious regret answered, "Humor."

Chapter 1

1. Camus, *L'Étranger* (Paris: Gallimard, 1942), translated as *The Stranger* by Stuart Gilbert (New York: Knopf, 1946). I have long preferred this more lyrical translation to the several others available, including the new, American, "more literal" translation by Matthew Ward, which has replaced Gilbert's translation in the Random House (Vintage) series (New York, 1989). The British translation, for instance, ends with the words "howls of execration"; the American, with "cries of hate."

2. Camus, *L'Étranger*, edited by Germaine Brée and Carlos Lynes, Jr. (New York: Appleton-Century-Crofts, 1955), vii.

3. Camus, *La Mort heureuse* (Paris: Gallimard, 1971), translated as *A Happy Death* by Richard Howard (New York: Knopf, 1995).

4. Camus, introduction to *The Stranger*, in 1955 edition by Brée and Lynes.

5. Rachel Bespaloff, in *Camus*, edited by Germaine Brée (Englewood Cliffs, N.J.: Prentice-Hall, 1962), 93; John Cruickshank, *Albert Camus and the Literature of Revolt* (Oxford: Oxford University Press, 1959); Breé, in her *Camus*, 7, 12.

6. Conor Cruise O'Brien, *Albert Camus* (New York: Viking, 1970), 21.

7. Ibid.

8. Jean-Paul Sartre, *Saint Genet*, translated by Bernard Frechtman (New York: George Braziller, 1981).

9. But see also, for a much clearer and more responsible treatment, Richard Moran, *Authority and Estrangement* (Princeton, N.J.: Princeton University Press, 2001).

10. G. W. F. Hegel, *The Phenomenology of Spirit*, translated by A. V. Miller (Oxford: Clarendon Press, 1977), ch. 1, "Sense Certainty," in which the notion of an unconceptualized particular ("this") is rejected.

11. J. L. Austin, "On Pretending," in *Essays in Philosophical Psychology*, edited by Donald F. Gustafson (New York: Anchor, 1964), 99–116. The essay (for the Aristotelian Society) was inspired by one of the few early analytic classics on the philosophy of emotions, Errol Bedford's "Emotions" (reprinted in the same volume, 77–98).

12. O'Brien, *Albert Camus*, 22–23.

13. David Sherman, "Camus's Meursault and Sartrian Irresponsibility," *Philosophy and Literature* 16 (1995): 60–77.

Chapter 2

This chapter was originally the first chapter of my favorite of all of my books, *The Passions* (New York: Doubleday,1976). I have tried to retain as much of that original as possible, updating some of the references (most of which concerned the magical delusions of the 1960s), filling in the arguments, and adding my reflections from thirty more years of reading and teaching Camus' book. In *The Passions*, the aim of the chapter was to set up what I called "the new romanticism" and a philosophy that would give the passions their due. Here, my aim is just to comment on and try to clarify Camus' *Myth of Sisyphus*. All references to *The Myth of Sisyphus* are to the Justin O'Brien translation (New York: Random House, 1955).

1. David Sherman, "The Absurd," in *The Blackwell Companion to Phenomenology and Existentialism*, edited by Hubert Dreyfus and Mark Wrathall (London: Blackwell, 2006).

2. Hayden Carruth, "Introduction," in Jean Paul Sartre, *Nausea* (New York: New Directions, 1964), vii.

3. This is actually rather confusing. Sisyphus (according to one tradition), snatched death away from the gods and thus rendered all men immortal. He was thwarted in this attempt, obviously, and in punishment for his crime he was condemned. So, in a sense, Sisyphus was already dead. He carried out his punishment in the afterlife, in what we would consider Hell. But in Hell, he is immortal, in the sense that he will never die and his punishment will never cease.

4. An excellent meditation on the agony of living forever is Bernard Williams's now classic essay, "The Makropulos Case: Reflections on the Tedium of Immortality," in his *Problems of the Self: Philosophical Papers* 1956–1972 (Cambridge: Cambridge University Press, 1973), 82–100.

5. Morris Raphael Cohen, *Preface to Logic* (New York: Meridian Books, 1956).

6. Thus Heidegger, following Kierkegaard, sharply distinguishes those "syllogisms" that merely give us the impersonal conclusion that we are going to die from the profound realization, "Being-unto-Death," that we are indeed going to die. The difference here, one might argue, is also the difference between sound argument and objective truth versus the intense subjectivity of the actual experience of confronting death.

7. Colin Wilson, *Anti-Sartre* (London: Borgos Press, 1981).

8. Ibid., 10.

9. I will make much of this distinction later on, when I discuss Sartre, who too willingly conflates the two. Sartre further confuses matters by insisting both that (1) the self appears only with reflection and (2) there is a kind of self-consciousness ("the pre-reflective cogito," "Being-for-Itself") on the pre-reflective level of consciousness. But Camus was not worried about any such distinctions.

10. Robert Meagher, ed., *Albert Camus: The Essential Writings* (New York: Harper Colophon, 1979).

11. Friedrich Nietzsche, *The Gay Science*, translated by Walter Kaufmann (New York: Random House, 1968).

12. Plato, of course, was already way ahead of the game in his understanding of the myriad options that were available in the understanding of "justice." But whether the concept of good and evil is as crass as "good for me, evil if not," or as enlightened as Socrates' high-flown defense of spiritual virtue, the "naturalness" of the demand for justice is not questioned, even by Thrasymachus, who puts forward the crassest and most cynical interpretation of it.

Chapter 3

1. As reported by Simone de Beauvoir. I have taken this account of the incident from Colin Wilson, *Anti-Sartre* (London: Borgos Press, 1981), 12.

2. Jean-Paul Sartre, *Being and Nothingness*, translated by Hazel E. Barnes (New York: Philosophical Library, 1956). The point about not reading back into *Nausea* the philosophical positions defended in *Being and Nothingness* has been ably defended by Ashok Kumar Malhotra in his book *Jean-Paul Sartre's Existentialism in Literature and Philosophy* (Oneonta: State University of New York Press, 1995).

3. The song title is "Me and Bobby McGee." Kristofferson claims that he came up with the idea, against the protest of his musician friends, when he had just suffered a near total setback in his life, including divorce and apparent failure. The song and the idea were memorably "covered" by Janice Joplin a few years later. This is a point on which I seriously disagree with Malhotra, who claims that freedom is treated as an important theme in *Nausea*. The freedom defended there is quite the opposite of what Sartre later defended for most of his life, that freedom is first of all responsibility. Few characters in literature, except perhaps Camus' Meursault, have been less responsible than Roquentin. Freedom, to him, means the realization that it is all meaningless and arbitrary, so that he has no ties or obligations.

4. Again, I respectfully disagree with Malhotra, who says that *Nausea* is all about emotional insight, whereas *Being and Nothingness* is thoroughly conceptual and philosophical. But Sartre had already thought through and published his "sketch" of a theory of emotions, and in that essay he makes it quite clear that this traditional duality is unsupportable.

5. As reported in Annie Cohen-Solal, *Sartre: A Life*, translated by Anna Cancogni, edited by Norman McAfee (New York: Pantheon, 1987), 116.

6. Edward R. Royzman and John Sabini, "Something It Takes to Be an Emotion: The Interesting Case of Disgust," *Journal for the Study of Social Behavior* 31, no. 1 (March 2001): 29–60.

7. Malhotra points out that one of Sartre's pervasive literary devices in *Nausea* is his more or less systematic switching of person, object, and animal descriptions, for instance, describing a hand as a crab (134), a man's face as the face of a dog or a young woman's mouth as looking like a chicken's backside (166), a house with a heart (168), a garden that smiles (181), and, most important of all, objects as living beasts (19). Malhotra, *Sartre's Existentialism*.

8. See, for example, Charles Hartshorne, *The Ontological Proof* [of God's Existence], reprinted, in part, in Robert C. Solomon, *Introducing Philosophy*, 8th ed. (New York: Oxford University Press, 2005).

9. Wilson, *Anti-Sartre*, 4.

10. One obvious way of understanding this—and sharply contrasting Roquentin's outlook with the author's—is to compare the famous passages from "Existentialism as a Humanism" in which Sartre says that since our "existence precedes our essence," we have no given purpose in life, but nevertheless have obligations not only to ourselves but to all humanity.

11. In current analytic jargon, Sartre's would be an "externalist" account of consciousness.

12. Jean-Paul Sartre, *Being and Nothingness*, translated by Hazel Barnes (New York: Philosophical Library, 1956).

13. Hazel Barnes writes in her introduction to *Being and Nothingness* that "a full explication of *Nausea* would require the whole of *Being and Nothingness*" (xi). But I will also suggest that Sartre is making at least one profound point in *Nausea* that he could not make in *Being and Nothingness*, for it is, to a significant extent, an argument against philosophy.

14. Edmund Husserl, *Ideas*, translated by W. R. Boyce Gibson (New York: Collier Macmillan, 1931), 76.

15. One consequence of this, very au courant in more recent postmodern circles, is the notion that there are no true stories. See, for example, Hayden White, *The Content of the Form: Narrative Discourse and Historical Representation* (Baltimore: Johns Hopkins University Press, 1987).

16. Robert Nozick, *Philosophical Explanations* (Cambridge, Mass.: Harvard University Press, 1981).

17. Jean-Paul Sartre, *Existentialism as a Humanism*, translated by Philip Mairet (New York: Philosophical Library, 1949).

18. This classic formulation is credited to Bertrand Russell, "On Denoting," *Mind* 14 (1905): 479–493.

19. Husserl, *Ideas*, 76.

20. Thus there was a rather tedious debate in the 1960s about whether the *cogito* was intended as an argument, an inference, or a "performative," a term that was much in vogue in those days from J. L. Austin. Jaakko Hintikka,

"Cogito ergo Sum: Inference, or Performative," *Philosophical Review* 71 (1962): 3–32.

21. I am (obviously) borrowing from Sartre's *Being and Nothingness* analysis of nothingness, replacing his friend Pierre with Roquentin's friend Anny (*Being and Nothingness*, 40ff.).

22. I will stick with the English "anxiety," despite the more dramatic connotations of "angst" and the more romantic perfume of *angoisse*. But the reader should keep in mind the unusually philosophical sense of the word, much like the unusually philosophical sense of "nausea" that Sartre employs.

23. Some of this rests on Sartre's peculiar but very deep philosophical conviction that consciousness itself is nothing, and so cannot be about itself in the way that it can be about any object. Thus he calls consciousness "Being-for-Itself," in order to indicate that its existence consists solely in its self-recognition *as opposed to* the cognition of objects or "Being-in-Itself." We need not get stuck on this or on Sartre's various reasons (historical, ontological, and those having to do with his insistence on freedom as the being of consciousness). It is enough to say that anxiety, as opposed to fear, involves an awareness of one's own consciousness rather than an awareness of anything in the world.

24. Charles Guignon points out that even though Sartre may think he's following Heidegger here, they in fact hold opposite theses. Heidegger thinks that the no-thing is an openness to future possibilities, while Sartre believes that the world is a "plenum," that existence is "full." See his *Heidegger's Theory of Knowledge* (Indianapolis, Ind.: Hackett, 1977).

25. I should qualify this in a surprising way. Carefully reading through *Being and Nothingness*, looking for statements denying the scientific standpoint, I was somewhat surprised to find that insofar as Sartre talks about science at all, it is quite positively, and I would even say that he presumes, if not defends, a weak version of scientific determinism.

26. I am thinking in particular of the distinguished English philosopher A. J. Ayer, who early on seems to have confused Sartre with Dr. Joyce Brothers and dismissed him out of hand for thinking that "if one tried, one could do anything."

27. Aristotle, *Nicomachean Ethics*, translated by W. D. Ross (Oxford: Oxford University Press, 1929), 109f.

28. *The Transcendence of the Ego*, originally published as *La Transcendance de l'égo* in 1937, translated by Forrest Williams and Robert Kirkpatrick (New York: Noonday Press, 1957).

29. *Being and Nothingness*, 315, 318.

30. Ibid., 319–321 and passim to 329.

31. Ibid., 330, 335.

32. John Stuart Mill, *A System of Logic* (Honolulu: University Press of the Pacific, 2002).

33. Most notably, Ludwig Wittgenstein has a now famous "private language argument" in which he takes on the problem and, through a series of still somewhat mysterious hints and suggestions, indicates the problem regarding even developing language of mental states if those states are in fact unavailable to anyone other than their subject. Language and its referents, he argues, must be public. So even if there are private mental states, the argument goes, we would not be in a position to name them or refer to them, and we could not identify or reidentify them and they could play no part in our psychological language. (Thus they are like "a wheel that is no part of the mechanism.")

Ludwig Wittgenstein, *Philosophical Investigations*, translated by G. E. M. Anscombe (Oxford: Blackwell, 1953). But, of course, this leaves the argument that the states themselves might nevertheless be "private" and inaccessible, and that one could ("logically") have learned the language of mental states with a group of properly acting and speaking mental state-invoking robots. A. J. Ayer, "The Private Language Argument," in Donald Gustafson, ed., *Essays in Philosophical Psychology* (Garden City, N.Y.: Anchor, 1963). See also Norman Malcolm, "The Private Language Argument," in the same collection. Even more recently, Daniel Dennett has introduced the notion of "the intentional stance," by means of which we can understand the behavior of everything from thermostats to Harvard professors. But the question of whether that "stance" actually refers to features of the being in question is not thereby resolved (presumably "no" for thermostats, "yes" for most Harvard professors). Daniel Dennett, *The Intentional Stance* (Cambridge, Mass.: MIT Press, 1987).

34. About the closest he comes to being *looked at* in the relevant sense is on page 43, where the Self-Taught Man surprises him. "I look at the Self-Taught Man with stupor. But he seems surprised at my surprise. . . . I have been slightly lowered in his estimation." On page 143, Roquentin notes, "What a curious look [the Self-Taught Man] gives me." But the look betrays him. It does not "catch" Roquentin. One might even say that Roquentin suffers mostly from *not* being looked at. He is *de trop*, superfluous, unwanted (164).

35. Many years ago, I remember an attempt to capture this in "dialogal phenomenology," in a book of that title by Stephen Strasser. Sartre himself attempts it in his *Critique of Dialectical Reason*.

36. Pederasty is a phenomenon that clearly intrigued Sartre, from *Nausea* to the chapter "Bad Faith" in *Being and Nothingness* to Daniel in *Age of Reason*.

37. There is a good deal to say about Sartre's seemingly callous attitude toward violence. A good study of his ambivalence is Ronald Santoni's *Sartre on Violence: Curiously Ambivalent* (University Park: Penn State University Press, 2003).

38. A sadistic image that Sartre repeats ten years later in *The Age of Reason*.

39. We are reminded of Gabriel Garcia Márquez's character Fiorentino in *Love in the Time of Cholera*, who maintains his "fidelity" to his beloved Fermina despite hundreds of such illicit liaisons over the years. But Roquentin, unlike Fiorentino, is neither lovable nor innocent.

Chapter 4

This sketch of Sartre's "Sketch" was originally published in *Sartre*, edited by Paul Schilpp, in the Library of Living Philosophers series edited by Paul Schilpp (La Salle, Ill.: Open Court, 1981), 211–228. All quotes from *Being and Nothingness* are from the 1972 printing of the Washington Square paperback edition, translated by Hazel Barnes (New York: Philosophical Library, 1956). This work is hereafter cited in parentheses as *B&N*.

1. See, for example, Freud's early "Project for a Scientific Psychology" in *The Standard Edition of the Complete Psychological Works of Sigmund Freud*, edited by James Strachey, vol. 3 (London: Hogarth, 1953–). See also his masterpiece, *The Interpretation of Dreams*.

2. *Esquisse d'une théorie des émotions*, Actualités Scientifiques et Industrielles, 838 (Paris: Hermann, 1939). This work, translated by Bernard Frechtman, first

appeared in English as *The Emotions: Outline of a Theory* (New York: Philosophical Library, 1948). All references here are to the 1948 (second) Hermann edition, and translations are based on the Frechtman 1971 Citadel Press edition. The page numbers that appear in parentheses in the text refer to the English edition.

3. According to Simone de Beauvoir, *Coming of Age* (New York: Putnam, 1973), 53, and Michel Contat and Michel Rybalka, *The Writings of Jean-Paul Sartre*, an extensive bibliography translated from the French by Richard C. McCleary, vol. 1 (Evanston, Ill.: Northwestern University Press, 1974), 65.

4. *Recherches philosophiques*, vol. 6, 1936–37, 85–123. Translated by Forrest Williams and Robert Kirkpatrick as *The Transcendence of the Ego* (New York: Noonday, 1957).

5. All quotes from *Being and Nothingness* are from the 1971 printing of the Citadel paperback edition, translated by Hazel Barnes (New York: Philosophical Library, 1956).

6. *St. Genet, comédien et martyr* (Paris: Gallimard, 1952), translated by Bernard Frechtman as *St. Genet, Actor and Martyr* (New York: Braziller, 1963).

7. *The Family Idiot* (Chicago: University of Chicago Press, 1981–1993).

8. William James, "What Is an Emotion?" *Mind* (1884). Reprinted in Robert Solomon, ed., *What Is an Emotion?* (New York: Oxford University Press, 2004).

9. Gilbert Ryle, *The Concept of Mind* (New York: Barnes & Noble, 1949), esp. ch. 6.

10. In philosophy, I have argued such a "cognitivist" thesis for thirty years, beginning with my book *The Passions* (New York: Doubleday, 1976) and most recently in *Not Passion's Slave* (New York: Oxford University Press, 2003). Other prominent "cognitivist" philosophers in the field include Ronald De Sousa, Peter Goldie, and Martha Nussbaum, among many others. In psychology, I would pick Magda Arnold, Richard Lazarus, and Nico Frijda as three exemplary defenders of the thesis Sartre is defending. Frijda, in particular, gives full credit to Sartre for setting him on the way.

11. I should note here that a neo—Jamesian movement in philosophy and psychology based on the new neuroscience is in full swing. Representatives are Joseph Le Doux and Antonio Damasio in neuropsychology and Paul Griffiths and Jesse Prinz in philosophy.

12. Major portions of *Being and Nothingness* are devoted to an attack on Freud. A late addition to that book introduces "existential psychoanalysis," which is an obvious attempt to compete with Freud. Sartre's later biographies (*Saint Genet, Baudelaire, Flaubert*) were heavily psychoanalytic but anti—Freudian. And late in life he undertook a film project with John Huston critical of Freud and his methods. (The film was never made, but Sartre's rough script has been published as *The Freud Scenario*, edited by J.-B. Pontalis, translated by Quintin Hoare [Chicago: University of Chicago Press, 1985].)

13. I argued this myself in an early essay, "Reasons as Causal Explanations," about the same time I was writing my dissertation on Freud. It was published in *Philosophy and Phenomenological Research* 34, no. 3 (March 1974).

14. Maurice Merleau-Ponty, *The Phenomenology of Perception* (Paris: Gallimard, 1945; Boston: Routledge, 2002).

15. Paul Ricoeur, to take but one prominent French example, retains the traditional view of the emotions, placing them on the "involuntary" side in his most important work, *Volontaire et l'involontaire* (Paris: Aubier, 1950); see his *Freedom and Nature*, vol. 1, *The Voluntary and the Involuntary*, translated by Erazim V. Kohak (Evanston, Ill.: Northwestern University Press, 1966).

16. *Not Passion's Slave*, ch. 12.

17. In this light, it is worth rereading Sartre's early "Faces," in *Essays in Phenomenology*, edited by Maurice Natanson (The Hague: Martinus Nijhoff, 1966). See also David Rapaport's *Emotions and Memory* (New York: International Universities Press, 1971).

18. See ch. 7 of this volume.

19. Similarly, Leibniz once argued that emotions were "confused intelligence."

20. Gilles Deleuze and Felix Guattari have argued this position in their *L'Anti-Oedipe: Capitalisme et schizophrénie* (Paris: Éditions de Minuit, 1972).

21. Friedrich Nietzsche, *Twilight of the Idols*, translated by Walter Kaufmann (New York: Viking, 1954).

22. To follow Sartre's understanding of this, see his *Between Existentialism and Marxism*, translated by John Mathews (New York: Pantheon, 1974).

23. There is a disagreement worth mentioning here. Peter Goldie, in *The Emotions: A Philosophical Exploration* (Oxford: Clarendon Press, 2000), distinguishes between the expressions of emotions, which are immediate, and actions *out of* emotion, which follow as courses of action, where the latter would be precisely what I am insisting we think of as expressions.

24. Wittgenstein employs such examples in his discussion of Fraser's *The Golden Bough* in *Synthèse* [1975]).

25. Fyodor Dostoevsky, *Notes from Underground*, translated by Ralph Matlaw (New York: Dutton, 1960).

Chapter 5

1. Albert Camus, *The Plague*, translated by Stuart Gilbert (New York: Knopf, 1948). I have also benefited from reading Steven G. Kellman's *The Plague: Fiction and Resistance* (New York: Twayne, 1993).

2. The real epidemic was in 1665 in England, when Defoe was five years old.

3. An excellent account of that part of France in which Camus was living and writing is Philip Hallie's superb book, *Lest Innocent Blood be Shed* (New York: Harper & Row, 1979).

4. Camus edited a paper aggressively called *Combat*. Sartre, of course, founded and edited *Les Temps modernes*.

5. For example, in his *Neither Victims nor Executioners* (Columbia, B.C.: New Society Publishers, 1986).

6. Camus, "Reflections on the Guillotine," in his *Resistance, Rebellion, and Death*, translated by Justin O'Brien (New York: Knopf, 1960), 173–234.

7. Kellman, *The Plague*.

8. On plague, see Barry, *The Great Influenza*. Also see Gewen, "Virus Alert." Robert Sullivan's *Rats* (New York: Bloomsbury, 2004) is eye-opening, as is the review by Sue Halpern, "City Folks," *New York Review of Books*, May 13, 2004, 13–15. See John M. Barry, *The Great Influenza: The Epic Story of the Deadliest Plague in History* (New York: Viking, 2004). See the review "Virus Alert," by Barry Gewen, in the *New York Times Book Review*, March 14, 2004, 10–11.

9. A. Langmuir, J. Solomon, T. Worthen, C. G. Ray, and E. Peterson, "The Thucydides Syndrome: A New Hypothesis for the Cause of the Plague of Athens," *New England Journal of Medicine*, October 17, 1985, 1027–1030.

10. See Robert C. Solomon, *In Defense of Sentimentality* (Oxford: Oxford University Press, 2004), ch. 6, "Real Horror."

Chapter 6

I especially want to thank David Sherman for his extensive review and comments on this chapter, as well as his perceptive conversations and observations over many years. I also want to thank Clancy Martin, who opened my eyes to some new complexities surrounding the notions of truthfulness and deception.

1. I take some responsibility for this. Walter Kaufmann included these two selections in his *Existentialism: From Dostoevsky to Sartre* (New York: Meridien, 1960), and I followed him in doing so (along with a few other selections) in my *Existentialism* (Oxford: Oxford University Press, 2004).

2. E.g., "quand un philosophe viendra me dire que les arbres sentent et que les rochers pensent, il aura beau m'embarrasser dans ses arguments subtils. Je ne puis voir en lui qu'un sophiste de *mauvaise foi*" ("when a philosopher comes to tell me that trees feel and that rocks think, he can embarrass me all he likes with his subtle arguments. I cannot see in him anything but a sophist of bad faith). *Oeuvres complètes*, edited by B. Gagnebin, vol. 4 (Paris: Pléïade), 585. But my dear friend and French Enlightenment scholar Jenene Alison suggests that Rousseau is playing with the notion of being "de bonne foi," meaning "according to received religion." But "un sophiste de mauvaise foi" is a way of saying rather agitatedly, "someone who doesn't write as honestly as I do." Thus Rousseau defends "good faith" in just the sense that Sartre denies it, as evidenced, supposedly, in Rousseau's own much misunderstood integrity.

3. Amelia Rorty, Perspectives on Self-Deception (Berkeley: University of California Press, 1988), 11.

4. H. Markus and S. Kitiyama, "Independent and Interdependent Cultures," in *Cross-Cultural Psychology* 33 (1991): 248–269.

5. See Mary Delvecchio, *Pain as Human Experience* (Los Angeles: University of California Press, 1994).

6. Herbert Fingarette, *Self-Deception* (London: Routledge and Kegan-Paul, 1963).

7. See Robert C. Solomon, *Not Passion's Slave* (New York: Oxford University Press, 2003); and Richard Moran, *Authority and Estrangement* (Princeton: Princeton University Press, 2001).

8. I think the main credit here goes first to Fingarette, but more recently to Alfred Mele, who in his book *Self-Deception Unmasked* (Princeton, N.J.: Princeton University Press, 2001) shows once and for all, I think, that the "lie to oneself" model is inappropriate here.

9. *Being and Nothingness*, pt. IV, ch. 2, sec. 1.

10. Bruno Bettelheim's *Freud and Man's Soul* (New York: Knopf, 1982).

11. See, for example, Fingarette, *Self-Deception*.

12. Fingarette offers a similar analysis of Freud and the "Unconscious," ibid., 111–135.

13. See "The Reiteration of Bad Faith" (pages 174–176 in this book).

14. Fingarette, *Self-Deception*; Mele, *Self-Deception Unmasked*; Moran, *Authority and Estrangement*.

15. Rorty, *Perspectives on Self-Deception*, 207.

16. Ibid., 208.

17. In her "Bad Faith and Kitsch as Models for Self-Deception," in *Self and Deception: A Cross-Cultural Philosophical Enquiry*, edited by Wimal Dissanayake and Roger Ames (Albany: State University of New York Press, 1996).

18. Dissanayake and Ames, *Self and Deception*, 126.

19. Ibid., 127.

20. Ibid., 128.

21. Ibid.

22. I have also been prompted to think about this with regard to the notion of "authentic emotions" by Mikko Salmela of the University of Helsinki. See his "What Is Emotional Authenticity?" in *Journal of the Theory of Social Behavior* 35 (September 2005).

23. Again, see Ronald Santoni, *Sartre on Violence: Curiously Ambivalent* (University Park: Penn State University Press, 2003).

24. For instance, Lionel Trilling, *Sincerity and Authenticity* (Cambridge, Mass.: Harvard University Press, 1972).

25. Sartre is particularly insightful on the nature of reflection in sec. 3, "Reflection," of ch. 2 ("Temporality"). There, he explains reflection as a (further) attempt of consciousness to "recover itself, to finally be to itself its own foundation." On love, he adds, "this reflection is in bad faith" (225).

26. Mele, *Self-Deception Unmasked*.

27. The notion of "twisted" self-deception has been ingeniously developed by Mele, *Self-Deception Unmasked*.

Chapter 7

1. Jean-Paul Sartre's play *Huis clos* was first performed at the Théâtre du Vieux-Colombier in Paris and published in Paris by Gallimard in 1945. It was translated as *No Exit* by Stuart Gilbert and published in Britain by H. Hamilton in 1946, and in New York by Knopf in 1947. Eric Bentley's essay on *No Exit* was published in his book *The Playwright as Thinker* (New York: Reynal & Hitchcock, 1946), 197–200.

2. I am not quite sure what to call them. "Characters (in the play)" begs too many interesting questions. "Inmates" seems a bit too institutional; "roommates," too cozy; and even "the deceased" and "the dead" are odd under the circumstances. Estelle's suggestion, "absentees," by contrast, is nothing but an evasive euphemism.

3. Daniel Maxwell, "SparkNote on *No Exit*," April 29, 2005, http://www.sparknotes.com/lit/noexit/.

4. C. A. J. Coady, "The Morality of Lying," in *To Tell a Lie: Truth in Business and the Professions*, edited by C. A. J. Coady (Sydney: St. James Ethics Center, 1992), 7–12, reprinted in *Res Publica* (Melbourne: Center for Philosophy and Public Issues, 1992).

5. Nietzsche, *Beyond Good and Evil*, translated by Walter Kaufmann (New York: Vintage, 1966).

6. This seeming inconsistency in Nietzsche is interpreted by Clancy Martin in his forthcoming book, *Nietzsche's Lies*.

7. Richard Rorty, *Philosophy and the Mirror of Nature* (Princeton, N.J.: Princeton University Press, 1979).

8. See Richard Moran, *Authority and Estrangement* (Princeton, N.J.: Princeton University Press, 2001).

9. *Being and Nothingness*, 315, 318.

10. See Robert C. Solomon, "Thinking Death in the Face," in his *The Joy of Philosophy* New York: Oxford University Press, 1999.

Chapter 8

1. Albert Camus, *La Chute* (Paris: Gallimard, 1956), translated as *The Fall* by Justin O'Brien (New York: Knopf, 1956). All references to the book are to the O'Brien edition and are in parentheses in the text.

2. Phillip L. Quinn, "Hell in Amsterdam: Reflections on Camus's *The Fall*," in *Midwest Studies in Philosophy* 16, *Philosophy and the Arts* (Notre Dame, Ind.: University of Notre Dame Press,1991), 89–103.

3. Albert Camus, *L'Étranger* (Paris: Gallimard, 1942), translated as *The Stranger* by Stuart Gilbert (New York: Vintage, 1946).

4. David Sherman, "Camus's Meursault and Sartrian Irresponsibility," *Philosophy and Literature* 19 (1995): 60–77.

5. David Hume, *Treatise of Human Nature*, edited by L. A. Selby-Bigge (Oxford: Clarendon Press, 1978), book II, sec. iii, 415.

6. Milan Kundera, *The Unbearable Lightness of Being* (New York: Harper & Row, 1984), 251, *Nietzsche's Lies.*

Conclusion

1. Reprinted in Solomon, *Phenomenology and Existentialism*, p. 513.

SELECTED BIBLIOGRAPHY

Since this book is primarily a selective reading of Camus and Sartre, a full bibliography would be pretentious and misleading. I have listed only those books I have (more or less) referred to in the text. For a full guide to the writings of the two philosophers, see Robert F. Roeming, comp. and ed., *Camus: A Bibliography* (Madison: University of Wisconsin Press, 1968); and Brian T. Fitch and Peter C. Hoy, *Essai de bibliographie des études en langue française consacrées à Albert Camus, 1937–1967*, 2nd ed. (Paris: Lettres Modernes, 1969).

A complete annotated bibliography of Sartre's works is Michel Contat and Michel Rybalka, comps., *The Writings of Jean-Paul Sartre* (Evanston, Ill.: Northwestern University Press, 1974), updated in *Magazine littéraire* 103–104 (1975): 9–49, and by Michel Sciard in *Obliques* 18–19 (May 1979): 331–347. Rybalka and Contat have an additional bibliography of primary and secondary sources published since Sartre's death: *Sartre: Bibliography, 1980–1992* (Bowling Green, Ohio: Philosophy Documentation Center; Paris: Éditions CNRS, 1993).

Camus

Novels and Short Stories

L'Étranger. Paris: Gallimard, 1942. Translated by Stuart Gilbert as *The Stranger.* New York: Vintage, 1946.
La Peste. Paris: Gallimard, 1947. Translated by Stuart Gilbert as *The Plague.* New York: Random House, 1948.
La Chute. Paris: Gallimard, 1956. Translated by Justin O'Brien as *The Fall.* New York: Knopf, 1957.

L'Exil et le royaume. Paris: Gallimard, 1957. Translated by Justin O'Brien as *Exile and the Kingdom.* New York: Knopf, 1958. Short stories.

La Mort heureuse. Paris: Gallimard, 1971. Translated by Richard Howard as *A Happy Death.* New York: Knopf, 1995.

Le Premier Homme. Paris: Gallimard, 1994. Translated by David Hapgood as *The First Man.* New York: Knopf, 1995.

Plays

Le Malentendu. Published with *Caligula* in *Le Malentendu, suivi de Caligula.* Paris: Gallimard,1944. Translated by Stuart Gilbert as *Caligula and Three Other Plays.* New York: Knopf, 1958.

Essays, Journalism, and Notebooks

L'Envers et l'endroit. Paris: Gallimard, 1937. Recollections of childhood and travel sketches.

Noces. Paris: Charlot, 1938. Four Algerian essays.

Le Mythe de Sisyphe: Essai sur l'absurde. Paris: Gallimard, 1942; enl. and rev. ed., 1945. Translated by Justin O'Brien as *The Myth of Sisyphus and Other Essays.* New York: Knopf, 1955.

Lettres à un ami allemand. Lausanne: Marguerat, 1946. Translated by Justin O'Brien in *Resistance, Rebellion, and Death.* New York: Knopf, 1960.

Actuelles. 3 vols. Paris: Gallimard, 1950–1958. Editorials and articles written for *Combat,* 1944–1945.

L'Homme révolté. Paris: Galllimard, 1951. Translated by Anthony Bower as *The Rebel.* New York: Knopf, 1954.

"Reflections on the Guillotine." In *Resistance, Rebellion, and Death.* Translated by Justin O'Brien. New York: Knopf, 1960.

Carnets: Mai 1935–février 1942. Paris: Gallimard, 1962. Translated by Philip Thody as *Notebooks, 1935–1942.* New York: Knopf, 1963.

Carnets: Janvier 1942–mars 1951. Paris: Gallimard, 1964. Translated by Justin O'Brien as *Notebooks, 1942–1951.* New York: Knopf, 1965.

Carnets: Avril 1951–décembre 1959. Paris: Gallimard, 1966. Translated by Philip Thody as *Notebooks, 1951–1959.* New York: Knopf, 1969.

Biographies

Lebesque, Morvan. *Portrait of Camus: An Illustrated Biography.* Translated by T. C. Sherman. New York: Herder and Herder, 1971. Originally published *as Albert Camus par lui-même.* Paris: Éditions du Seil, 1963.

Lottman, Herbert R. *Albert Camus: A Biography.* Garden City, N.Y.: Doubleday, 1979; reissued 1997.

McCarthy, Patrick. *Camus.* New York: Random House, 1982.

Selected Essays and Books on Camus

Bespaloff, Rachel. In *Camus.* Edited by Germaine Brée. Englewood Cliffs, N.J.: Prentice-Hall, 1962.

Brée, Germaine. *Camus.* Rev. ed. New York: Harcourt, Brace and World, 1964. Reissued New Brunswick, N.J.: Rutgers University Press, 1972.

Brisville, Jean-Claude. *Camus.* Paris: Gallimard, 1959; reissued 1969.

Cruickshank, John. *Albert Camus and the Literature of Revolt.* New York: Oxford University Press, 1959. Reprinted, Westport, CT: Greenwood, 1978.

Fitch, Brian T. *The Narcissistic Text: A Reading of Camus' Fiction.* Toronto: University of Toronto Press, 1982.

Kellman, Steven G. *The Plague: Fiction and Resistance.* New York: Twayne, 1993.

King, Adele. *Albert Camus.* New York: Grove Press, 1964. Reissued, New York: Capricorn, 1971.

King, Adele, ed. *Camus's L'Étranger: Fifty Years On.* New York: St. Martin's, 1992.

Knapp, Bettina L., ed. *Critical Essays on Albert Camus.* Boston: G. K. Hall, 1988.

McBride, Joseph. *Albert Camus: Philosopher and Littérateur.* New York: St. Martin's, 1992.

McCarthy, Patrick. *Albert Camus, The Stranger.* Cambridge, U.K.: Cambridge University Press, 2004.

O'Brien, Conor Cruise. *Camus.* In the Modern Masters series. New York: Viking, 1970.

Parker, Emmett. *Albert Camus: The Artist in the Arena.* Madison: University of Wisconsin Press, 1965.

Quilliot, Roger. *The Sea and Prisons: A Commentary on the Life and Thought of Albert Camus.* University: University of Alabama Press, 1970.

Rhein, Philip H. *Albert Camus.* Rev. ed. Boston: Twayne, 1989.

Sherman, David. "Camus's Meursault and Sartrian Irresponsibility." *Philosophy and Literature* 19 (1995): 60–77.

Sprintzen, David. *Camus: A Critical Examination.* Philadelphia: Temple University Press, 1988.

Tarrow, Susan. *Exile from the Kingdom: A Political Rereading of Albert Camus.* University: University of Alabama Press, 1985.

Thody, Philip. *Albert Camus, 1913–1960.* New York: Macmillan, 1961.

Thody, Philip. *Albert Camus.* New York: St. Martin's, 1989.

Sartre

Biographies

Beauvoir, Simone de. *Adieux: A Farewell to Sartre.* Translated by Patrick O'Brian. New York: Pantheon, 1984.

Cohen-Solal, Annie. *Sartre: A Life.* Translated by Anna Cancogni. Edited by Norman McAfee. New York: Pantheon, 1987.

Gerassi, John. *Jean-Paul Sartre: Hated Conscience of His Century.* Chicago: University of Chicago Press, 1989.

Hayman, Ronald. *Sartre: A Life.* New York: Simon & Schuster, 1992.

Selected Plays and Novels

Huis clos. Paris: Gallimard, 1945. Translated as *No Exit* by Stuart Gilbert. London: Hamish Hamilton, 1946; New York: Knopf, 1947.

The Age of Reason. Translated by Eric Sutton. London: Hamish Hamilton, 1947; New York: Vintage, 1992.

The Reprieve. Translated by Eric Sutton. New York: Knopf, 1947; New York: Vintage, 1992.

Nausea. Translated by Lloyd Alexander. New York: New Directions, 1964.

"The Wall." In *The Wall and Other Short Stories.* Translated by Lloyd Alexander. New York: New Directions, 1975.

Selected Philosophical Works

The Transcendence of the Ego. Translated by Forrest Williams and Robert Kirkpatrick. New York: Noonday Press, 1957; New York: Hill and Wang, 1990.

L'imagination. Paris: Alcan, 1936. Translated by Forrest Williams as *Imagination.* Ann Arbor: University of Michigan Press, 1962.

L'imaginaire. Paris: Gallimard, 1940.

The Emotions: Outline of a Theory. Translated by Bernard Frechtman. New York: Philosophical Library, 1948. First published as *Esquisse d'une théorie des émotions.* Actualités Scientifiques et Industrielles, no. 838. Paris: Hermann, 1939.

Being and Nothingness. Translated by Hazel E. Barnes. New York: Philosophical Library, 1943; 1956, 1948.

Existentialism Is a Humanism. Translated by Bernard Frechtman. New York: Philosophical Library, 1947. Reprinted in *Existentialism.* Edited by Robert C. Solomon. New York: Oxford University Press, 2005.

Existentialism as a Humanism. Translated by Philip Mairet. New York: Philosophical Library, 1949.

Anti-Semite and Jew. Translated by George J. Becker. New York: Schocken, 1948.

Saint Genet, comedién et martyr. Paris: Gallimard, 1952. Translated by Bernard Frechtman as *St. Genet, Actor and Martyr.* New York: Braziller, 1963, 1981.

Between Existentialism and Marxism. Translated by John Mathews. London: New Left Books, 1959; New York: Pantheon, 1974. Essays and interviews.

Critique of Dialectical Reason. Vol. 1, *Theory of Practical Ensembles.* Translated by Alan Sheridan-Smith. London: New Left Books, 1960; Atlantic Highlands, N.J.: Humanities Press, 1976.

"Materialism and Revolution." In Sartre's *Literary and Philosophical Essays.* Translated by Annette Michelson. New York: Crowell-Collier, 1962.

The Words. Translated by Bernard Frechtman. New York: Braziller, 1964.

"Faces." In *Essays in Phenomenology.* Edited by Maurice Natanson. The Hague: Martinus Nijhoff, 1966.

Search for a Method. Translated by Hazel E. Barnes. New York: Vintage Books, 1968.

"Kierkegaard: The Singular Universal." In Sartre's *Between Existentialism and Marxism.* Translated by John Mathews. New York: Pantheon, 1974.

Sartre on Theater. Edited by Michel Contat and Michel Rybalka. Translated by Frank Jelinek. New York: Pantheon, 1976.

Life/Situations: Essays Written and Spoken. Translated by Paul Auster and Lydia Davis. New York: Pantheon, 1977.

The Family Idiot: Gustave Flaubert, 1821–1857. Translated by Carol Cosman. 5 vols. Chicago: University of Chicago Press, 1981–1993.

The War Diaries. Translated by Quintin Hoare. New York: Pantheon, 1984.

"What Is Literature?" And Other Essays. Translated by Bernard Frechtman et al. Cambridge, Mass.: Harvard University Press, 1988.

Critique of Dialectical Reason. Vol. 1, *Theory of Practical Ensembles.* Translated by Alan Sheridan-Smith. Edited by Jonathan Rée. London: Verso, 1991.

Critique of Dialectical Reason. Vol. 2, *The Intelligibility of History.* Translated by Quintin Hoare. London: Verso, 1991.

The Psychology of the Imagination. Translated by Bernard Frechtman. New York: Citadel Press, 1991.

Notebook for an Ethics. Translated by David Pellauer. Chicago: University of Chicago Press, 1992.

Quiet Moments in a War: The Letters of Jean-Paul Sartre to Simone de Beauvoir, 1940–1963. Edited by Simone de Beauvoir. Translated by Lee Fahnestock and Norman MacAfee. New York: Scribner's, 1993.

Hope, Now: The 1980 Interviews. Translated by Adrian van den Hoven. Chicago: University of Chicago Press, 1996.

Selected Secondary Sources

Anderson, Thomas C. *Sartre's Two Ethics: From Authenticity to Integral Humanity.* Chicago: Open Court, 1993.

Aronson, Ronald. *Sartre's Second Critique.* Chicago: University of Chicago Press, 1987.

Barnes, Hazel E. *Sartre and Flaubert.* Chicago: University of Chicago Press, 1981.

Beauvoir, Simone de. *Force of Circumstance.* Translated by Richard Howard. New York: Putnam's, 1964–.

Beauvoir, Simone de. *The Ethics of Ambiguity.* Translated by Bernard Frechtman. New York: Putnam's, 1965.

Beauvoir, Simone de. *Adieux: A Farewell to Sartre.* Translated by Patrick O'Brian, New York: Pantheon, 1984.

Beauvoir, Simone de. *Letters to Sartre.* Translated and edited by Quintin Hoare. New York: Arcade, 1992.

Bell, Linda A. *Sartre's Ethics of Authenticity.* Tuscaloosa: University of Alabama Press, 1989.

Bentley, Eric. *The Playwright as Thinker,* 197–200. New York: Reynal & Hitchcock, 1946. Essay on *No Exit.*

Busch, Thomas. *The Power of Consciousness and the Force of Circumstances in Sartre's Philosophy.* Bloomington: Indiana University Press, 1990.

Catalano. Joseph S. *A Commentary on Jean-Paul Sartre's Being and Nothingness.* Chicago: University of Chicago Press, 1980.

Catalano, Joseph S. *A Commentary on Jean-Paul Sartre's Critique of Dialectical Reason.* Vol. 1, *Theory of Practical Ensembles.* Chicago: University of Chicago Press, 1986.

Caws, Peter. *Sartre.* London: Routledge and Kegan Paul, 1979.

Danto, Arthur C. *Jean-Paul Sartre.* London: Fontana Press, 1991.

Detmer, David. *Freedom as a Value: A Critique of the Ethical Theory of Jean-Paul Sartre.* La Salle, Ill.: Open Court, 1988.

Dobson, Andrew. *Jean-Paul Sartre and the Politics of Reason.* Cambridge: Cambridge University Press, 1993.

Fell, Joseph P. *Emotion in the Thought of Sartre.* New York: Columbia University Press, 1965.

Fell, Joseph P. *Heidegger and Sartre: An Essay on Being and Place.* New York: Columbia University Press, 1979.

Flynn, Thomas R. "Praxis and Vision: Elements of a Sartrean Epistemology." *Philosophical Forum* 8 (1976–1977).

Flynn, Thomas R. *Sartre and Marxist Existentialism: The Test Case of Collective Responsibility.* Chicago: University of Chicago Press, 1984.

Flynn, Thomas R. *Sartre, Foucault and Historical Reason*. Vol. 1, *Toward an Existentialist Theory of History*. Chicago: University of Chicago Press, 1997.

Fretz, Leo. "An Interview with Jean-Paul Sartre." In *Jean-Paul Sartre: Contemporary Approaches to His Philosophy*. Edited by. Hugh Silverman and Frederick Elliston. Pittsburgh, Pa.: Duquesne University Press, 1980.

Grene, Marjorie. *Sartre*. Washington, D.C.: University Press of America, 1983.

Hartmann, Klaus. *Sartre's Ontology*. Evanston, Ill.: Northwestern University Press, 1966.

Jeanson, Francis. *Sartre and the Problem of Morality*. Translated by Robert V. Stone. Bloomington: Indiana University Press, 1980.

Kenevan, Phyllis Berdt. "Self-Consciousness and the Ego in the Philosophy of Sartre." In *The Philosophy of Jean-Paul Sartre*. Edited by Paul Arthur Schilpp. La Salle, Ill.: Open Court, 1981.

Malhotra, Ashok Kumar. *Jean-Paul Sartre's Existentialism in Literature and Philosophy*. Oneonta: State University of New York Press, 1995.

McBride, William L. *Sartre's Political Theory*. Bloomington: Indiana University Press, 1991.

McBride, William L., ed. *Sartre and Existentialism*. 8 vols. New York: Garland, 1997.

McCulloch, Gregory. *Using Sartre*. London: Routledge, 1994.

Rybalka, Michel, et al. "An Interview with Jean-Paul Sartre." In *The Philosophy of Jean-Paul Sartre*. Edited by Paul Arthur Schilpp. La Salle, Ill.: Open Court, 1981.

Santoni, Ronald E. *Bad Faith, Good Faith, and Authenticity in Sartre's Early Philosophy*. Philadelphia: Temple University Press, 1995.

Santoni, Ronald E. *Sartre on Violence: Curiously Ambivalent*. University Park: Penn State University Press, 2003.

Schilpp, Paul Arthur, ed. *The Philosophy of Jean-Paul Sartre*. La Salle, Ill.: Open Court, 1981.

Schroeder, William. *Sartre and His Predecessors*. Boston: Routledge and Kegan Paul, 1984.

Silverman, Hugh J. *Inscriptions: Between Phenomenology and Structuralism*. London: Routledge and Kegan Paul, 1987.

Stone, Robert, and Elizabeth Bowman. "Dialectical Ethics: A First Look at Sartre's Unpublished 1964 Rome Lecture Notes." *Social Text* no. 13–14 (Winter—Spring 1986): 195–215.

Taylor, Charles. *The Ethics of Authenticity*. Cambridge, Mass.: Harvard University Press, 1992.

Wilder, Kathleen V. *The Bodily Nature of Consciousness: Sartre and Contemporary Philosophy of Mind*. Ithaca, N.Y.: Cornell University Press, 1997.

Other Works Referred to in the Text

Aristotle. *Nicomachean Ethics*. Translated by W. D. Ross. Oxford: Oxford University Press, 1929.

Austin, J. L. "On Pretending." In *Essays in Philosophical Psychology*, 99–116. Edited by Donald Gustafson. New York: Anchor, 1964. The essay (for the Aristotelian Society) was inspired by one of the few early analytic classics on the philosophy of emotions, Errol Bedford's "Emotions."

Beauvoir, Simone de. *Coming of Age*. New York: Putnam, 1972.

Coady, C. A. J. "The Morality of Lying." In *To Tell a Lie: Truth in Business and the Professions*, 7–12. Edited by C. A. J. Coady. Sydney: St. James Ethics Center, 1992. Reprinted in *Res Publica*. Melbourne: Center for Philosophy and Public Issues, 1992.

Cohen-Solal. Annie. *Sartre: A Life*. Translated by Anna Cancogni. Edited by Norman MacAfee. New York: Pantheon, 1987.

Deleuze, Gilles, and Felix Guattari. *L'Anti-Oedipe: Capitalisme et schizophrénie*. Vol. 1. Paris: Editions de Minuit, 1972.

Dennett, Daniel. *The Intentional Stance*. Cambridge, Mass.: MIT Press, 1987.

Dostoevsky, Fyodor. *Notes from Underground*. Translated by Ralph Matlaw. New York: Dutton, 1960.

Fingarette, Herbert. *Self-Deception*. London: Routledge and Kegan Paul, 1963.

Freud, Sigmund. "Project for a Scientific Psychology." In *The Standard Edition of the Complete Psychological Works of Sigmund Freud*. Edited by James Strachey. Vol. 3. London: Hogarth, 1953.

Goldie, Peter. *The Emotions: A Philosophical Exploration*. Oxford: Clarendon Press, 2000.

Guignon, Charles. *Heidegger's Theory of Knowledge*. Indianapolis, Ind.: Hackett, 1977.

Hallie, Philip. *Lest Innocent Blood Be Shed*. New York: Harper & Row, 1979.

Hegel, G. W. F. *The Phenomenology of Spirit*. Translated by A. V. Miller. Oxford: Clarendon Press, 1977.

Heidegger, Martin. *Being and Time*. Translated by Joan Stambaugh. Albany: State University of New York Press, 1997.

Husserl, Edmund. *Ideas: General Introduction to Pure Phenomenology*. Translated by W. R. Boyce Gibson. New York: Macmillan/Collier, 1931.

James, William. "What Is an Emotion?" *Mind* (London) (1884).

Kellman, Steven G. *The Plague: Fiction and Resistance*. New York: Twayne, 1993.

Kundera, Milan. *The Unbearable Lightness of Being*. Translated by Michael Henry Heim. New York: Harper & Row, 1984.

Meagher, Robert, ed. *Albert Camus: The Essential Writings*. New York: Harper Colophon, 1979.

Mele, Alfred. *Self-Deception Unmasked*. Princeton, N.J.: Princeton University Press, 2001.

Merleau-Ponty, Maurice. *The Phenomenology of Perception*. Translated by Colin Smith. Paris: Gallimard, 1945; Boston: Routledge, 2002.

Mill, John Stuart. *A System of Logic*. Honolulu: University Press of the Pacific, 2002.

Nagel, Thomas. *Mortal Questions*. New York: Cambridge University Press, 1979.

Nietzsche, Friedrich. *Twilight of the Idols*. Translated by Walter Kaufmann. New York: Viking, 1954.

Nietzsche, Friedrich. *Beyond Good and Evil*. Translated by Walter Kaufmann. New York: Vintage, 1966.

Nietzsche, Friedrich. *The Gay Science*. Translated by Walter Kaufmann. New York: Random House, 1968.

Nozick, Robert. *Philosophical Explanations*. Cambridge, Mass.: Harvard University Press, 1981.

Quinn, Phillip L. "Hell in Amsterdam: Reflections on Camus's *The Fall*." In *Philosophy and the Arts*, 89–103. *Midwest Studies in Philosophy*, 16. University of Notre Dame Press, 1991.

Ricoeur, Paul. *Volontaire et l'involontaire.* Paris: Aubier, 1950. Translated by Erazim V. Kohák as *The Voluntary and the Involuntary.* Vol. 1, Freedom and Nature. Evanston, Ill.: Northwestern University Press, 1966.

Royzman, Edward R., and John Sabini. "Something It Takes to Be an Emotion: The Interesting Case of Disgust." *Journal for the Study of Social Behavior* 31, no. 1 (March 2001): 29–60.

Russell, Bertrand. "On Denoting." *Mind* (1905).

Salmela, Mikko. "What Is Emotional Authenticity?" *Journal of the Theory of Social Behavior* 35 (2005).

Santoni, Ronald. *Sartre on Violence: Curiously Ambivalent.* University Park: Penn State University Press, 2003.

Sherman, David. "Camus's Meursault and Sartrian Irresponsibility." *Philosophy and Literature* 19 (1995): 60–77.

Sherman, David. "The Absurd." In *The Blackwell Companion to Phenomenology and Existentialism.* Edited by Hubert Dreyfus and Mark Wrathall. London: Blackwell, 2005.

Solomon Robert C. *The Passions.* New York: Doubleday, 1976.

Solomon, Robert C. *From Hegel to Existentialism.* New York: Oxford University Press, 1987.

Solomon, Robert C. "The Emotions in Phenomenology and Existentialism." In *The Blackwell Companion to Phenomenology and Existentialism.* Edited by Hubert Dreyfus and Mark Wrathall. London: Blackwell, 2005.

Trilling, Lionel. *Sincerity and Authenticity.* Cambridge, Mass.: Harvard University Press, 1972.

White, Hayden. *The Content of the Form: Narrative Discourse and Historical Representation.* Baltimore: Johns Hopkins University Press, 1987.

Williams, Bernard. "The Makropulos Case: Reflections on the Tedium of Immortality." In his *Problems of the Self: Philosophical Papers 1956–1972.* Cambridge: Cambridge University Press, 1973.

Wilson, Colin. *Anti-Sartre.* London: Borgo Press, 1981.

Wittgenstein, Ludwig. *Philosophical Investigations.* Translated by G. E. M. Anscombe. Oxford: Blackwell, 1953.

INDEX

Responsibility, 154, 218
Roquentin (in Sartre's *Nausea*), 60–92, 179
Rorty, Amelie, 132
Rorty, Richard, 190–91
Rousseau, Jean-Jacques, 184–85, 201
Russell, Bertrand, 185

Saint-Genet (Sartre), 149
Schopenhauer, Arthur, 214
Second Sex, The (Beauvoir),195
Self-consciousness, 139–144, 191, 207, 213–19
Self-deception, 132, 138, 144–47, 150, 154–55, 183–89
Self-taught man, the, 89–92
Shame, 86–89
Sherman, David 33

Sincerity, 163, 168–69
Sisyphus, 38–59
Sophocles, 198
Stekel, Willhelm 150, 156, 163–64
Stoics, the 163
Stranger, The (Camus), 11–33, 41, 48, 69, 70, 72, 114, 117–18, 128, 137, 178, 198–202, 215
Subconscious, 148

Thus Spoke Zarathustra (Nietzsche), 205
Transcendence, 133–39, 158, 160–61, 163–64, 167, 175
Transcendence of the Ego, 191

Wilson, Colin, 47, 65
Wittgenstein, Ludwig, 102
Wood, Allen, 155–56, 161